The Politics of Extraction

STUDIES IN COMPARATIVE ENERGY AND ENVIRONMENTAL POLITICS

Series editors: Todd A. Eisenstadt, American University, and Joanna I. Lewis, Georgetown University

A Good Life on a Finite Earth: The Political Economy of Green Growth
Daniel J. Fiorino

Democracy in the Woods: Environmental Conservation and Social Justice in India, Tanzania, and Mexico
Prakash Kashwan

Who Speaks for Nature? Indigenous Movements, Public Opinion, and the Petro-State in Ecuador
Todd A. Eisenstadt and Karleen Jones West

The Politics of Extraction

Territorial Rights, Participatory Institutions, and Conflict in Latin America

Maiah Jaskoski

OXFORD
UNIVERSITY PRESS

OXFORD
UNIVERSITY PRESS

Oxford University Press is a department of the University of Oxford. It furthers the University's objective of excellence in research, scholarship, and education by publishing worldwide. Oxford is a registered trade mark of Oxford University Press in the UK and certain other countries.

Published in the United States of America by Oxford University Press
198 Madison Avenue, New York, NY 10016, United States of America.

Library of Congress Cataloging-in-Publication Data
Names: Jaskoski, Maiah, 1977- author.
Title: The politics of extraction : territorial rights, participatory institutions, and conflict in Latin America / Maiah Jaskoski.
Description: 1 Edition. | New York, NY : Oxford University Press, [2022] |
Series: Studies compar energy environ pol series |
Includes bibliographical references and index.
Identifiers: LCCN 2022000769 (print) | LCCN 2022000770 (ebook) |
ISBN 9780197568927 (hardback) | ISBN 9780197568941 (epub)
Subjects: LCSH: Mineral industries—Political aspects—Latin America. |
Political participation—Latin America. | Communities—Latin America.
Classification: LCC HD9506.L292 J37 2022 (print) | LCC HD9506.L292
(ebook) | DDC 338.2098—dc23/eng/20220304
LC record available at https://lccn.loc.gov/2022000769
LC ebook record available at https://lccn.loc.gov/2022000770

DOI: 10.1093/oso/9780197568927.001.0001

For Jacob and Sam

CONTENTS

ACKNOWLEDGMENTS

This research began with exploratory fieldwork that I carried out in Lima in 2012 on mining conflict. During that visit, I became aware of how powerfully the environmental impact study, including participation built into it, structured conflict over new extraction—often in ways not planned or desired by state or company actors.

I am indebted to the individuals in Bolivia, Colombia, and Peru who generously gave me their time and shared with me their knowledge for this study. Many of them spoke with me at length, multiple times, to orient me and put me in contact with other experts. In Peru I received guidance from Jacqueline Fowks, Carlos Monge, Maritza Paredes, Cynthia Sanborn, Martin Scurrah, and John Youle Sr. In Colombia, I benefited from the help of Julio Fierro, Juan Diego Prieto, Gloria Amparo Rodríguez, Diana Rodríguez-Franco, and Yamile Salinas Abdala. Elizabeth Huanca, José Martínez, Patricia Molina, and Wilfredo Plata Quispe met with me during my fieldwork in Bolivia. Carla Alberti, Matt Amengual, Denise Humphreys Bebbington, Benjamin Dangl, Bret Gustafson, Derrick Hindery, Andrea Marston, and Tom Perreault helped me prepare for fieldwork in Bolivia, through conversations and correspondence.

Numerous colleagues provided insightful suggestions on the project as it evolved, in many cases through detailed comments on draft portions of the research: Arun Agrawal, Felipe Agüero, Michaël Aklin, Carla Alberti, Moisés Arce, Javiera Barandiarán, Naazneen Barma, Tony Bebbington, Paúl Cisneros, Gonzalo Delamaza, Tasha Fairfield, Tulia Falleti, Riccarda Flemmer, Candelaria Garay, Maria-Therese Gustafsson, Veronica Herrera, Kathy Hochstetler, Tony Lucero, Juan Pablo Luna, Lindsay Mayka, John-Andrew McNeish, Stephanie McNulty, Eduardo Moncada, Françoise Montambeault, Martin Papillon, Maritza Paredes, Juan Diego Prieto, Jessica Rich, Thea Riofrancos, María Paula Saffon, Almut Schilling-Vacaflor, Bettina Schorr, Eduardo Silva, Carie Steele, and Stephen Wright. Todd Eisenstadt, Cynthia McClintock, and two anonymous reviewers through Oxford University Press read and provided indispensable feedback on the full book manuscript. Kent Eaton saw the research as a book project long before I did. I am thankful for his feedback on the research throughout its evolution.

I received research assistance from Sara Caicedo and Nathan Edenhofer, who compiled parts of the conflict timelines for the Afrodita, Block 116, Conga, Gasoducto del Sur, and Tía María cases. Diego Esparza assisted with gathering secondary sources in Colombia. Yu Cao, Joseph Chirwa, Alena Gross, Mara Pfeffer, and Kassidy Sanders provided editorial assistance.

I had wonderful opportunities, by the invitation of colleagues, to present and receive invaluable comments on different phases of the research, at the Pontifical Catholic University of Chile, the University of Los Lagos, and the University of Montreal. Conversations during those events helped me clarify further the book's argument.

I thank Angela Chnapko, my editor at Oxford University Press, and the editors of the Studies in Comparative Energy and Environmental Politics series, Todd Eisenstadt and Joanna Lewis, for their enthusiasm for the project. I appreciate the excellent work of Alexcee Bechthold and the rest of the Oxford production team.

I received support for this research in the form of multiple grants through Northern Arizona University and the US Department of Defense Threat Reduction Agency Advanced Systems and Concepts Office. Portions of the research are published, as "Environmental Licensing and Conflict in Peru's Mining Sector: A Path-Dependent Analysis," *World Development* 64 (December 2014): 873–883; "Participatory Institutions as a Focal Point for Mobilizing: Prior Consultation and Indigenous Conflict in Colombia's Extractive Industries," *Comparative Politics* 52, no. 4 (July 2020): 537–556; and "Conflicto y estrategia social en la minería y los hidrocarburos peruanos: Los usos variados de la participación en la evaluación de impacto ambiental," *Revista de Ciencia Política* 41, no. 3 (December 2021): 587–609.

From early drafts of conflict analyses, to the sorting of the conflicts across chapters, and continuing through the final revisions, I kept one book on hand to serve as a model for medium-*n* analysis using qualitative case studies: Ruth Berins Collier's *Paths Toward Democracy: The Working Class and Elites in Western Europe and South America*.

Finally, I am grateful to my family for their support. My husband John and our sons Sam and Jacob embraced the project as something that would develop alongside the other facets of our lives. They accompanied me to Colombia one summer for research, tolerated my absence during other research trips, and accepted without complaint many months of "final" revisions.

NOTE TO THE READER

Unless otherwise indicated, all quotations from interviews are the author's translation from Spanish, as are all quotations from Spanish-language written sources.

ABBREVIATIONS

BG	British Gas
DS	Decreto Supremo (Supreme Decree)
EIA	estudio de impacto ambiental (environmental impact study)
FPIC	free, prior, and informed consent
FTA	free trade agreement
GDP	gross domestic product
IACHR	Inter-American Commission on Human Rights
ILO	International Labour Organization
PB	participatory budgeting
NGO	nongovernmental organization
OAS	Organization of American States
UN	United Nations
UNDRIP	United Nations Declaration on the Rights of Indigenous Peoples
UNOPS	United Nations Office for Project Services

Bolivia

APG	Asamblea del Pueblo Guaraní (Assembly of the Guaraní People)
CCGT	Consejo de Capitanes Guaraníes de Tarija (Council of Guaraní Captains of Tarija)
CIDOB	Confederación de Pueblos Indígenas de Bolivia (Confederation of Bolivian Indigenous Peoples)
COMIBOL	Corporación Minera de Bolivia (Bolivian Mining Corporation)
CONAMAQ	Consejo Nacional de Ayllus y Markas del Qullasuyu (National Council of Ayllus and Markas of Qullasuyu)
CPIB	Central de Pueblos Indígenas del Beni (Beni Indigenous People's Council)

CPILAP	Central de Pueblos Indígenas de La Paz (La Paz Indigenous People's Council)
CSUTCB	Confederación Sindical Única de Trabajadores Campesinos de Bolivia (Unified Syndical Confederation of Rural Workers of Bolivia)
EEIA	Estudio de Evaluación de Impacto Ambiental (Environmental Impact Evaluation Study)
INC	Instituto Nacional de Colonización (National Colonization Institute)
INRA	Instituto Nacional de Reforma Agraria (National Agrarian Reform Institute)
LPP	Ley de Participación Popular (Law of Popular Participation)
MAS	Movimiento al Socialismo (Movement for Socialism)
MNR	Movimiento Nacionalista Revolucionario (Nationalist Revolutionary Movement)
OPIM	Organización del Pueblo Indígena Mosetén (Organization of the Mosetén Indigenous People)
ORCAWETA	Organización de Capitanes Weenhayek (Organization of Weenhayek Captains)
SERNAP	Servicio Nacional de Áreas Protegidas (National Service for Protected Areas)
SNRA	Servicio Nacional de Reforma Agraria (National Agrarian Reform Service)
TCO	Tierra Comunitaria de Origen (Traditional Communal Lands)
TIPNIS	Territorio Indígena Parque Nacional Isiboro-Sécure (Isiboro Sécure Indigenous Territory and National Park)
YPFB	Yacimientos Petrolíferos Fiscales Bolivianos (Bolivian State Oil Fields; the Bolivian state oil company)

Colombia

ACIYA	Asociación de Capitanes Indígenas de Yaigojé Apaporis (Association of Yaigojé Apaporis Indigenous Leaders)
ACP	Asociación Colombiana de Petróleo (Colombian Oil Association)
ANH	Agencia Nacional de Hidrocarburos (National Hydrocarbon Agency)
ANLA	Agencia Nacional de Licencias Ambientales (National Environmental Licensing Agency)

ASCATIDAR	Asociación de Cabildos y Autoridades Tradicionales Indígenas del Departamento de Arauca (Association of Traditional Indigenous Councils and Authorities of the Arauca Department)
ASOU'WA	Asociación de Autoridades Tradicionales y Cabildos U'wa (Association of U'wa Traditional Authorities and Councils)
AUC	Autodefensas Unidas de Colombia (United Self-Defense Forces of Colombia)
BACRIM	bandas criminales (criminal bands)
CAR	corporación autónoma regional (regional autonomous corporation)
CDMB	Corporación Autónoma Regional Para la Defensa de la Meseta de Bucaramanga (Regional Autonomous Corporation for the Defense of the Bucaramanga Plateau)
CINEP/PPP	Centro de Investigación y Educación Popular Programa por la Paz (Center for Research and Popular Education Peace Program)
CORDATEC	Corporación Defensora del Agua, Territorio y Ecosistemas (Corporation for the Defense of Water, Territory, and Ecosystems)
ECOPETROL	Empresa Colombiana de Petróleos (Colombian Petroleum Company)
ELN	Ejército de Liberación Nacional (National Liberation Army)
EPL	Ejército Popular de Liberación (Popular Liberation Army)
FARC	Fuerzas Armadas Revolucionarias de Colombia (Revolutionary Armed Forces of Colombia)
INDERENA	Instituto de Desarrollo de los Recursos Naturales Renovables (Institute for the Development of Renewable Natural Resources)
INGEOMINAS	Instituto Nacional de Investigaciones Geológico-Mineras (National Institute of Geological-Mining Research)
M-19	Movimiento 19 de Abril (April 19 Movement)
MAVDT	Ministerio de Ambiente, Vivienda y Desarrollo Territorial (Ministry of Environment, Housing, and Territorial Development)
ONIC	Organización Nacional Indígena de Colombia (National Indigenous Organization of Colombia)
PNNYA	Parque Nacional Natural Yaigojé Apaporis (Yaigojé Apaporis National Park)
SPNN	Sistema de Parques Nacionales Naturales (National Parks System)

Peru

AIDESEP	Asociación Interétnica de Desarrollo de la Selva Peruana (Inter-Ethnic Association for the Development of the Peruvian Amazon)
ANA	Autoridad Nacional del Agua (National Water Authority)
CAN	Confederación Nacional Agraria (National Agrarian Confederation)
CCP	Confederación Campesina del Perú (Peasant Confederation of Peru)
CECONAMA	Central de Comunidades Nativas Machiguengas (Council of Native Machiguenga Communities)
CEPPAW	Comisión Especial Permanente de los Pueblos Awajún y Wampis (Permanent Special Commission of the Awajún and Wampis Peoples)
COMARU	Consejo Machiguenga del Río Urubamba (Machiguenga Council of the Urubamba River)
CONACAMI	Confederación Nacional de Comunidades del Perú Afectadas por la Minería (National Confederation of Peruvian Communities Affected by Mining)
CONAP	Confederación de Nacionalidades Amazónicas del Perú (Confederation of Amazonian Nationalities of Peru)
CORECAMI	Coordinadora Regional de Comunidades Afectadas por la Minería (Regional Coordinating Committee of Communities Affected by Mining)
DGAA	Dirección General de Asuntos Ambientales (General Directorate of Environmental Affairs)
DGAAM	Dirección General de Asuntos Ambientales Mineros (General Directorate of Environmental Affairs in Mining)
DIA	Declaración de Impacto Ambiental (Environmental Impact Statement)
DINOES	Dirección Nacional de Operaciones Especiales (National Directorate of Special Operations)
DREM	Dirección Regional de Energía y Minas (Regional Directorate of Energy and Mines)
EA	Evaluación Ambiental (Environmental Assessment)
FDRNZS	Frente de Defensa de los Recursos Naturales de la Zona Sur de Puno (Southern Puno Natural Resources Defense Front)
FDSFNP	Frente por el Desarrollo Sostenible de la Frontera Norte del Perú (Front for the Sustainable Development of the Northern Border of Peru)

FDVSLT	Frente de Defensa del Valle de San Lorenzo y Tambogrande (San Lorenzo and Tambogrande Valley Defense Front)
FECONAYY	Federación de Comunidades Nativas Yine Yane (Federation of Yine Yane Indigenous Communities)
FOSBAM	Fondo Social Las Bambas (Las Bambas Social Fund)
FUDIE	Frente Unido de Defensa de los Intereses de Espinar (United Defense Front of the Interests of Espinar)
GNCDPA	Grupo Nacional de Coordinación para el Desarrollo de los Pueblos Amazónicos (National Coordinating Group for the Development of Amazonian Peoples)
GRUFIDES	Grupo de Formación e Intervención para el Desarrollo Sostenible (Training and Intervention Group for Sustainable Development)
INGEMMET	Instituto Geológico, Minero y Metalúrgico (Geological, Mining, and Metallurgical Institute)
INRENA	Instituto Nacional de Recursos Naturales (National Institute of Natural Resources)
ITS	Informe Técnico Sustentatorio (Supporting Technical Report)
MEIA	Modificación del Estudio de Impacto Ambiental (Modification of the Environmental Impact Study)
MINAM	Ministerio de Ambiente (Ministry of Environment)
MINEM	Ministerio de Energía y Minas (Ministry of Energy and Mines)
MRTA	Movimiento Revolucionario Túpac Amaru (Tupac Amaru Revolutionary Movement)
ODECINAC	Organización de Desarrollo de las Comunidades Indígenas Numpatkaim y Alto Comaina (Organization for the Development of the Numpatkaim and Alto Comaina Indigenous Communities)
ODECOAC	Organización de Desarrollo de las Comunidades del Alto Comaina (Organization for the Development of the Alto Comaina Communities)
ODECOFROC	Organización de Desarrollo de las Comunidades Fronterizas del Cenepa (Organization for the Development of the Border Communities of El Cenepa)
OEFA	Organismo de Evaluación y Fiscalización Ambiental (Office of Environmental Evaluation and Auditing)
OGCS	Oficina de Gestión de Conflictos Sociales (Office of Social Conflict Management)

ONAMIAP	Organización Nacional de Mujeres Indígenas Andinas y Amazónicas del Perú (National Organization of Amazonian and Andean Indigenous Women of Peru)
ONDS	Oficina Nacional de Diálogo y Sostenibilidad (National Office of Dialogue and Sustainability)
ONPE	Oficina Nacional de Procesos Electorales (National Office of Electoral Processes)
ORPIAN	Organización Regional de los Pueblos Indígenas de la Amazonía Norte (Regional Organization of the Northern Amazonian Indigenous Peoples)
OSINERG	Organismo Supervisor de la Inversión en Energía (Supervising Body for Energy Investment)
OSINERGMIN	Organismo Supervisor de la Inversión en Energía y Minería (Supervising Body for Energy and Mining Investment)
PCM	Presidencia del Consejo de Ministros (Presidency of the Council of Ministers)
PNIMCC	Parque Nacional Ichigkat Muja—Cordillera del Condor (Ichigkat-Muja Condor Mountain Range National Park)
PROINVERSIÓN	Agencia de Promoción de la Inversión Privada (Private Investment Promotion Agency)
RD	Resolución Directoral (Chief Resolution)
RM	Resolución Ministerial (Ministerial Resolution)
SBN	Superintendencia Nacional de Bienes Nacionales (National Superintendency of State Assets)
SERNANP	Servicio Nacional de Áreas Naturales Protegidas del Estado (National Service for Natural Protected Areas of the State)
SNA	Sistema Nacional Ambiental (National Environmental System)
SNMPE	Sociedad Nacional de Minería, Petróleo y Energía (National Society of Mining, Oil, and Energy)
UAC	Unidad de Análisis de Conflictos (Unit of Conflict Analysis)
UAEPCS	Unidad de Análisis Estratégico y Prevención de Conflictos (Unit of Strategic Analysis and Conflict Prevention)
ZRSC	Zona Reservada Santiago Comaina (Santiago Comaina Reserve)

Figure 0.1 Map of Peru
Source: University of Texas Libraries

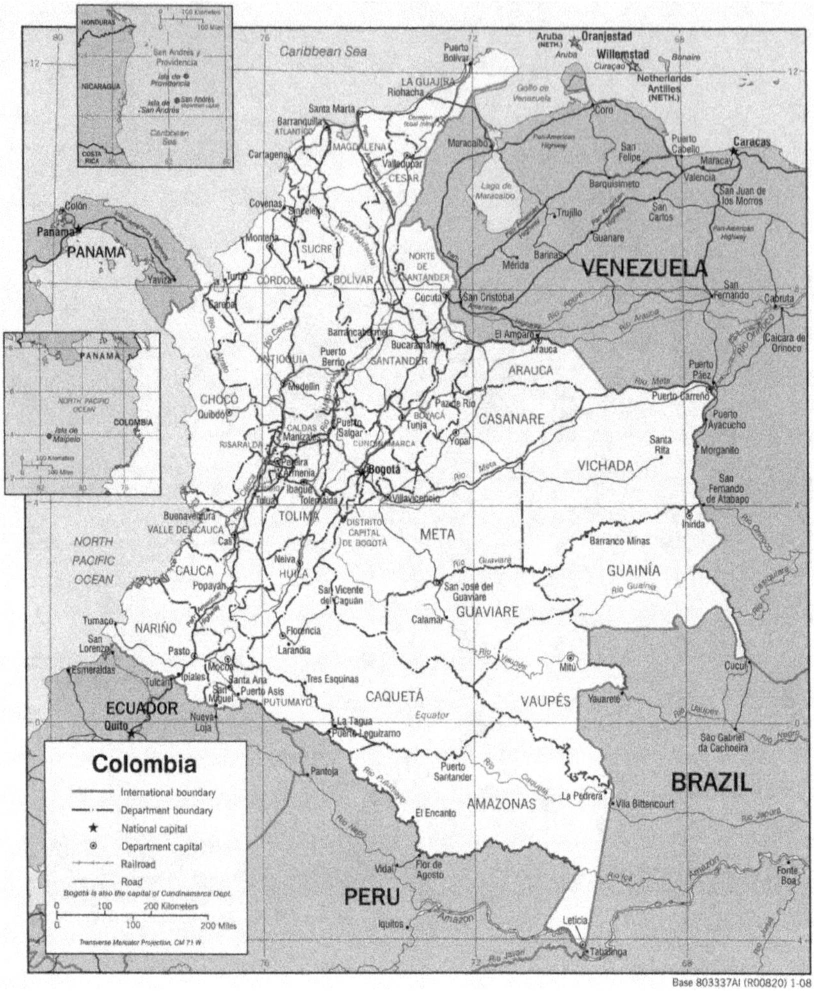

Figure 0.2 Map of Colombia
Source: University of Texas Libraries

Figure 0.3 Map of Bolivia
Source: University of Texas Libraries

The Politics of Extraction

PART I

Introduction

CHAPTER 1

Participatory Institutions and Extractive Conflict

In Latin America, development in mining and hydrocarbons is high stakes for extractive firms, communities in resource-rich zones, and states. Amid liberal economic policies and global commodity price increases, the two sectors expanded during the 1990s–2010s, making private investors and Latin American governments ever more committed to extraction. For their part, communities have organized to protest about the social and environmental impacts of mining and hydrocarbon activities and to reap associated material benefits (De Echave et al. 2009; Arellano Yanguas 2011; Bebbington and Bury 2013; Arce 2014; Henao and Gonzáles Espinosa 2016; Delamaza et al. 2017; Pellegrini and Arsel 2018). Social conflict that pits communities against extractive companies and the state manifests as legal battles, local standoffs in which activists block project sites, and large-scale, sometimes violent, demonstrations. These struggles have had significant ramifications for production, as well as for local socioeconomic realities and the environment.

Communities affected by hydrocarbons and mining have formal opportunities to communicate their reservations about extraction and its impacts. In accordance with environmental licensing—pervasive across Latin America since the 1990s (Orihuela 2014a)—the state informs the public of proposed extraction. That process often involves a public hearing on the environmental impact study (*estudio de impacto ambiental*, EIA), which identifies anticipated impacts of development, and measures to mitigate them. In addition, Latin America and the Caribbean are home to fifteen of the twenty-four governments worldwide that have ratified the 1989 Indigenous and Tribal

The Politics of Extraction. Maiah Jaskoski, Oxford University Press. © Oxford University Press 2022.
DOI: 10.1093/oso/9780197568927.003.0001

People's Convention (International Labour Organization Convention 169, "ILO 169"), which requires the state to consult Native peoples affected by proposed development. National regulations in several Latin American countries now detail procedures for these "prior consultations." Communities impacted by extraction also have voted it down through local "popular consultations," or referendums. The introduction of local popular consultations was part of the larger wave of decentralization that swept the region in the 1980s and 1990s (Montero and Samuels 2004; Walter and Urkidi 2017, 266).

This book identifies and explains variation in how communities use participatory institutions in extractive conflict. It analyzes thirty important cases of social mobilizing over new hydrocarbon and mining development in Bolivia, Colombia, and Peru. While in some cases communities engaged in formal processes of participation, in others they organized "around" or "in reaction" to those institutions, using institutional procedures as a focal point in the escalation of conflict. By examining how participatory institutions channel and exacerbate mobilizing over new extraction, this study sheds light on the relationship between participation and conflict, and on the versatility of institutions. In particular, it shows how communities can utilize institutions that formally do not grant them the power to affect development outcomes, in their fights to alter, stall, block, and/or benefit from extraction.

Communities employed participatory institutions to navigate three distinct challenges to participation. Those challenges arose or increased due to contestation over the boundaries that determined access to the institutions. First, contestation over the line between subnational authority and the central state's jurisdiction heightened communities' challenge of initiating a participatory process. Second, disagreement over the territorial delineation of the communities impacted by extraction produced the challenge of gaining inclusion in participatory events for formally nonimpacted communities. Third, disputes over the boundary that set representatives of impacted communities apart from the communities at large intensified the challenge of conveying positions on extraction.

USES OF PARTICIPATORY INSTITUTIONS IN MINING AND HYDROCARBON MOBILIZING

A brief summary of four conflicts illustrates some of the variation in how communities used participatory institutions in this study's conflict sample. Protests over the Peruvian Tía María mine project led to police repression and activist deaths. In that case, local communities opposed a project design that threatened critical freshwater sources, and they resented the poor transparency of company communications. As part of their organizing, communities protested violently during an EIA hearing, causing the meeting's suspension and helping to stall the project. In another Peruvian conflict, over the immense Las Bambas mine, communities displeased by their share of compensation also staged large-scale mobilizations. However, rather than interfering with the EIA hearing, they conveyed their complaints within the meeting structure.

Communities used prior consultation in varying ways, as well. During 2011–12, the Takovo Mora Indigenous community of the Bolivian Guaraní nation delayed the $160 million Río Grande natural gas plant. The project raised serious environmental concerns for the community, which wanted to be consulted about the plant and compensated for its impacts. When Takovo Mora saw that the project owner was moving forward without consulting them, community members occupied the plant site and achieved a prior consultation process.

In contrast to the Río Grande conflict, when the Colombian state failed to consult the Nasa, that Indigenous nation demanded prior consultation later, using the courts. At issue was the 2014 approval of expanded production in three major oil fields in Colombia's southern department (just below the national level) of Putumayo. The project alarmed local Nasa communities that feared adverse socioenvironmental impacts, having already experienced high levels of contamination from oil production. After the state issued an environmental license for the project, the Nasa installed a blockade to force a negotiation with the government about the impacts of oil development. However, to defend their right to prior consultation, they filed a legal complaint. That action resulted in a Constitutional Court decision in their favor.

Why did groups organize around the Tía María EIA hearing, interrupting it to use it as a device to delay extraction, whereas in the Las Bambas conflict, groups worked through the established participatory process? Why, in the case of the Río Grande plant, did communities take direct action to force prior consultation, whereas communities used the judicial system to secure a consultation on the Putumayo project, after the state approved the development?

Community strategies in these four cases exemplify trends in the study's larger conflict sample. As summarized in Table 1.1, communities utilized participatory institutions in four ways: (1) they took part in formal participatory events, (2) they refused to participate in or interfered with those meetings, (3) they challenged the absence of or their exclusion from participatory processes after the fact, and (4) they physically blocked projects to demand participation, at or directly following the participatory stage. This book explains these different strategies.

Table 1.1 COMMUNITY USES OF PARTICIPATORY INSTITUTIONS IN THIRTY MAJOR CONFLICTS OVER NEW EXTRACTION IN BOLIVIA, COLOMBIA, AND PERU, 2001–2020

Dominant participatory institution	Sector	Mobilizing through the institution	Mobilizing around the institution		
			Refusal to participate/ interference	Contestation of process after the fact	Direct action to demand participation
Prior consultation	Hydrocarbons		*Bolivia*: San Antonio *Colombia*: Samoré	*Colombia*: Putumayo oil fields *Peru*: Block 116	*Bolivia*: El Dorado wells, Gran Chaco plant, Percheles and El Dorado fields, Río Grande plant, Timboy X-2 *Colombia*: Magallanes
	Mining		*Colombia*: diversion of Ranchería	*Colombia*: Mandé Norte *Peru*: Afrodita	
EIA hearing	Hydrocarbons	*Colombia*: fracking in San Martín*, Lorito 1, Nogal	*Peru*: Camisea Block 56		
	Mining	*Colombia*: Angostura *Peru:* Las Bambas, Quellaveco	*Peru*: Tambo Grande, Tía María	*Peru*: Conga, Santa Ana	
Popular consultation	Hydrocarbons	*Colombia*: fracking in San Martín*, Odisea 3D			
	Mining	*Colombia*: La Colosa			

Note: In four outlier cases, mobilized communities did not use the relevant participatory institution in their organizing: the Colombian Cosigo mining conflict and the Peruvian Gasoducto del Sur hydrocarbon and Quilish and Río Blanco mining conflicts.

* In the San Martín case, the EIA hearing and the popular consultation were equally influential in organizing conflict.

EXISTING RESEARCH

The study builds on three literatures. Research on participatory institutions that incorporate citizens in local policymaking, and scholarship on participation and social conflict in extractive industries, analyze how participatory institutions promote citizen participation and influence. The two literatures do not, however, ask why organized communities might use a single institution in different ways. A third research tradition, on institutional change, addresses that question but does not account for the variation identified in this book.

A prevailing finding across the three research traditions is that state actors, the nature of civil society, and/or institutional design can give activists the ability to employ an institution to their advantage. The present research incorporates these insights into a new, broader paradigm for explaining alternative uses of participatory opportunities in extractive conflict.

Local Participatory Institutions

The literature on local participatory institutions in Latin America offers causal explanations for citizen participation in and influence through subnational committees, councils, and other bodies that have brought regular people into policy debates, within decentralized political contexts (Goldfrank 2011; Mayka 2019). Scholars often explain citizen empowerment in the face of political parties that otherwise might absorb or co-opt them (e.g., Goldfrank 2011; Montambeault 2016; Herrera 2017). Prominent causal factors in these studies are institutional design and characteristics of the state and of civil society.

Much of the literature focuses on civil society. Veronica Herrera argues that local citizen boards in Mexican urban water delivery suffered partisan capture due to "the absence of societal groups that exhibit[ed] strong, coordinated support for participatory institutions and simultaneously possess[ed] the political clout to superimpose their preferences onto new mayoral leadership" (Herrera 2017, 480). In their comparative study of Brazilian cases of "participatory budgeting" (PB)—which brings residents into municipal (comparable to county-level) spending discussions—Baiocchi et al. (2011, 35–38, ch. 5) identify participation and policy influence only where civil society had autonomy relative to the state. Lindsay Mayka's (2019) research on Brazil and Colombia attributes the performance of participatory institutions in health, social assistance, and planning to civil-society organizing during institutional genesis.

The impact of organized civil society may depend on the behavior or characteristics of state actors, specifically at the subnational level. For Rebecca

Neaera Abers (2000), state actions together with civil society explained the significant participation and impact of residents in PB in Porto Alegre, Brazil. The Workers Party administration in that city helped organize civil society, and the resulting civic groups then took on a life of their own, acting independently of the state and affecting policy (Abers 2000, 14–18). In his research on PB in Brazil, Brian Wampler concludes that for citizens to have a voice in PB, citizens and civil-society organizations must cooperate with one another and with the local government enough to ensure that the process functions, but not so much that they lose their footing. "If groups are unwilling or unable to vigorously defend their interests against those of other groups and government officials, then PB will weaken because the participants will likely be steamrolled by the government or other groups" (Wampler 2007, 38). Wampler further underscores mayoral actions that decentralize local administration such that it better reaches citizens (Wampler 2007, 35–36; see also Wampler and Avritzer 2004). Stephanie McNulty's research on Peruvian PB and "coordination councils" stresses organized civil society and subnational state support, but at the regional level, above the municipality (McNulty 2011, 129–40).

Added to this emphasis on the power of civil society and state actors, scholars also have devoted considerable attention to the design of participatory institutions. Leonardo Avritzer values a basic design element of Brazilian PB and citizen elections monitoring in Mexico: the formal placement of members of the public in the policy arena. That facet of the two institutions eliminated the gap between citizens and their interests, on one hand, and policy outcomes, on the other (Avritzer 2002). Yanilda Gonzalez's research on Argentine, Brazilian, and Colombian community-police crime prevention programs finds that a program's effectiveness depended on its inclusivity and on whether it obliged the state to comply with community wishes (Gonzalez 2016). In his study of PB in Brazil, Uruguay, and Venezuela, Benjamin Goldfrank locates greater citizen engagement where more issues are open to debate, the rotation of representatives is frequent, meetings are public and numerous, and, as in Gonzalez's work, results are binding (Goldfrank 2011, 7, 31).

Some scholars ascribe causal weight to both institutional design and civil society. Gianpaolo Baiocchi's "relational approach" to PB in three Porto Alegre districts considers whether there is harmony between civil society and PB. PB was most successfully implemented where civil society was *weakest* (Baiocchi 2005, especially 17–20, ch. 3); and a preexisting vibrant civil society contributed to success only "where established activists and organizations blended with the new structures of [PB]" (Baiocchi 2005, 51). In her analysis of state-society relations in municipal cases of PB in Brazil and of participatory urban planning in Mexico, Françoise Montambeault finds that mobilization patterns and societal autonomy in the participatory spaces were influenced by the "configuration of civil society" and whether the participatory institution was designed to create "incentives for collective mobilization and demand making" (2016, 9–10).

In sum, research on participatory institutions in Latin America reveals how civil society, institutional design, and state characteristics or actions affect citizen participation and influence on policy. While illuminating, these studies address only participation through institutions, without also analyzing how people mobilize around them.

Participation and Conflict in Extraction amid Power Asymmetries

The interdisciplinary literature on participation and conflict in extraction is similar to scholarship on local participatory institutions in that it explains community mobilizing and its impacts by focusing on civil society, institutional design, and state actors. While studies in this second literature observe organizing both through and in reaction to participatory institutions, they have not (1) explored variation in the ways communities mobilize around prescribed participatory channels or (2) tried to identify the conditions under which communities act in accordance with institutional procedures or, alternatively, organize outside of them.[1]

It is useful to begin this review of work on participatory institutions in extractives by recognizing the extreme power asymmetries that are intrinsic to hydrocarbons and mining. As observed by experts on extractive conflict, this dynamic makes community organizing difficult, including during participatory moments.

At the forefront of conversations about these asymmetries is the question of whether communities can retain cohesion and/or take a stance against development. Communities contend with national governments that enthusiastically transfer exploration and extraction rights to companies (Bebbington 2009), and state-backed, wealthy firms have fractured communities and limited their development options. It is the EIA, developed by private consultants, that defines the impacts of large-scale hydrocarbon and mining projects and in that way frames debates about development to center on mitigable impacts and not on whether extraction should take place at all (Li 2015, ch. 5). The EIA also demarcates a project's "area of influence" and therefore, in discussions

1. Exceptions are Jaskoski 2014, 2020, and 2021, which are based on the research for the present book. An excellent collection of studies that depicts mobilizing around different participatory institutions in extractive industries is Leifsen et al. 2017a.

about project impacts, who "matters"—that is, communities within the area of influence—and who does not (O'Faircheallaigh 2017, 1182–84).

Company investments to obtain local community support for projects can be especially divisive. These initiatives tend to favor some communities over others (A. Bebbington 2010, 106–7). Where extraction affects Native peoples, firms have negotiated compensation agreements with individual communities, excluding higher-level Indigenous organizations (Pellegrini and Ribera Arismendi 2012). More fundamentally, when discussions about extraction and its impacts are oriented around compensation, communities might be unable to maintain cohesion, due to the nature of impacts from extraction. Maria-Therese Gustafsson observes the following, in mining: "As being affected is related to specific issues—pollution of water, construction of roads, purchases of land, price increases—it becomes difficult for different communities to define common interests in relation to the mining project" (2016, 96–97).

These concerns about community cohesion and goals serve to ground research on participation and conflict in hydrocarbons and mining. Studies have asked whether and how communities that contend with powerful companies and extractivist states, might find and articulate positions, and ultimately influence development outcomes, by using available participatory institutions built into state approval processes.

Mobilizing through Participatory Institutions

One position in research on participation and conflict in extraction is that by working through participatory institutions, communities can form interests and make demands. In their medium-*n* analysis of conflict over large-scale pipeline projects in the developing world, Doug McAdam and collaborators conclude that the mere presence of a participatory stage in project approvals facilitates activism: "Consultation grants opponents entrée to the project, thereby encouraging mobilization" (McAdam et al. 2010, 423; see also 407).

Other research has observed great effort and setbacks in the process of making participatory institutions meaningful (e.g., Schilling-Vacaflor 2017b). Scholars argue that institutional design, support from state actors, and/or societal cohesion can inject substance into otherwise empty procedures, echoing the previously discussed literature on local participatory institutions. As for societal cohesion, more unified Indigenous populations, represented by organizations above the community level, may have greater influence in prior consultations (Schilling-Vacaflor 2013a, 209, 214; Schilling-Vacaflor and Flemmer 2015, 835).

Communities that organize through participatory institutions have received crucial assistance from state institutions. Kathryn Hochstetler's research on large-scale energy projects in Brazil finds that, whereas some state agents may support energy projects, others—in particular the Ministério Público—have been important members of antiproject "blocking coalitions," for instance by ensuring proper EIA hearing procedures (Hochstetler 2011, 355, 357). Similarly, the Peruvian national ombudsman (Defensoría del Pueblo) has helped communities in some prior consultations, as an observer (Schilling-Vacaflor and Flemmer 2015, 833).

Given the power imbalances built into resource extraction, perhaps it is unsurprising that scholars emphasize not only state support but also community allies more generally. Intellectuals have helped communities take advantage of environmental assessment, including associated participatory opportunities (Devlin and Yap 2008). The involvement of nongovernmental organizations (NGOs) in individual prior consultations might increase their transparency (Schilling-Vacaflor and Flemmer 2015, 833).

Finally, for the specific institution of prior consultation, institutional design has affected the strength of participating communities. In their extensive research on Bolivia and Peru, Riccarda Flemmer and Almut Schilling-Vacaflor identify several design elements of prior consultation that they maintain strengthen, or would strengthen, communities' capacity within consultations. The authors aver that consultations should be led by impartial state agencies (Schilling-Vacaflor 2013a, 215; Schilling-Vacaflor and Flemmer 2015, 832; see also Haarstad and Campero 2011, 38–40, 55), occur before a project is designed in detail (Schilling-Vacaflor 2013a, 209), be planned with community participation (Schilling-Vacaflor and Flemmer 2015, 829; Flemmer and Schilling-Vacaflor 2016, 177–78), include communities' regional or national Indigenous leaders (Schilling-Vacaflor and Flemmer 2015, 834), and produce agreements that participants are obliged to follow (Schilling-Vacaflor and Flemmer 2015, 835–36).

Design *processes* also can affect the quality of prior consultations. Indigenous participation in developing national prior consultation institutions has infused legitimacy into actual consultations (Falleti and Riofrancos 2018; see also Schilling-Vacaflor and Flemmer 2015, on the negative case of Peru).

Mobilizing around Participatory Institutions

Alongside research on community participation in and influence through participatory institutions in extractives, are studies that view communities as having little if any potential impact using these formal avenues. From this more pessimistic perspective, prior consultation and EIA hearings mainly divide and control communities and expedite extraction (e.g., Pellegrini and Ribera Arismendi 2012; Merino 2018; Barandiarán and Rubiano-Galvis 2019; Eisenstadt and West 2019, ch. 3; Torres Wong 2019). Yet some scholars writing in this vein have found that these institutions *indirectly* can encourage activism within communities that feel unrepresented in those processes: the institutions cause groups to organize *in reaction to* participatory opportunities.

For example, communities have protested extractive projects by refusing to be consulted and by interfering with or boycotting hearings. Fabiana Li describes as follows a protest outside the site of an EIA hearing held on an expansion of the massive Yanacocha mine in northern Peru:

> The protesters' statement was clear: they were not interested in the information that was to be presented or the meeting's proceedings, because nothing they could say would prevent the EIA from being approved. Not only would their intervention in the meeting be futile, but the company would use their attendance to legitimate the EIA with the claim that it was democratically accepted. They decided that their best course of action was to *step outside the document*. (Li 2015, 208)

Similarly, Mariana Walter and Joan Martinez-Alier write of activists' refusal to attend an EIA hearing for a planned open-pit gold and silver mine in Mendoza, Argentina: "The perceived lack of opportunity for participation via official channels led the [Autonomous People's Assembly] to boycott the event" (Walter and Martinez-Alier 2010, 298).[2]

Communities also have organized around formal participatory processes by demanding that participation be made available in a more robust form, or at all. In the case of the large-scale Mirador mining project in Ecuador, by failing to follow the (weak) national prior consultation requirements, the state unwittingly brought on a legal battle. "The lack of application of formal participatory instruments . . . lays the ground for alternative and unintended uses . . . formal procedural resources are detached from the control of public authorities and re-used politically by the affected population" (Leifsen et al. 2017b, 1097–98). In her research on popular consultations to vote down mining in Guatemala and Peru, Amanda Fulmer (2014) argues that the absence of a strong prior consultation framework may lead communities to demand the withheld rights, by staging popular consultations.

Indeed, local popular consultations to stop large-scale extraction have become common in Latin America.[3] Consistent with the literature on EIA

2. For another example of communities preventing a participatory event from taking place as a means to impede extraction, see Rodríguez-Garavito 2011, 296, on prior consultation in Colombia.

3. Walter and Urkidi (2017) identify and analyze sixty-eight mining consultations in Latin America between 2002 and 2012. See also Szablowski 2010, 120–21; Costanza 2015; Riofrancos 2017; and Rodríguez-Franco 2017, 70–73.

hearings and prior consultation, research that offers causal explanations for popular consultations in extractives also points to societal cohesion, support from the state or other allies, and institutional design—specifically, the existence of legal scaffolding for local referendums (McNeish 2017, 1132; Walter and Urkidi 2017, 275–76; Shenk forthcoming).

As a whole, then, research on social conflict in extraction has identified different ways that groups mobilize within and around participatory institutions. Although studies have not tried to explain variation in community uses of the institutions, we can pull from the literature certain expectations about what might account for organizing through, versus organizing around, participatory opportunities. One set of expectations parallels writings on local participatory institutions: communities that (1) are cohesive, (2) have access to local participatory processes that exhibit certain design traits, and/or (3) receive support from sympathetic or at least impartial state agents or from nonstate allies, will take part in and have influence through participatory processes.

We also might construct a very different possible pattern of community behavior from scholarship on participation and extractive conflict. This second logic overlaps with the first in that it, too, emphasizes community cohesion and institutional design; but it emerges specifically from studies that are skeptical about community organizing through prior consultation and EIA hearings. Cohesive communities might be less likely to participate in those participatory processes, which are designed merely to inform communities. Rather, greater cohesion may encourage organizing around the institutions, to include possibly coordinating alternative participatory events such as popular consultations. Community goals also enter: communities that want to hold up extraction might resist participating in processes that do not give them veto power, and thus might be more likely to organize around and not through the institutions.

As this book will demonstrate, neither set of expectations fully explains community strategies in the study's conflict sample. For instance, some communities that exhibited a great deal of cohesion engaged in formal participatory processes, whereas others refused to do so.

Institutional Ambiguities and Change

Scholarship on institutional change is a third research tradition germane to understanding variation in communities' uses of participatory institutions in hydrocarbons and mining. Unlike studies of extractive conflict and participatory institutions, the institutional change literature addresses the phenomenon of an institution serving more than one function. In particular, actors might use a formal institution in ways not intended by its designers during "conversion," one path to institutional change (Mahoney and Thelen 2010, 17–18; Hacker et al. 2015).

Research on institutional change takes seriously civil society, institutional design, and the state, like the other two literatures reviewed. Greater ambiguity in institutions—an aspect of institutional design—facilitates the use of a formal institution in new ways (Mahoney and Thelen 2010, 21; Hacker et al. 2015, 189). As for civil society, well-organized, motivated societal groups often pursue institutional change (Mahoney and Thelen 2010, 27; Hacker et al. 2015, 186, 197). The roles of state entities include blocking change (Mahoney and Thelen 2010, 18–20); assisting with it—when, for example, civil-society actors turn to public agencies or the courts (Hacker et al. 2015, 192, 196–97)—and even initiating change (Hacker et al. 2015, 191).

The present study aligns with scholarship on institutional change, in that it analyzes societal actors that took advantage of uncertainties within participatory institutions, to hold up extraction. Moreover, a process of institutional change was underway in some cases. For example, by contesting the absence of prior consultation for certain extractive projects, Colombian and Peruvian Indigenous communities helped make the prior consultation institution more accessible to other communities in the future. Communities in Colombia that interpreted popular consultation rules so as to hold municipal consultations on hydrocarbon and mining development, paved the way for other communities to do the same.

Notwithstanding these congruencies, this book diverges from the institutional change literature. Contradicting the conversion model, in this study several communities that confronted *less* ambiguity in procedures and had a *stronger* guarantee of participation were *more* likely to organize around rather than through available participatory institutions, by interrupting participatory events or refusing to participate in them. Additionally, in many cases, activists that employed participatory institutions creatively did not appear to be effecting institutional change.

BOUNDARIES AND ASSOCIATED CHALLENGES TO COMMUNITY PARTICIPATION

In following with the literatures examined in the previous section, this book, too, finds that civil society, the state, and institutional design matter—specifically, for helping to explain varying community uses of participatory institutions in extractive conflict. The three factors stand out not for altering the power balance between participating communities, on one hand, and companies and the state, on the other; nor for helping to predict institutional change or change paths. Rather, they affected which uses of participatory institutions were available to communities, as part of this book's broader paradigm. This discussion introduces the paradigm and reflects on how it incorporates civil society, institutional design, and the state.

At the core of this study are the inherently fraught boundaries that determine access to participatory institutions in extraction. Contestation over those boundaries caused or exacerbated certain participatory challenges for communities. These challenges explain how mobilized communities used the institutions in the book's conflict sample. The research identifies three boundary fights and associated participatory challenges. First, there is the question of which level of government has jurisdiction in extractives. Contestation over the delineation of subnational authority vis-à-vis the central state's jurisdiction heightened the *event initiation challenge*, to begin a participatory process. Second is the matter of who experiences the impacts of extractive development. Many conflicts involved disputes about the geographic border around impacted communities, and therefore about which communities were invited to participatory events. That contestation caused the *inclusion challenge* for communities that rejected their classification as not impacted. Third is the issue of who speaks on behalf of impacted communities. In some cases, members of these communities disagreed about the line that set their representatives apart from the communities at large—that is, it was unclear who legitimately could speak on behalf of the communities. That disagreement intensified communities' *articulation challenge*, or the task of conveying a position on extraction at the participatory stage.

Figure 1.1 summarizes the book's argument, including the causal relationships between contested boundaries and community challenges.

Event Initiation Challenge, Heightened by Contested Policy Jurisdictions

Communities faced the *event initiation challenge*, of spurring participatory events, in the Colombian conflicts that involved the municipal popular consultation or the EIA hearing—processes activated only by formal request. Petitioning could be cumbersome. In Colombia, the municipal popular consultation required mayoral backing or signature drives, and only certain public officials or civil-society representatives, or a minimum of one hundred members of the public, could request the EIA hearing. That a participatory event was not automatic affected how communities employed it in the larger conflict: they were limited to requesting and taking part in the participatory stage—that is, working through the formal institutional structures.

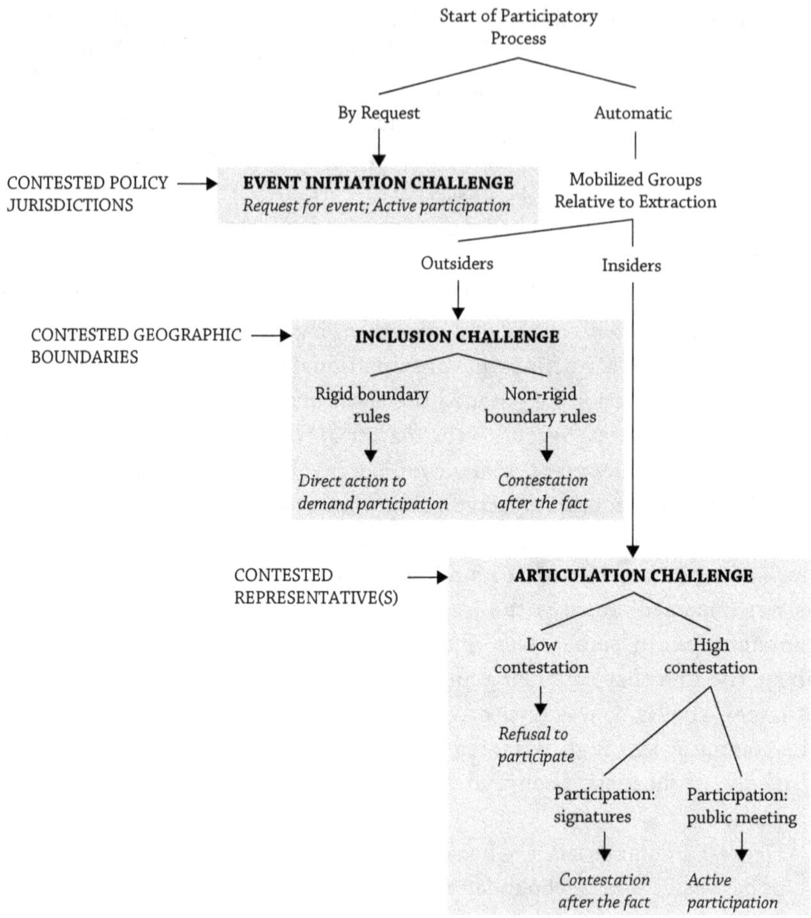

Figure 1.1 Participatory Institutions in Extractive Conflict: Pathways to Community Strategies

Contested policy jurisdictions heightened the event initiation challenge. When a municipality's right to host a participatory event was in doubt, communities might only achieve a public hearing through substantial activism (while also following the formal request process). Specifically, intensive organizing was required where groups outside of a planned mine's area of influence asked for an EIA hearing in their municipality, and when communities sought a hearing about a component of a previously approved oil exploration project. Contestation over policy jurisdictions was most evident in conflicts that involved the popular consultation. In those cases, municipalities claimed the right to hold votes on extraction, whereas national government officials and extractive firms argued that the central state owned and controlled subsoil resources.

Inclusion Challenge, Caused by Contested Geographic Boundaries

Different from the Colombian EIA hearing and popular consultation, the other institutions analyzed in this book mandated participatory opportunities for communities impacted by development—in this study, "insider" communities, as opposed to unaffected "outsiders."

In many cases, communities still struggled to access these participatory processes. Specifically, communities defined as outsiders disputed that status. Some communities asserted that the EIA defined too narrowly project impacts, incorrectly placing the communities outside of impacted areas. Indigenous communities claimed rights to more territory than their state-recognized lands. In short, contestation over the geographic border around impacted communities created the *inclusion challenge* for outsiders who viewed themselves as impacted and who, on those grounds, contended that they should have access to participatory institutions.

The lines that defined communities as outsiders could be "rigid" or "nonrigid." The latter signified that there was formal room for interpretation when drawing a boundary. The placement of the border around a project's area of influence often could be questioned, due to disparate definitions of impacts. In Colombia and Peru, the state considered multiple forms of Indigenous presence and land use when determining whether a project affected Indigenous communities and thus whether to hold prior consultations. Assessments along these dimensions often could be—and were—deliberated. In settings of nonrigid borders, outsiders contested their exclusion after the participatory stage, putting forth technical or legal-administrative justifications.

Distinct from the Colombian and Peruvian cases, borders around Bolivian Indigenous communities for purposes of prior consultation were rigid, in that communities needed title to affected land in order to be consulted. Indigenous outsiders in Bolivia hence did not have legal footing to defend their right to participate after the prior consultation moment had passed. Instead, they took direct action to hold up development and demand prior consultation at the time of their exclusion from project approvals. Colombian communities also harnessed this strategy in one hydrocarbon case. In that conflict, a previous legal process had determined that the land rights of an Indigenous nation did not extend beyond its formal communal landholding; communities therefore had the sole option of using direct action, to prompt negotiations with the state.

Articulation Challenge, Intensified by Contested Community Representation

Insiders, who had guaranteed access to participatory processes, encountered the challenge of expressing their positions on extraction—the *articulation challenge*. They could either discuss planned development within participatory processes or organize around them, in different ways. The articulation challenge was greater for communities in which mobilized insiders competed with community members amenable to the planned development—that is, where the boundary that distinguished community representatives from the rest of the community was contested.

In the absence of competition, unified insider communities delayed extraction by refusing to be consulted or by preventing or interfering with the EIA hearing. By contrast, competition helped participatory processes advance, with activists' strategies depending on the rules of participation. Where participation involved the holding of a meeting for residents—as was true of EIA hearings—groups on all sides participated, defending their respective positions. Unlike EIA hearing procedures, participation in prior consultation entailed community leaders signing off on the process. That institutional design characteristic encouraged the state to consult only sympathetic groups, causing activists to challenge the legitimacy of the consultation.

We now can consider how this study's paradigm—based on participatory challenges that were caused or amplified by boundary contestation—includes civil society, institutional design, and the state. Civil society, especially insider cohesion, mattered. With regard to institutional design, the book's focus on contested boundaries brings to the fore rules about policy jurisdictions and impacted populations. Also crucial are the steps necessary to prompt a participatory process, the rigidity of boundaries between insiders and outsiders, and how regulations define participation. State institutions, at the subnational and national levels, enter in several ways. Due to politicized, biased decisions by Bolivia's agrarian reform agency, many Indigenous communities did not hold title to lands impacted by extraction and hence found themselves excluded from project approvals. Colombia's Constitutional Court helped ensure community access to popular consultation and prior consultation. For Colombian popular consultations, municipal government support also was important.

CASE SELECTION

This medium-*n* analysis of thirty hydrocarbon and mining conflicts builds on existing research on conflict and participation in extraction. The richness of that scholarship has come with trade-offs when it comes to comparative leverage: the literature mainly is composed of single-case studies and small-*n* comparisons within a single country and/or sector; and overall, it has supported an artificial separation among analyses of EIA participation, prior consultation, and popular consultation.[4] Although this book's relatively large sample necessarily precludes the in-depth treatment of cases that is characteristic of small-*n* research, its vantage point allows for analysis of multiple participatory institutions at work in conflicts that span hydrocarbons and mining and three countries.

Country Level: Most Different Systems Design

Bolivia, Colombia, and Peru offer excellent settings for this study. Each of the countries has relied on hydrocarbons and mining, and in each case the national government has adopted aggressive, extractivist policies, including measures to open the sectors to private investment.[5] In addition, in all three cases the state has channeled extractive revenue to producing regions, such that local communities may anticipate environmental impacts and also material benefits from production. Furthermore, community participation in hydrocarbons and mining is institutionalized; formal structures govern prior consultation in the three countries, EIA hearings in Colombia and Peru, and popular consultation in Colombia. And in each country, community organizing has stalled—and in some cases led to the cancellation of—new mining and hydrocarbon development.

The countries also diverge, in their national political trajectories and in dominant forms of extractive conflict. This variation makes possible the book's most different systems design (Przeworski and Teune 1970, 34–39): the study's single causal framework explains the roles of participatory institutions in extractive conflict, in the different national contexts.

Peru is a case of large-scale protests, especially in mining, in the wake of redemocratization. Individual conflicts have brought tens of thousands of protesters to the streets and have resulted in intensive police repression, deaths of activists and security personnel, and the resignation of ministers. The Colombian regime is famously paradoxical. On one hand, Colombia's stable democracy deepened in the early 1990s, through extensive

4. There are exceptions to the latter trend. Leifsen et al. (2017b) analyze how communities impacted by the Mirador mining project in Ecuador used prior consultation and EIA participatory structures. Rodríguez-Franco (2017) studies two Colombian cases, one involving prior consultation and the other, popular consultation. Schilling-Vacaflor's (2017a) examination of two hydrocarbon project approval processes in Bolivia incorporates both prior consultation and a company-run EIA participatory process.

5. In Bolivia, private hydrocarbon companies remained important even following nationalization in the 2000s, as discussed further in Chapter 2.

decentralizing reforms and the creation of a progressive Constitutional Court that has advocated for the individual and communal rights of the country's popular sectors. On the other hand, from the mid-twentieth century to the 2000s, an internal armed conflict that impacted hydrocarbon and mining zones threatened Colombian citizens' civil and human rights. The waning of the civil war facilitated environmental and social organizing. Mobilized communities often used the judiciary, with the Constitutional Court proving an important ally.

Bolivia enables us to examine social mobilizing in extraction with the Left in power at the national level.[6] Highly organized Indigenous communities that initially aligned with the ruling party developed strong critiques of President Evo Morales's (2006–19) development policies, leading to the fracturing of the government's support base.[7] Communities frequently resorted to direct action to block physically, and in doing so postpone, hydrocarbon projects.

The country cases also differ in how Indigenous communities contributed to formal prior consultation norms. In all three countries, Indigenous mobilizing caused the government to institute prior consultation. However, only in Bolivia did Indigenous communities participate throughout the development of the formal prior consultation procedures. In Peru, Indigenous communities initially took part in drafting prior consultation regulations but then, feeling unrepresented, gave up. The Colombian government regulated prior consultation swiftly, through a top-down process. This cross-national variation is useful, considering the finding that Indigenous involvement in the design of prior consultation institutions can result in more legitimate consultations (see the section "Existing Research" in this chapter).

The Conflicts

Each of the thirty conflicts in this book occurred before, during, and/or shortly after the approval process for new, large-scale extractive plans.[8] The study omits negative cases—that is, where conflict did not occur—because it seeks to explain not conflict itself but, rather, variation in the role of participatory

6. Peruvian president Ollanta Humala (2011–16) was elected on a leftist platform. However, because he governed on the right, this study does not treat his administration as left leaning, consistent with other comparative research on Peru (e.g., Eaton 2017).

7. For an in-depth analysis of another case in which splits emerged in the Left over extractivism, see Riofrancos 2020 on Ecuador.

8. In most cases, the author easily discerned whether a conflict evolved during that time frame. The Peruvian Tintaya/Antapaccay case required more extensive examination. The author ultimately excluded that conflict, because noteworthy organizing began well after the state approved the EIA for the Antapaccay expansion project. On this case, see Appendix A.

institutions in conflict.[9] The author selected conflicts from the periods in which (a) a country-sector had been liberalized, and (b) regulations structured the EIA hearing and/or prior consultation. Within those parameters, the author chose the most important conflicts over new extraction (see Table 1.2), informed by her review of secondary sources and her interviews during 2016–17 with experts on extractive conflict, in the three countries.[10]

The conflict sample consists of twenty-six cases that fit within the book's paradigm and four outliers. In three of the outlier cases, conflict unfolded before the state would have scheduled a prior consultation or an EIA hearing. In the fourth case, mobilizing took place within communities that resided outside of the project's area of influence but that did not challenge their outsider status or otherwise employ participatory institutions in their struggle.

State-led hearings were absent from the Bolivian EIA framework, and no major mining conflict emerged in Bolivia between the introduction of prior consultation in that sector in 2015, and the author's most recent field research in the country, in 2017. The case-selection process for Bolivia thus produced only hydrocarbon conflicts in which the relevant participatory institution was prior consultation.

Over the course of multiple research trips in 2012 and 2016–18, the author collected data on the thirty conflicts through interviews and through her review of secondary sources and primary sources—including laws, judicial decisions, executive measures, and news outlets.

Treatment of the Popular Consultation

A final note about case selection pertains to popular consultation. This institution does not enjoy widespread legitimacy in Latin American hydrocarbons or mining, in contrast to the EIA hearing and prior consultation. Activists and their local government allies have embraced popular consultation in extractives, based on their interpretations of subnational policymaking powers. That approach runs against a common assertion of extractive companies and national governments: that the central state alone controls subsoil resources (Walter and Urkidi 2017, especially 275).

Because of this controversy, this study defines the time periods for the conflict case selection using the date that the EIA hearing or prior consultation

9. In this way, the book resembles Ruth Berins Collier's medium-*n* study of democratic transitions, which identifies and explains the roles of working classes and elites, across transitions (Collier 1999).

10. For information on the study participants, see Appendix B.

Table 1.2 CONFLICT CASE SELECTION

Country	EIA hearings	Hydrocarbons				Mining			
		Liberalization	Prior consultation	Period	No. of Cases	Liberalization	Prior consultation	Period	No. of Cases
Peru	2002–	1991	2012–	2002–17	3	1991	2015–	2002–17	9
Colombia	2007–	2003	1998–	2003–16	7	2001	1998–	2001–16	5
Bolivia	n/a	1996	2007–	2007–17	6	1997	2015–	2015–17	0

was introduced and not based on when laws or regulations about popular consultations were implemented.

Nonetheless, in the book's sample, communities did use the municipal popular consultation strategically, and for a period in Colombia, the institution operated formally in hydrocarbons and mining and helped structure several conflicts that are analyzed in Chapter 4. Given the formal status of Colombian municipal popular consultations on extraction, it is noteworthy that the Colombian country-sector periods used for selecting cases—2003–16 in hydrocarbons and 2001–16 in mining (see Table 1.2)—include 2013, the year that Colombian municipalities began holding (formal) popular consultations in extractives. Alongside Colombia's formal consultations, communities organized informal popular consultations in several cases (the conflicts over Mandé Norte in Colombia, and Río Blanco, Tambo Grande, and Tía María in Peru). Those consultations are analyzed in the respective case studies.

PLAN OF THE BOOK

Chapter 2 examines in more detail the Bolivian, Colombian, and Peruvian national political contexts to help ground the book's analysis of the thirty conflicts. It focuses on government and regime changes, mining and hydrocarbon policies, and social conflict in extractives. Chapter 3 continues the country-level analysis by reviewing the development and implementation of the formal participatory institutions under study: prior consultation in the three countries, EIA hearings in Colombia and Peru, and the Colombian municipal popular consultation. The chapter also explores the contested nature of the boundaries that underlie those institutions—the lines defining local policy jurisdictions, impacted communities, and community representatives.

The empirical portion of the study treats each conflict pathway in turn, addressing the twenty-six cases that fit within the causal framework as well as the four outliers. Chapter 4 analyzes the Colombian conflicts in which communities confronted the event initiation challenge. In those cases, communities organized to request participatory processes and then condemned planned extraction through them. The chapter further reveals how the event initiation challenge was heightened by contested policy jurisdictions—especially disagreement about whether municipalities could determine the fate of subsoil resources, in cases involving popular consultation.

Chapter 5 investigates the plight of outsider communities. They denounced geographic borders that defined them as not impacted by planned development and thus ineligible to participate in approval processes. The chapter first treats cases in which outsiders left out of participatory processes subsequently decried that exclusion, using legal-administrative and/or technical arguments. It then examines how communities formed blockades and occupied project sites to hold up development and demand participation, at the participatory stage or immediately afterward.

Chapter 6 turns to the last set of conflicts, in which insider communities confronted the articulation challenge. It begins by analyzing how cohesive communities used participation as a procedural lever to hold up extraction, either by interrupting the participatory process or by refusing to take part in it. The chapter subsequently analyzes the strategies of insiders in fragmented settings. In two conflicts, activists participated in the EIA hearing to compete with other insiders. In one prior consultation case, the state consulted community members who accepted a mine project, after which excluded groups questioned the consultation's legitimacy.

Although the book sorts conflicts across and within Chapters 4–6 according to the principal ways that communities utilized participatory institutions, in many cases, groups employed multiple strategies. The case studies describe the additional uses of participatory institutions, which generally fit within the book's paradigm. For example, the overriding dynamic in the Block 116 oil conflict in Peru was one of impacted Indigenous communities denouncing the state for not consulting them about planned development (see Chapter 5). However, within that larger conflict—and as discussed in the Block 116 case study—the state invited communities that opposed the oil development to a hearing on the transfer of the oil block. Consistent with the pattern of active participation in public hearings by divided insiders, those communities engaged in the meeting to compete with pro-development groups.

Chapter 7 explores relationships in the conflict sample among several important themes in the literature on extractive conflict: community goals, cohesion, uses of participatory institutions, and previous experience with extraction. It then addresses the book's contributions to our understanding of how institutions can serve multiple purposes simultaneously. In a concluding section, the chapter situates the study within research on state building by highlighting how the introduction of participation in extraction has created new challenges for state builders who seek order and control in Latin America's hydrocarbon and mining regions.

PART II

National Political Dynamics

CHAPTER 2

Extraction and Conflict in Bolivia, Colombia, and Peru

During the 1990s–2010s, Bolivian, Colombian, and Peruvian governments encouraged private investment in hydrocarbons and mining, and the resulting growth in extractives brought social conflict. This chapter presents an overview of these phenomena. For each of the three countries, it analyzes policies that fostered development in mining and hydrocarbons, the significance of the sectors for the economy, and social mobilizing around extraction. The chapter highlights cross-national variation in political dynamics and in dominant forms of extractive conflict that facilitates this study's most different systems design.

PERU: LARGE-SCALE PROTEST IN THE WAKE OF AUTHORITARIANISM

Mobilizing over resource extraction in Peru escalated beginning in the 2000s, when the country was undergoing redemocratization. Much of that social conflict took the form of explosive protests that were met by government coercion and negotiation efforts.

Redemocratization

Peru transitioned to democracy in 1980, as part of Latin America's third wave of democracy. However, that democracy soon fell. President Alberto Fujimori

The Politics of Extraction. Maiah Jaskoski, Oxford University Press. © Oxford University Press 2022.
DOI: 10.1093/oso/9780197568927.003.0002

(1990–2000), who came to office through democratic elections, staged a "self-coup" in April 1992 to push through liberal economic reforms and hard-line security policies against two leftist insurgencies, Shining Path (Sendero Luminoso) and the Tupac Amaru Revolutionary Movement (Movimiento Revolucionario Túpac Amaru, MRTA; Jaskoski 2013, 26, 52–54). Fujimori was reelected in 1995 in accordance with a new constitution, but his government continued nondemocratic practices that spanned electoral manipulation, coercion of the political opposition, and a legally questionable extension of term limits (McClintock 2006).[1] Fujimori resigned amid scandal in November 2000 while in exile in Japan. His departure from office marked the start of redemocratization, which included decentralizing reforms in the early 2000s (McNulty 2011).

Extraction-Reliant Economy

Historically, the Peruvian economy has depended appreciably on hydrocarbons and mining. The sectors increased in prominence starting in the 1990s, when the government promoted private investment, reversing a trajectory of state-led development in extractives.[2]

Fujimori privatized mining and hydrocarbons as part of his government's neoliberal policies (Bury and Norris 2013, 99–100). Perhaps most salient was the 1991 Legislative Decree 757, which removed state privilege in the two sectors (Barrera-Hernández 2009, 159; Orihuela 2014a, 255; 2014b, 163). The Peruvian government continued taking a liberal approach in extractives after Fujimori resigned. For instance, in the first two years of his (second) presidency, President Alan García (2006–11) issued ninety-nine decrees that encouraged mining and hydrocarbon development. Among other things, the decrees reduced environmental standards in protected areas and undermined communal property rights (Bebbington 2009, 12; Stetson 2012, 78; see also analysis of the "Baguazo" conflict in Chapter 3). A 2013–15 series of laws and regulations known as the "environmental packages" (*paquetazos ambientales*) streamlined bureaucratic processes and weakened oversight in environmental matters, to attract investment (Defensoría del Pueblo, Adjuntía del Medio Ambiente, Servicios Públicos y Pueblos Indígenas 2016, 29; Gamboa Balbín

1. See also Levitsky and Way 2010, 163–70, on nondemocratic tendencies of Peru's regime during 1992–2000.

2. On the importance of hydrocarbons and mining in Peru and their expansion during the military government of Juan Velasco Alvarado (1968–75), see Guasti 1983, 187–92; and Stallings 1983, 158–59, 164–65, 174.

2017, 9). The specific norms in question were Laws 30327 and 30230 and two decrees: Supreme Decree (Decreto Supremo, DS) 054-2013-PCM and DS 060-2013-RCM.[3]

Backed by policies that favored development, economic activity in mining and hydrocarbons expanded from the 1990s to the 2010s. Investment in mining exploration increased by 2,000 percent between 1990 and 1997 (A. Bebbington 2010, 100). Total annual investment in mining surged from $1.09 billion in 2005 to $9.7 billion in 2013 (CooperAcción 2018c, 5), and the number of new annual mining claims leapt from under one thousand in 2002 to nearly eight thousand in 2007 (Bebbington et al. 2010, 309). Mineral production grew most years during 2003–17, the exceptions being 2009–11 and 2014 (Banco Central de Reserva del Perú 2012, 32; 2017, 22).

In hydrocarbons, the proportion of Peru's Amazon covered by oil and gas concessions shot up from approximately 13 percent in 2004 to 70 percent in 2007. Private investment in the sector totaled $797 million in 2009 (Stetson 2012, 78). Notably, in 2015 hydrocarbons experienced their biggest contraction in decades, with production down 11.5 percent from the previous year due to low international crude oil prices (Banco Central de Reserva del Perú 2015, 25). Production dropped again in 2016 and 2017, by 5.1 percent and 2.4 percent, respectively (Banco Central de Reserva del Perú 2017, 22).

The allocation of state revenue from extraction favored producing subnational entities. According to Peru's *canon* system, subnational governments of producing regions, provinces, and districts received 50 percent of profit taxes from mining and gas companies and 50 percent of royalties paid by gas companies (Munilla 2010, 32; Arellano Yanguas and Mejía Acosta 2014, 24–25).[4]

3. For a description of the four norms, see Red Muqui and GRUFIDES 2015, 3, 23–25. The term paquetazos ambientales by and large has been used in reference to Laws 30327 and 30230, and DS 054-2013-PCM and DS 060-2013-RCM. However, during 2013–15, other norms also reduced environmental standards for new investment. Red Muqui and GRUFIDES 2015; Defensoría del Pueblo, Adjuntía del Medio Ambiente, Servicios Públicos y Pueblos Indígenas 2016, 29; and Interview with César Gamboa Balbín, Executive Director, Derecho, Ambiente y Recursos Naturales; by Skype, Lima, July 30, 2018 (Interview P1).

4. The levels of subnational government in Peru, from highest to lowest, are the region, the province, and the district. The canon system for mining was instituted in 1992. In 2001, it was extended to include the gas sector, and the proportion of taxes allocated to subnational governments increased from 20 percent to 50 percent (Arellano Yanguas and Mejía Acosta 2014, 24–25).

Socioenvironmental Conflict: Massive Protest and Centralized Government Reactions

Communities located in extractive areas of Peru mobilized over mining and hydrocarbon development, often in the form of protests. That activism was made possible by democratization at the national level. Subnational electoral politics also proved important: political parties were too weakly institutionalized at the regional level to contain voter demands in the electoral system, driving people to the streets to express their policy preferences (Arce 2014, 45–64).

The overall level of protest activity in Peru became so alarming that the Defensoría del Pueblo began tracking and publicizing data on conflicts in the country in monthly reports, as part of its duty to monitor situations that could threaten human rights and social peace. It then created a special unit to follow civil unrest and, in 2009, a permanent office for that function. The Defensoría also engaged in conflict mediation; in 2013, it participated in one-half of the government's national roundtables (*mesas de diálogo*) for resolving conflicts (Paredes and de la Puente 2017, 135–37).

According to the Defensoría del Pueblo's records of conflict during 2006–11, the number of monthly active conflicts rose from 73 in January 2006 to peak at 286 in September 2009, and then followed a trend of decline, to 215 conflicts in September 2011. Protest and violence were pervasive. Each month from January 2009 through September 2011, the number of active conflicts ranged from 197 to 286, and between 98 and 129 conflicts involved at least one act of violence (Defensoría del Pueblo, Adjuntía para la Prevención de Conflictos Sociales y la Gobernabilidad 2012, 37, 40, 41). From 2006 to the end of October 2016, violence in social conflict caused 270 deaths and injured 4,614 people. Based on death tolls during those years, the most violent year was 2009, when fifty-two people died as a consequence of social conflict (De Echave C. 2018, 535).[5]

Socioenvironmental mobilizing was notable. Activists protested about the environmental impacts of hydrocarbons and mining on community livelihoods and local economies, and to obtain more funds from extraction for their communities and subnational governments (De Echave et al. 2009; Arellano Yanguas 2011; Ponce and McClintock 2014). As of late 2011, natural resource issues accounted for 41.7 percent of all conflicts—the largest category.[6] The number of socioenvironmental conflicts fell in 2010, increased again in 2011 and 2012—when it surpassed the 2009 level—and then declined slightly in

5. The particularly violent Baguazo, a conflict analyzed in Chapter 3, occurred in 2009.
6. Local government issues were second, at 17 percent (Defensoría del Pueblo, Adjuntía para la Prevención de Conflictos Sociales y la Gobernabilidad 2012, 38).

2013, 2014, and 2015 (Dargent et al. 2017, 8). These struggles constituted a sizable percentage of total conflicts throughout the 2010s, comprising 88 percent of the 211 conflicts monitored by the Defensoría in March 2015 (*Servindi* 4/10/2015) and 65 percent of the 198 social conflicts that the office followed in May 2018 (CooperAcción 2018b, 2).

The Peruvian government responded to protest through centralized, reactive methods that included repression. The García administration notoriously used rhetoric that sought to criminalize activists, and employed police force (Flórez Unzaga 2016, 17).

Added to coercion, the national government also led negotiations. At first, it addressed protest by convening ad hoc roundtables between local populations and senior executive representatives, often ministers. In part, roundtables responded to community calls for dialogue with the government. Communities wanted "to assure a more serious compromise would be reached," relative to outcomes produced through the typical practice at the time: negotiations between communities and extractive firms (Paredes and de la Puente 2017, 128).

The government attempted to institutionalize conflict management, mainly under the Presidency of the Council of Ministers (Presidencia del Consejo de Ministros, PCM), through a series of offices dedicated to social conflict. The first three units, pursued by the Alejandro Toledo (2001–6) and García administrations, had weak capacity and failed—the Unit of Strategic Analysis and Conflict Prevention (Unidad de Análisis Estratégico y Prevención de Conflictos, UAEPCS), the Unit of Conflict Analysis (Unidad de Análisis de Conflictos, UAC), and the Coordination Secretariat (Secretaría de Coordinación; Flórez Unzaga 2016, 16–17; Paredes and de la Fuentes 2017, 138).

President Ollanta Humala's (2011–16) government achieved greater institutionalization with the National Office of Dialogue and Sustainability (Oficina Nacional de Diálogo y Sostenibilidad, ONDS), created in 2012 from the previous Office of Social Conflict Management (Oficina de Gestión de Conflictos Sociales, OGCS; Flórez Unzaga 2016, 16–17). "Looking to be an official mediator between the state and communities," ONDS participated in roundtables—a total of fifty by the end of 2013—and collected data on conflicts (Paredes and de la Fuentes 2017, 139). In 2017, the new Secretariat of Social Management and Dialogue (Secretaría de Gestión Social y Diálogo) replaced ONDS (Montoya 2018). Within the secretariat, the Undersecretariat of Dialogue and Sustainability (Subsecretaría de Diálogo y Sostenibilidad) was participating in 196 dialogues as of mid-2017.[7]

7. Interview with an official in the Undersecretariat of Dialogue and Sustainability, Secretariat of Social Management and Dialogue, Presidency of the Council of Ministers; Lima, May 8, 2017 (Interview P2).

COLOMBIA: CIVIL WAR, THE RENTIER STATE, AND ACTIVISM THROUGH THE COURTS

Similar to the Peruvian case, extractives contributed substantially to Colombia's economy and expanded in the 2000s and 2010s, as successive administrations implemented policies friendly to private investors. Also as in Peru, communities in Colombian hydrocarbon and mining regions mobilized around new development due to its threats to the environment and to livelihoods, even as the state directed extractive revenue to producing regions. However, whereas Peru was a case of redemocratization, Colombia experienced a civil war in which hydrocarbon and mining regions served as strongholds or battle zones for violent nonstate groups that benefited financially from extraction.

Concurrent with the civil war, Colombia enjoyed stable formal democracy that had deepened in the 1980s–1990s, with the end of a pacted democracy, the implementation of decentralizing reforms, and the creation of an independent, progressive Constitutional Court. In this context, extractive conflict—which became more common when civil-war violence subsided—often played out in the judiciary, in contrast to the large protests characteristic of Peru.

Armed Conflict Linked to Extraction

Colombia's civil war can be traced to 1958, the start of the "National Front," a period during which the Liberal and Conservative parties shared power (e.g., see Bejarano and Pizarro 2005). In the 1960s, leftist actors that were frustrated by the exclusionary democracy took up arms to pursue their political goals through warfare. Most notable were the Maoist Popular Liberation Army (Ejército Popular de Liberación, EPL); and the Marxist Revolutionary Armed Forces of Colombia (Fuerzas Armadas Revolucionarias de Colombia, FARC) and National Liberation Army (Ejército de Liberación Nacional, ELN). Alleged fraud in the country's 1970 elections fed radicalization, and the April 19 Movement (Movimiento 19 de Abril, M-19) insurgency formed. Self-defense paramilitaries organized in response to the armed Left—some organically and others by the Colombian military or large landowners. Paramilitaries grew in numbers and in power in the 1990s as hired security for vast stretches of land owned by drug traffickers. In 1997, paramilitary groups came together under the national organization United Self-Defense Forces of Colombia (Autodefensas Unidas de Colombia, AUC; Chernick 2003, 198; Bejarano and Pizarro 2005, 244, 251–54).

Policymakers hoped that the enhancement of political inclusion would help resolve the armed conflict. The National Front concluded formally in 1974 when restrictions on competition in legislative and presidential elections were lifted. In 1986, power sharing in the executive branch ended (Bejarano and Pizarro 2005, 239–40 n. 9). The 1991 constituent assembly produced a new constitution, a main goal of which was to encourage democratic participation and thereby reduce violence. The charter contributed to an ongoing trajectory of decentralization that had begun in the 1980s (Bejarano and Pizarro 2005, 245; Eaton 2006, 541–43; Nunes 2010, 73).

Despite this political opening, the civil war continued, and Colombia's weak state could not guarantee basic protections of civil liberties. Drug traffickers corrupted, threatened, and assassinated judges at an alarming rate, and voters regularly confronted coercion (Bejarano and Pizarro 2005, 242, 250–51, 255–56). Between 1994 and 1998, there were 7,022 kidnappings, and on average twenty-six thousand homicides per year. One hundred thirty-eight mayors, 569 other elected politicians at the national and subnational levels, and 174 other public officials were assassinated between 1989 and 1999 (Bejarano and Pizarro 2005, 241, 242). More than six million people in Colombia were displaced from the late 1980s to the end of 2014 (Quiroga Ángel 2018, 231).

The armed conflict waned in the late 2000s, due to the Álvaro Uribe Vélez (2002–10) government's aggressive counterinsurgency policy and public education and health programs. The country's number of homicides per one hundred thousand residents dropped from eighty in 1991 to thirty-two in 2012 (Rettberg et al. 2018b, 16). The AUC demobilized in 2005, although that process was followed by the emergence of criminal successor groups (*bandas criminals*, or *bacrim*), often made up of former paramilitaries who continued using previous tactics and who worked within inherited paramilitary structures (Human Rights Watch 2010).[8] Another critical benchmark was the 2016 signing of a peace agreement between the Colombian government and the FARC, the country's most powerful insurgency.

Extractive industries helped sustain the civil war, principally through a rentier-state logic: money from hydrocarbons and mining contributed to a cycle of, on one hand, state weakening, and on the other, the enrichment of private international extractive firms. Companies financed public and private security forces and paid off illicit armed groups on different sides of the conflict, for security provision—frequently through extortionary relationships.

8. As of the late 2010s, bacrim were operating in 149 municipalities, in twenty-two departments (Rettberg et al., 2018b, 17).

For its part, the Colombian state lowered tax rates on companies to attract their business in the otherwise unfriendly investment climate of civil war (Richani 2005).

Examples of connections between extraction and armed conflict abound. Illegal armed groups extorted from firms in the coal and gold sectors (Quiroga Ángel 2018, 213; Rettberg et al. 2018a, 356). The ELN grew starting in the 1980s due to its ties to oil, particularly in the department of Arauca; by sabotaging infrastructure, the insurgency established a lucrative system according to which it refrained from staging attacks in exchange for company payments. The FARC, paramilitaries, and bacrim also engaged in extortion in hydrocarbons (Rettberg and Prieto 2018, 169–71). Added to their participation in extortionary arrangements, companies hired private security firms and subsidized the national military, which assigned units to oil security. Public security personnel performed operations to protect extractive development and also served as a contact point between companies and paramilitaries, which themselves provided security to the firms (e.g., Quiroga Ángel 2018, 227–30; Rettberg and Prieto 2018, 171–74).

Finally, illegal armed groups' relationship to extraction extended to financing gold operations (Massé 2016); tapping pipelines to steal and then sell refined hydrocarbon products (Rettberg and Prieto 2018, 164–65); and capturing royalties that had been distributed subnationally (Eaton 2006; Rettberg and Prieto 2018, 174–79).[9]

Extraction-Reliant Economy

Mining and hydrocarbons have a long history in Colombia. Colombian oil extraction dates to 1921, when the US Tropical Oil Company began operating in the country. In 1951, the state oil company (Empresa Colombiana de Petróleos, Ecopetrol) took control of extraction and, a decade later, the Tropical Oil refinery (Rettberg and Prieto 2018, 147). As a proportion of national exports, oil and its derivatives grew from approximately 8 percent in the early 1970s, to 13 percent in the 1980s, to 30 percent in the 1990s (Pérez-Rincón 2014, 7). Mining, too, was significant by the late twentieth century, with the large-scale production of nickel and coal starting in the 1970s and 1980s, respectively (Caballero Argáez and Bitar 2016, 121).

9. After the 2011 adoption of a royalty distribution structure that no longer favored producing departments—a change discussed in this section, under "Extraction-Reliant Economy"—there were no further reports of illegal armed groups obtaining royalties in this way (Rettberg and Prieto 2018, 180).

Colombia's government welcomed investment in extraction in the 2000s and 2010s. President Uribe's Plan Visión Colombia 2019 sought, by 2019, to boost coal exports to 100 million tons per year (up from 50.9 million tons) and to expand gold production by nearly seven times. In hydrocarbons, the plan aimed to enlarge the natural gas sector and increase new oil reserves by 3.5 billion barrels, to add to the existing 1.473 billion (Departamento Nacional de Planeación, Colombia 2005, 17–18, 188–90; see also Roa Avendaño and Navas 2014, 28). President Juan Manuel Santos's (2010–18) Plan Nacional de Desarrollo 2010–14 development plan identified mining and energy as one of five "locomotives" (*locomotoras*) that would drive Colombian development (Roa Avendaño and Navas 2014, 28–29). It also introduced the concept of strategic mining reserves—geographic areas where mining would be prioritized (Law 1450, Article 108; Urrea and Rodríguez Maldonado 2014, 98). Santos's Plan Nacional de Desarrollo 2014–18 retained this concept (Law 1753, Article 20).

In following with the government's extractivist orientation, targeted measures opened hydrocarbons and mining to private investment. A 2003 reform removed the requirement that private hydrocarbon companies work in partnership with the state, by making Ecopetrol a competing firm (Rettberg and Prieto 2018, 152). The liberalization of mining took place through the 2001 mining code, which simplified the titling process, thereby encouraging exploration (Toro Pérez 2012, 23; Rettberg et al. 2018a, 348). The 2010 Law 1382 further encouraged private investment in mining, granting more time for exploration and reducing payments to the state during that stage (Toro Pérez 2012, 23–24).[10]

In a controversial move, the state authorized mining in Colombia's *páramos*, a type of wetlands found at high altitudes. Colombia was home to thirty-four páramos—nearly one-half of all páramos in Latin America—which provided 70 percent of the water consumed by Colombians (Flórez Flórez 2012, 466). Formally, the state had in place unambiguous safeguards for páramos. The country's 1993 environmental law (Law 99, discussed in Chapter 3) established protections for the wetlands. Law 1382 and the Plan Nacional de Desarrollo 2010–14 declared páramos off limits to extractive activities (Buitrago 2016, 143–45).

Despite those norms, as of 2012 the Colombian state had issued 391 titles for coal, gold, and silver mining in concessions that overlapped with twenty-two páramos (Flórez Flórez 2012, 466). The overlap generated a complex,

10. In 2010, the same year that Law 1382 was passed, the Constitutional Court declared the law unconstitutional for not having undergone a prior consultation process, but that decision took two years to come into force (Toro Pérez 2012, 23–24; Buitrago 2016, 145).

drawn-out process of delineating páramo boundaries (Buitrago 2016, 149–55). A 2016 Constitutional Court decision blocked mining in Colombian páramos, effectively negating 473 granted concessions and potentially impacting more than three hundred mining operations, in twenty-five páramos (Guidi 3/15/2016).

With government support, mining and hydrocarbons expanded. From 1994 to 2012, mining, oil, agriculture, energy, gas, and water went from representing 14 to 55 percent of foreign direct investment, which rose from US$1.4 billion to US$15.6 billion during that same period (Pérez-Rincón 2014, 9–10). Daily oil production climbed from 578,000 barrels in 2002 to more than 1 million in 2013 (Caballero Argáez and Bitar 2016, 128). As of 2018, twenty of the country's thirty-two departments had producing oil fields (Rettberg and Prieto 2018, 148). Whereas 20 new wells were drilled annually in the early 2000s, 124 wells were drilled in 2012, and 159 in 2013 (Roa Avendaño and Navas 2014, 31). Notably, a plunge in oil prices that began in 2014 caused a diminution in hydrocarbon exploration (Rettberg and Prieto 2018, 151).

In mining, coal production surged from 3.9 million metric tons in 1980 to 88.5 in 2014. During 2001–14, coal was second only to hydrocarbons in the export sector, measured as a percentage of gross domestic product (GDP; Quiroga Ángel 2018, 201–3). International investment in mining increased overall during 1996–2013, with peaks in 2005, 2009, and 2013. Between 2000 and 2010, on average, mining made up 25.7 percent of all annual international investment in Colombia. Gold stood out. Between 1990 and 1999, the state issued an average of 160 mining titles per year, 19 (12 percent) of which were for gold exploration. The average annual titles issued between 2000 and 2009 was 633, 136 (22 percent) of which were for gold. Low international prices impacted Colombian mining in the 2010s: foreign investment in the sector fell abruptly in 2014 (Rettberg et al. 2018a, 349–50).

A large proportion of Colombian royalties from extraction was channeled to subnational governments in producing areas of the country. Until 2011, the state allocated more than 80 percent of royalties in mining and hydrocarbons to producing departments and municipalities, and to the municipalities that had ports used for the transport of the resources. Under that system, three departments (Arauca, Casanare, and Meta) in which 3.5 percent of the population resided, received 46.8 percent of royalties (López-Murcia 2017, 77–78, 168). A 2011 constitutional reform distributed royalties more evenly across producing and nonproducing regions and centralized investment decisions about the funds (López-Murcia 2017, especially 168–78).

Socioenvironmental Conflict: Legal Activism

Given the reliance of both the state and illegal armed groups on hydrocarbons and mining, environmental activism was risky in Colombia during the civil war. The abatement of violence allowed for a rise in organizing in extractives (Henao and González Espinosa 2016; Ulloa and Coronado 2016). Consistent with that trend, most of the Colombian conflicts analyzed in this book took place after the civil war had calmed. Experts interviewed for this research attributed this clustering precisely to the fact that violence connected to the armed conflict had deterred social mobilizing until the late 2000s.

This assessment by study participants is reinforced by quantitative data on social conflict managed by the Colombian research institute Centro de Investigación y Educación Popular Programa por la Paz (CINEP/PPP). CINEP/PPP data on all collective action events in public spaces—for example, marches, strikes, protests, occupations, and roadblocks—show a rise in conflict related to the extraction of oil, coal, and gold in 2006 and 2007, a decline in 2008, and then a steep three-year increase (CINEP/PPP 2012, 4, 10).[11] Much of the 2009–11 organizing over extraction was by rural communities (CINEP/PPP 2012, 10–11).

A study by Mario Alejandro Pérez-Rincón of seventy-two major environmental conflicts over development in Colombia from the 1950s through 2011 also observes a swell in social conflict beginning in the late 2000s. All but three of the conflicts occurred during or after the 1980s. The 2000s exhibited an upward trend, from two conflicts in 2001 to peaks in 2003–4 (four conflicts each year), 2006 (seven conflicts), and 2008–9 (ten conflicts each year; Pérez-Rincón 2014, 20–21, 34). The most conflict-ridden sectors in the sample were mining (thirty conflicts—twenty-three over gold) and fossil fuels (fourteen conflicts—eleven over coal and three over oil; Pérez-Rincón 2014, 35–37).

Conflicts in Pérez-Rincón's study tended to take place in rural areas and involve campesinos (peasants) or Indigenous populations; each of the two groups was the primary population impacted in eighteen of the seventy-two conflicts. Those thirty-six cases were concentrated in mining (fourteen conflicts) and fossil fuels (ten conflicts; Pérez-Rincón 2014, 44–46). In the conflict sample, and in the subsample of mining and fossil-fuel conflicts, the main natural resource impacted by development was water, and the main ecosystem, rivers (Pérez-Rincón 2014, 41–43).

Peaceful tactics were common in the seventy-two conflicts. Organized groups took a total of 266 actions, 80 percent of which consisted of court filings, media activism, NGO advocacy, written requests, and the

11. Of the total collective action events, 274, or 3.7 percent, were in extractives (CINEP/PPP 2012, 10).

presentation of alternative proposals (Pérez-Rincón 2014, 49). Activists used legal instruments in mining and fossil fuels more than in the other sectors. For instance, they relied on environmental legal structures, ILO 169, and Law 70, which protected rights of Afro-Colombian communities (Pérez-Rincón 2014, 53–54). More generally, mining and hydrocarbons were contentious: mining experienced the most protest events (thirteen), followed by fossil fuels and energy generation (eight protests in each sector; Pérez-Rincón 2014, 49).

BOLIVIA: DIRECT ACTION BY OCCASIONAL ALLIES OF A LEFTIST GOVERNMENT

Bolivia resembled Colombia and Peru in that its government supported extractive industries, which saw social conflict. However, Bolivia differs in that the Left was in power—specifically, a leftist government with ties to Indigenous peoples impacted by hydrocarbon development. As shown in this section and throughout the book, Indigenous communities in Bolivia's eastern lowlands, where hydrocarbons were concentrated, participated in a collapsed alliance with leftist president Evo Morales's (2006–19) party, the Movement for Socialism (Movimiento al Socialismo, MAS). The tensions between the party and lowland groups were brought on by the Morales administration's pursuit of development, even to the detriment of Indigenous peoples (Schilling-Vacaflor 2017a). Indigenous communities protested hydrocarbon projects through marches, blockades, and other extrainstitutional acts.

The Left in Power

The MAS's connection to lowland Indigenous groups can be traced to its ascent to the national political scene.

As of the 1990s, Bolivia's traditional political parties suffered from "weak, almost nonexistent linkages with civil society" (Mayorga 2005, 159). Popular sectors resented that many Bolivians had not benefited from the country's neoliberal economic reforms, introduced in the 1980s. Furthermore, parties had not created new means of reaching constituents after neoliberalism had weakened previous structures, to include unions (Mayorga 2005, 158–59, 167–68; Madrid 2011, 242–44). President Gonzalo Sánchez de Lozada's (1993–97) government implemented the 1994 decentralizing Law of Popular Participation (Ley de Participación Popular, LPP) in an effort to strengthen societal ties to and support for his party, the long-standing Nationalist Revolutionary Movement (Movimiento Nacionalista Revolucionario, MNR). Instead, the LPP benefited grassroots parties and movements, which performed well in local elections. Support for the MAS enabled the party to scale up, gaining impressive representation in the legislature in 2002 (Mayorga 2005, 156, 158–59, 168–70; Madrid 2011, 244).

The MAS's rise also was aided by the party's strategy of appealing to many groups in society. The party's original base consisted of the powerful coca growers' (*cocaleros*) unions in the highlands and the Unified Syndical Confederation of Rural Workers of Bolivia (Confederación Sindical Única de Trabajadores Campesinos de Bolivia, CSUTCB)—the main highland peasant union organization, which the cocaleros controlled by the early 1990s. In the 2000s, the MAS diversified its membership by incorporating urban mestizo groups (Madrid 2008, 487–89; 2011, 241).

Morales's national victory occurred following the 2003 and 2005 "gas wars." These protests were rooted in frustrations over the distribution of gas wealth, and nationalist sentiment surrounding hydrocarbons. The sector had undergone multiple shifts in its public-private balance since serious exploration began in the 1920s, by Standard Oil (Perreault and Valdivia 2010, 694–96), and had been liberalized most recently in 1996. Through that capitalization scheme, the government sold off 50 percent of the state oil company (Yacimientos Petrolíferos Fiscales Bolivianos, YPFB) to multinational corporations and set transnational royalties for new discovery sites at the low level of 18 percent (Hindery 2004, especially 281, 288, 292; Kaup 2010, 127).

Further moves toward augmenting the role of foreign firms in hydrocarbons proved too much for many Bolivians. The October 2003 gas war was an expression of outrage over the government's plan to allow a transnational consortium to move gas from landlocked Bolivia through Chile—a longtime rival—for export to Mexico and the United States. Labor unions, neighborhood associations, campesino groups, and students took to the streets, primarily in the city of El Alto (near La Paz). They protested the export plan and then, as the conflict escalated, all gas exportation. They also insisted on more state participation in the gas sector; the industrialization of gas for domestic use; and the resignation of President Sánchez de Lozada, then in his second presidency. More than seventy people were killed in four days of violent protests quelled by the police and armed forces. Protest continued, and on October 16, 2003, two hundred thousand people mobilized in La Paz's San Francisco Plaza to demand that Sánchez de Lozada resign. He did so the following day (Postero 2007, 206–10; Perreault 2008, 14–15).

Sánchez de Lozada's replacement, Vice President Carlos Mesa, tried to resolve the gas question but instead ignited a second gas war. Mesa held a national referendum in July 2004 on a new hydrocarbon law. The referendum questions addressed plans for the production of gas for export and the internal market, the renegotiation of gas contracts with transnational companies, and an increase in royalty rates for future concessions. Mesa's project passed the referendum, but many groups thought it did not go far enough in either industrializing or strengthening state control of gas. Mesa resigned in March 2005, during strikes and blockades across the country. The legislature denied his resignation. He stepped down, in June 2005, during more national strikes (Postero 2007, 213–14).

Following the gas wars, Morales was elected president with Indigenous support. The "Unity Pact" had formed in 2004, bringing together the MAS's highland base and the country's two largest Indigenous organizations: the national organization that represented lowland communities, the Confederation of Bolivian Indigenous Peoples (Confederación de Pueblos Indígenas de Bolivia, CIDOB); and the highland National Council of Ayllus and Markas of Qullasuyu (Consejo Nacional de Ayllus y Markas del Qullasuyu, CONAMAQ; Anria 2018, 93). Once in power, the Morales government nationalized hydrocarbons with the May 1, 2006, "Heroes of the Chaco" decree, DS 28701 (Perreault 2008, 16–17).

Consolidated Indigenous support for the MAS did not last, as the government prioritized development over Indigenous rights. In 2011, CIDOB and CONAMAQ broke from the Unity Pact over the government's plan to construct a highway through a national park that overlapped with Indigenous lands, the Isiboro Sécure Indigenous Territory and National Park (Territorio Indígena y Parque Nacional Isiboro Sécure, TIPNIS; McNeish 2013, 225).[12] Shortly thereafter, CIDOB and CONAMAQ suffered divisions. Parallel organizations formed in each case, with factions taking opposing positions vis-à-vis the Morales administration. The government backed the parallel CONAMAQ and participated in the creation of the parallel CIDOB (Tockman and Cameron 2014, 65 n. 12; Achtenberg 2/2/2014; Alberti 2019, 54–56). Morales reinstated the Unity Pact in 2013, with the sympathetic CONAMAQ and CIDOB factions (Alberti 2019, 55).

Extraction-Reliant Economy

Leading up to the period of focus in this research, the 1996 capitalization of hydrocarbons encouraged investment in that critical sector. Proven and probable gas reserves increased from 5.69 trillion cubic feet in 1997 to 54.86 trillion cubic feet as of 2003. Whereas oil reserves totaled 200.9 million barrels in 1997, in 2003 they amounted to 956.9 million barrels (Kaup 2010, 128). Hydrocarbons continued to be productive in the late 2000s, after nationalization. Annual gas production in 2009 was nearly twice that of 2001 (Schilling-Vacaflor 2013a, 207), and between 2006 and 2010, annual gas revenue rose

12. On the TIPNIS conflict, see Chapter 3.

from $2.9 billion to $10.6 billion. In 2008, gas contributed to 52 percent of government revenue and more than 16 percent of GDP (Radhuber 2012, 173).

Growth in hydrocarbons after nationalization took place with the participation of private companies:

> What the Morales administration nationalized was the natural gas itself. Whereas previously investing firms had been able to claim the natural gas they extracted once it left the ground, the legal changes gave the state control of the natural gas until it reached its point of sale. In this context, extraction and transport firms, including YPFB, performed a service for the state and received a certain percentage of the sale price for this service. (Kaup 2010, 130)

Petrobras, of Brazil, and the Spanish firm Repsol YPF—which together controlled more than 70 percent of Bolivia's hydrocarbon production—reluctantly accepted the terms established with nationalization, by signing new contracts (Perreault 2008, 18).

Nationalization meant greater wealth for the state, due to renegotiated prices for gas exported to Argentina and Brazil and hikes in taxes and royalties (Perreault 2008, 17–18; Kaup 2010, 129–30). Much of the state's gas revenue went to hydrocarbon departments; the eastern lowland department of Tarija, which produced more than 60 percent of the country's natural gas, received 30 percent of Bolivia's total royalties and revenue from the direct tax on hydrocarbons (Bebbington and Bebbington 2010, 147).[13]

The Morales administration energetically supported the gas sector. For example, the government authorized exploration in national parks, subject to the approval of the National Service for Protected Areas (Servicio Nacional de Áreas Protegidas, SERNAP). With an October 2010 decree, DS 0676, Morales permitted hydrocarbon development in vast stretches of protected lands. A May 2015 decree, DS 2366, opened additional protected areas to exploration. As of early 2018, fourteen YPFB blocks overlapped with seven of the country's twenty-two national protected areas. The government issued the 2015 decree at a time when Bolivia's gas reserves were being depleted; since nationalization, the results of exploration had been disappointing, and there had been intensive extraction from the country's three "megafields" (*megacampos*)—Margarita, San Alberto, and San Antonio—and a drop in San Antonio's production.[14]

13. On the distribution of hydrocarbon wealth in Bolivia, see also Arellano Yanguas and Mejía Acosta 2014, 11–12, 21–23.

14. Powęska 2017, 451; *Revista jubileo* 2017, 11–13; López Camacho 4/22/2018; and Interview with Raúl Velásquez Guzmán, Fundación Jubileo; La Paz, June 14, 2017 (Interview B1).

Although this study's case-selection parameters produced a sample of Bolivian conflicts solely in hydrocarbons (see Chapter 1), it is noteworthy that mining also was vital to Bolivia's economy and, as in hydrocarbons, the state's role in mining varied across time. With a crash in global tin prices in the 1980s and neoliberal restructuring, the state-owned Bolivian Mining Corporation (Corporación Minera de Bolivia, COMIBOL) was dismantled (Marston and Perreault 2017, 260). The government encouraged private investment in mining with a 1997 mining code (Arsel et al. 2014, 117). The Morales administration subsequently forced contract renegotiations to capture more revenue for the state (Amengual 2018, 35). However, the government did not nationalize mining. As much of the sector was controlled by the politically influential mining cooperatives—which had inherited former COMIBOL mine sites and equipment—the May 2014 mining code strengthened cooperatives, as well as private firms (Marston and Perreault 2017; see also Gandarillas G. 2014).

Mining boomed beginning in the second half of the 2000s. Production in Bolivian medium-scale mining (comprising the country's largest mining operations, to include open-pit mines) increased from 112,000 fine metric tons in 2006 to 364,000, in 2009. That growth was due mainly to the operations of private international firms, which dominated medium-scale mining. Annual mineral and metal exports jumped from under $500 million in the 1990s and the early 2000s, to $1.073 billion in 2006, to $2.405 billion in 2010 (Díaz Cuellar 2011, 22–24).

Socioenvironmental Conflict: Direct Action

With gas development ongoing and Morales's Indigenous alliances strained, lowland Indigenous communities protested about the environmental impacts of hydrocarbons and to press for compensation. In particular, they frequently created blockades to hold up projects. Bolivia lacked institutions that might have advocated on behalf of communities in hydrocarbon conflicts (Schilling-Vacaflor 2017b, 1062). More generally in Bolivia, the ongoing weakness of state institutions that otherwise could have managed public demands led societal groups to use mobilizations or threats thereof to secure policy change under Morales (Anria 2016, especially 99, 104).

Examining the years 2000–2011, Mähler and Pierskalla (2015) find that the annual number of Bolivian social conflict events—defined as violent or nonviolent collective activity outside of formal governmental institutions—rose starting in 2006. That year the number of conflict events surpassed 450, up from fewer than 125 in 2005. Conflict peaked at more than 700 events in 2007 and then fell slightly in 2008 and then dramatically in 2009, to approximately 300 events. Conflict increased again in 2010 and in 2011, when the number of events exceeded 400 (Mähler and Pierskalla 2015, 312, 313).

In hydrocarbons, Indigenous groups were prone to organize. Social conflict in gas-rich provinces (below the department level) during 2000–2011 was positively related to the size of the Indigenous population. The relationship loses statistical significance if only the Bolivian Guaraní nation, of the eastern lowlands, are considered, a finding that can be explained by the Guaraní's small size relative to other Bolivian Indigenous groups (Mähler and Pierskalla 2015, especially 320–23). Further discussion of the Guaraní is in order, given that they were heavily impacted by gas development, the most organized and autonomous Indigenous group in the eastern lowlands, and the nation involved in the six Bolivian cases in this book.

Indigenous mobilizing in Bolivia's lowlands began in the 1980s, especially around territorial rights. The 1990 March for Territory and Dignity (Marcha por el Territorio y la Dignidad), led by the Beni Indigenous People's Council (Central de Pueblos Indígenas del Beni, CPIB), of CIDOB, was a landmark event in lowland groups' struggle for state recognition of Indigenous territories. The 650-kilometer trek from the Bolivian Amazon to La Paz, in the highlands, succeeded in pressing President Jaime Paz Zamora (1989–93) to issue three decrees recognizing Indigenous territories. The march also set off a series of negotiations that effected the proliferation of state-recognized Indigenous lands, which by 1992 covered more than 2.5 million hectares (Yashar 2005, 204, 211–13). As discussed in Chapter 3, CIDOB subsequently helped craft major land reform legislation, passed in 1996.

In the lowlands, the Guaraní were exceptional for their organizational capacity. The Guaraní made up approximately 25 percent of the total population in the dry Bolivian Chaco region, located in the departments of Chuquisaca, Santa Cruz, and Tarija. They helped create CIDOB in 1982,[15] and in 1987 they formed their own organization, the Assembly of the Guaraní People (Asamblea del Pueblo Guaraní, APG). Organizationally, below the APG was the *capitanía*, which was headed by a *capitán grande* and was composed of several individual communities, each led by a *capitán* (Perreault 2008, 10). When this research was being conducted, the APG consisted of twenty-eight capitanías (Schilling-Vacaflor 2017a, 659 n. 2, 666).

Though structurally the APB was one of CIDOB's largest component organizations (known as *regionales*), it maintained a degree of independence. Unlike the other regionales and CIDOB itself, the APG as an organization avoided splintering under Morales. The fracturing of CIDOB was visible. In mid-2012, the national police removed CIDOB's elected president from the organization's main office, in the eastern city of Santa Cruz. The parallel

15. On the formation of CIDOB, see Yashar 2005, 198–204.

CIDOB was installed immediately in that same location. Subsequently, schisms emerged in regionales: by August 2012, government meddling to build support for the TIPNIS highway had led to the development of parallel structures for four of the thirteen regionales.[16] Most of the regionales had parallel leadership structures as of late 2020 (*El Deber* 11/1/2020). Yet the APG remained a single, cohesive organization. In the words of Celso Padillo, president of the Continental Council of the Guaraní Nation and former head of the APG and of the Takovo Mora capitanía, "APG is still united, still strong, not divided, which is unlike CIDOB and unlike CONAMAQ. But this is a hard time [for the organization]."[17]

The APG's autonomy was evident not only in its organizational strength but also in the electoral arena. The Guaraní supported the MAS in elections during the Morales administration, and Guaraní leaders seeking election at different levels of government were MAS candidates. However, Guaraní backing of the MAS was weaker than that of the party's historical stronghold, the cocalero-dominated Chapare province, in the department of Cochabamba; and unlike cocaleros, the Guaraní frequently formed alliances with other parties to win elections (Schilling-Vacaflor 2017a, 667).

The Guaraní resisted Morales's hydrocarbon policies.[18] For example, the APG disagreed with the government's opening of parks to extraction through DS 2366 (Schilling-Vacaflor 2017b, 1065). Consistent with the APG's position on the issue, in a 2015 conflict over the drilling of four gas wells (see Chapter 5), Takovo Mora and Morales sparred publicly: while Takovo Mora called for the abolishment of DS 0676 and DS 2366, Morales repeated the government's plan for YPFB to conduct exploration in seven national protected areas (*ERBOL* 8/21/2015).

Overall, the Guaraní believed blocking hydrocarbon projects was an unrealistic goal. Instead, they focused largely on obtaining compensation for the impacts of gas development (Schilling-Vacaflor and Kuhn 2015, 134–45; Schilling-Vacaflor 2017b). Schilling-Vacaflor describes the Guaraní's approach to extraction as follows:

> While many Guaraní aspire to stronger territorial rights than they currently legally have, in practice they generally adopt a pragmatic stance. This stance is

16. *ERBOL* 7/27/2012, 11/20/2012; and Interview with Magalí Barba, a specialist (*técnico*) who had worked in the APG for twenty-five years on themes of community-company-state relations in hydrocarbons, including prior consultation; Santa Cruz, September 6, 2012 (Interview B2).
17. Interview, Santa Cruz, June 23, 2017 (Interview B3).
18. For in-depth analysis of clashes between the Morales government's extractivism and Guaraní interests, see D. H. Bebbington 2010; and Anthias 2018.

> characterised by the Guaraní people's acceptance of the state's formal ownership of non-renewable natural resources—together with their insistence on strong participatory and collective rights, environmental protection, compensation payments for negative impacts, and a considerable share of benefits. (2017b, 1066)

The Guaraní communities that resided in traditional hydrocarbon areas skillfully drew on their past experiences with extraction to negotiate compensation for new projects. Those communities included the Itika Guasu, Takovo Mora, and Yaku Igua capitanías (Schilling-Vacaflor and Kuhn 2015, 144), which organized in the Bolivian gas conflicts in this study. One of the Yaku Igua conflicts serves as an exception to the Guaraní's emphasis on compensation: in that case, Yaku Igua fought to block entirely the Timboy X-2 well project, which was in a national park (see Chapter 5).

SUMMARY

This chapter has established Bolivia, Colombia, and Peru as excellent cases for a comparative study on social conflict over development in mining and hydrocarbons. It discussed key laws and other measures during the 1990s–2010s that encouraged the further growth of these already important sectors, and how that expansion came with social conflict in producing regions.

The chapter also emphasized cross-country variation in national political realities and in extractive conflict. It presented the Peruvian dynamic of protests set loose by redemocratization. The chapter then turned to Colombia, a case of complex extractive interests in civil-war regions and, simultaneously, reforms that encouraged political participation and more broadly deepened democracy. After the height of the armed conflict, activists objected to the environmental and social impacts of mining and hydrocarbons, frequently through legal filings. Finally, the chapter examined direct action by Bolivian Indigenous groups that wavered in their relationship to a leftist government.

The thirty hydrocarbon and mining case studies in this volume will illustrate these different forms of extractive conflict. They also will reveal a conflict pattern that cuts across country-level differences: in all three countries, communities' uses of participatory institutions in their mobilizing depended on the participatory challenges that they confronted. Those challenges were caused or exacerbated by contestation over certain boundaries that determined institutional access. Chapter 3 will introduce the participatory institutions and the fraught boundaries.

CHAPTER 3

Participatory Institutions and Their Underlying Boundaries

This chapter examines formal structures that govern participation in new extraction and that mobilized communities in Bolivia, Colombia, and Peru used, powerfully: the EIA hearing (*audiencia pública*, in Colombia and Peru), prior consultation (*consulta previa*, in all three countries), and popular consultation (*consulta popular*, in Colombia). The chapter describes these institutions and their evolution, and analyzes the boundaries that establish access to them. Specifically, it considers (1) boundaries between subnational and central state authority, (2) the geographic delineation of communities impacted by planned extractive development, and (3) the lines distinguishing representatives of affected communities from the communities at large. The chapter shows how contestation over the three boundaries has led to debates about which communities can be included in participatory events, who speaks on behalf of participating communities, and whether a participatory process is even appropriate. The discussion grounds the empirical analysis of thirty conflicts in Chapters 4–6, which will trace the implications of the boundary struggles for extractive conflict.

PUBLIC HEARINGS FOR ENVIRONMENTAL IMPACT STUDIES

In Latin America, the public hearing about the EIA is a common means for the state to inform local residents about planned large-scale development, to help fulfill the participatory component of environmental licensing (Rodríguez-Becerra and Espinoza 2002, 135–36, 149). The introduction of environmental licensing

The Politics of Extraction. Maiah Jaskoski, Oxford University Press. © Oxford University Press 2022.
DOI: 10.1093/oso/9780197568927.003.0003

in the region was a component of institution building in environmental matters that took place in the wake of the June 1992 United Nations (UN) Conference on Environment and Development, in Rio de Janeiro, Brazil (the "Rio Summit"; Rodríguez-Becerra and Espinoza 2002; Orihuela 2014a, 244–45).

This section analyzes regulations in Colombia and Peru that supported state-led, local hearings in mining and hydrocarbon areas, during the EIA approval process. It then briefly discusses the absence of such hearings in Bolivia.

Peru: Mandatory EIA Public Hearing

The EIA public hearing is required in Peruvian hydrocarbons and mining. It was regulated starting in the 1990s, as part of a larger shift toward heightened environmental standards.[1] The 1990 national environmental code, which established environmental licensing in Peru, was passed at the start of the Fujimori government in response to advocacy by environmental groups (Li 2015, 191; Orihuela and Paredes 2017, 102–3). Environmental institutions were bolstered later in the decade due to the Rio Summit and pressures from international lenders that conditioned loans on the enactment of higher environmental standards (Orihuela and Paredes 2017, 102–3).

Despite these developments, because the Fujimori government aggressively courted private investment, Peru lagged behind other Latin American countries when it came to implementing environmental protections (Orihuela and Paredes 2017, 102–3). More significant environmental institution building took place with the turn of the century, including in EIA oversight and public participation, as discussed in this section.

National Environmental Governance Structures: 1990s to 2010s

In the 1990s, environmental protections in Peru progressed by sector. Mining took the lead, with the 1992 creation of the General Directorate of Environmental Affairs (Dirección General de Asuntos Ambientales, DGAA) within the Vice Ministry of Mines, in the Ministry of Energy and Mining (Ministerio de Energía y Minas, MINEM). Two years later, in 1994, the National Environment Council (Consejo Nacional del Medio Ambiente, CONAM) was established, but regulatory authority in mining remained with DGAA (Orihuela and Paredes 2017, 101, 104; see also Orihuela 2014a, 254–55).

1. Peru's minimal, weak environmental structures prior to the 1990s included some formally protected areas and a national office to provide information about natural resources (Orihuela and Paredes 2017, 101–2).

Centralized environmental oversight—that is, beyond the sector level—advanced beginning in the 2000s. Mining was key in that progression, due to a particularly alarming case of regulatory failure on the part of DGAA, which did little to monitor Doe Run Peru's smelter outside La Oroya, a city east of Lima. The Doe Run case led to the transfer of environmental regulatory functions in mining from MINEM to the new Supervising Body for Energy and Mining Investment (Organismo Supervisor de la Inversión en Energía y Minería, OSINERGMIN), in 2006. OSINERGMIN replaced the Supervising Body for Energy Investment (Organismo Supervisor de la Inversión en Energía, OSINERG), which had overseen electricity and oil companies, including in environmental matters. When OSINERG converted to OSINERGMIN, the agency's purview expanded to encompass most of the regulatory functions of DGAA, though the latter continued reviewing EIAs (Orihuela 2014b; Orihuela and Paredes 2017, 100, 107–9).

National environmental oversight strengthened in the late 2000s with the Peru-US Free Trade Agreement (FTA), which encouraged greater environmental protections. In that context and to attract Inter-American Development Bank financing to develop Peru's enormous Camisea natural gas reserves, the García government created an environment ministry (Ministerio de Ambiente, MINAM) in 2008 and, within the ministry, the Office of Environmental Evaluation and Auditing (Organismo de Evaluación y Fiscalización Ambiental, OEFA). OEFA began functioning in 2009 as the national body in charge of environmental regulation, through the new National Environmental Control System (Sistema Nacional de Evaluación y Fiscalización Ambiental). In 2010, OSINERGMIN's environmental functions were transferred to OEFA (Orihuela and Paredes 2017, 100, 110–11).[2]

The reassignment of EIA oversight from individual ministries to a national environmental agency began in 2015. The National Service for Environmental Certification (Servicio Nacional de Certificación Ambiental, SENACE), a specialized body created in 2012 and attached to MINAM, was to take on all EIA reviews, in stages. The transfer process began with the "detailed EIAs" (EIA-d, often simply EIA), for development projects with "significant environmental impacts"; and later was to extend to the "semidetailed EIAs" (EIA-sd), for projects with "moderate environmental impacts." (Projects with minimal impact required the Environmental Impact Statement, or Declaración de Impacto Ambiental [DIA].) By December 2016, SENACE was reviewing the EIA-d in mining, transportation, and energy (i.e.,

2. OEFA was later weakened by the 2014 Law No. 30230 (one of the paquetazos ambientales mentioned in Chapter 2), which reduced the fines OEFA could issue for environmental harms and blocked OEFA from issuing fines for a first infraction (Red Muqui and GRUFIDES 2015, 10–11; Orihuela and Paredes 2017, 112).

hydrocarbons and electricity), and the transfer of EIA-d in other sectors was underway.[3]

Local EIA Hearings

Citizen participation in Peru's EIA has been traced to the 1990 environmental code, which granted "all people" the right to participate in defining environmental policy and to be informed of measures that might affect the environment, natural resources, or people's health (Legislative Decree 613, "Título preliminar" and ch. 7; and Solano 1999, 41). In energy and mining, the hearing was instituted through 1996 regulations (with Ministerial Resolution [Resolución Ministerial, RM] 335-96-EM/SG). That early framework limited participation. Hearings did not need to take place in the area of extraction and in practice were in Lima. Participation was restricted to company and state officials, and to representatives of civil-society organizations that formally asked to participate in advance. Those representatives were not provided the full EIA; they received an executive summary of the document, at the hearing.[4] In 1999, new regulations enhanced participation in hearings and access to project information. Members of the public now could participate and were given the EIA executive summary before the hearing. The public also could access the full draft EIA, through the national and regional energy and mining offices (RM 728-99-EM/VMM, Articles 5, 7; see also Barrera Ayala 2008, 321).

December 2002 regulations that supplanted the 1999 rules moved the hearing to the area of extraction.[5] The state implemented this change in response to social conflict over several hydrocarbon projects and, especially, the Tambo Grande mining project, analyzed in Chapter 6; by making the hearing more accessible to impacted populations, MINEM hoped to preempt future conflict that could interfere with extraction.[6]

The 2002 regulations detailed public hearing procedures for mining and hydrocarbon extraction, and for hydrocarbon exploration. They called for at least one hearing for a given project. DGAA led hearings, although it could delegate that role to the appropriate regional energy and mining office (Dirección Regional de Energía y Minas, DREM; RM 596-2002-EM/DM, Articles 3.2, 4, 11). Representatives of the project owner, and of the firm contracted to develop the EIA, were invited to the hearing. In advance of the hearing, its

3. Defensoría del Pueblo, Adjuntía del Medio Ambiente, Servicios Públicos y Pueblos Indígenas 2016, 17, 210–11, 214–15; and Interview P1.

4. Solano 1999, 40–42; Glave and Kuramoto 2002, 554 n. 9; and Interview with Manuel Glave Testino, Senior Researcher, Grupo de Análisis para el Desarrollo (GRADE); via Skype from Arizona, August 10, 2018 (Interview P3).

5. RM 596-2002-EM/DM; and Interview P3.

6. Interview P3.

location, date, and time were to be advertised, and the EIA and its summary were to be made available (Article 8). The event itself included two rounds of questions and answers, with each question lasting up to five minutes. The public could submit observations, proposals, and recommendations in writing within thirty days after the event. DGAA "evaluated" all comments, questions, and responses, in writing; and DGAA, the DREM, and the relevant municipal government stored the evaluations (Article 6.13). A "fortuitous event" or "overwhelming force" could cause the suspension and rescheduling of a hearing (Article 7). The regulations also required company-led EIA workshops (*talleres*). At those meetings, held during the drafting of the EIA, the extractive firm delivered a presentation on the project to the public.[7]

Sector-specific norms accompanied the 2002 regulations for EIA participation. Those additional regulations were implemented in 2004 (RM 535-2004-MEM-DM) and 2008 (DS 028-2008-EM, RM 304-2008-MEM-DM) in hydrocarbons and mining, respectively. In February 2008, a new set of rules in hydrocarbons (DS 012-2008-EM) replaced the 2004 structure, increasing participation in hydrocarbons so as to reduce social conflict and expedite extraction. The regulations detailed an early participatory phase before the licensing of a hydrocarbon block (Barrera Ayala 2008, 320–25).

Mining exploration entailed a degree of public participation, though not through EIA hearings. Regulations implemented in 1998 mandated an Environmental Assessment (Evaluación Ambiental, EA) for mining exploration. Beginning in 2008, either a DIA or an EIA-sd applied to mining exploration, depending on its impacts (DS 020-2008-EM; and SPDA n.d.a.). The public had access to the documents and could submit written comments about exploration projects. In addition, workshops were held for exploration.[8]

Participation in Project Modifications

Relative to new project approvals, project modifications in Peru offered little room for citizen engagement. The EIA modification (Modificación del Estudio de Impacto Ambiental, MEIA) process took up to 120 days.[9] Project changes that impacted new areas necessitated at least one workshop and one public hearing (CooperAcción 2015, 7).

7. Interview P3. Although companies directed workshops, regulations permitted companies, DGAA, or the DREM to lead them. DGAA—in coordination with the DREM—determined the number of workshops for a project (RM 596-2002-EM/DM, Article 3.1).

8. RM 596-2002-EM/DM, Article 11; DS 028-2008-EM, Article 13; RM 304-2008-MEM-DM, Articles 4–11; and DS 020-2008-EM, Article 8.

9. Calle and Mora 2016, 5; and Defensoría del Pueblo, Adjuntía del Medio Ambiente, Servicios Públicos y Pueblos Indígenas 2016, 32.

The 2013 environmental paquetazo DS 054-2013-PCM restricted participation in project revisions, through the Supporting Technical Report (Informe Técnico Sustentatorio, ITS). Companies submitted the ITS for technological improvements to project operations, and for project modifications the environmental impacts of which were "insignificant." (Firms continued making other types of project changes using the MEIA.) Modifications proposed in an ITS received automatic approval if the state did not raise concerns about them within fifteen days of the ITS submission.[10] The ITS did not oblige citizen participation, nor did companies include the public in the ITS voluntarily; of the 214 mining ITSs submitted as of 2016, only two mentioned citizen participation, and of the fifty-three in hydrocarbons, none mentioned it (Calle and Mora 2016, 21, 22, 28).

Colombia: EIA Public Hearing by Request

Like the Peruvian case, in Colombia the EIA public hearing was introduced in the 1990s along with other environmental reforms. Different from in Peru, the Colombian hearing was offered only through an application process, as detailed here.

National Environmental Governance Structures: 1990s to 2010s

Environmental institutions installed in Colombia during the 1990s built on a relatively strong foundation. The country's first protected areas were inaugurated between 1940 and 1960. A natural resources division was created in 1952 in the Ministry of Agriculture. In 1968, the division became the Institute for the Development of Renewable Natural Resources (Instituto de Desarrollo de los Recursos Naturales Renovables, INDERENA), still within Agriculture (Mance 2008, 131). INDERENA's approach to conservation, based on the exclusion of human populations, "crystalized" in the national parks system (Sistema de Parques Nacionales Naturales, SPNN; Andrade 2008, 481). The 1974 environmental code, though weakly implemented, put in place regulations for the management of all renewable resources (Mance 2008, 132–33).

Added to national institutions, Colombia had a subnational environmental regulatory regime. The first "regional autonomous corporations" (*corporaciones autónomas regionales*, CARs) were instated between 1954

10. Calle and Mora 2016, 5–6, 21; and Defensoría del Pueblo, Adjuntía del Medio Ambiente, Servicios Públicos y Pueblos Indígenas 2016, 31–32.

and 1968 (Canal Albán and Rodríguez Becerra 2008, 306; Mance 2008, 131–32).

The 1990s brought new opportunities for actors who wanted to strengthen environmental protections in Colombia, especially through the constitutional reform project. Influenced by the environmental movement, the 1991 constitution contained seventy-nine articles related to the environment (Mance 2008, 135–37), including requirements for citizen participation. Article 79 guaranteed the right of a healthy environment to all people, and participation by communities in decisions that might affect them (Rodríguez and Muñoz Ávila 2009, 39–43).

In the aftermath of the Rio Summit, the 1993 environmental law (Law 99) created Colombia's environment ministry (Ministerio de Medio Ambiente), which presided over the new national environmental system (Sistema Nacional Ambiental, SNA). SNA included SPNN, the now thirty-three CARs, and the country's four urban environmental authorities (*autoridades ambientales urbanas*), which operated in cities of more than one million people (Mance 2008, 138–39, 142–43). The existing environment ministry fused with parts of the Ministry of Economic Development in 2003, to form the new Ministry of Environment, Housing, and Territorial Development (Ministerio de Ambiente, Vivienda y Desarrollo Territorial, MAVDT; Mance 2008, 110). Another reorganization, in 2011, produced the Ministry of Environment and Sustainable Development (Ministerio de Ambiente y Desarrollo Sostenible; Tuval Antonio 2017, 11).

Article 50 of Law 99 established environmental licensing in Colombia (Rodríguez and Gómez Rey 2013, 94). Licenses for large-scale projects were issued at the national level, while CARs regulated smaller projects (SPDA 2016, 86). The environment ministry granted national environmental licenses until September 2011, when the newly created National Environmental Licensing Agency (Agencia Nacional de Licencias Ambientales, ANLA), attached to the environment ministry, took on that role (SPDA 2016, 90 n. 11).

In hydrocarbons, national regulations governed all activity and required an environmental license for extraction and certain exploration work—drilling outside of existing oil fields, and seismic exploration that entailed road construction or that was in marine areas less than two hundred meters deep. In mining, there was no environmental license for exploration, and the planned amount of minerals to be extracted determined whether permissions to extract would be issued at the national or regional level (Negrete Montes 2013, 39; SPDA 2016, 87).

Colombian environmental licensing has been characterized as exhibiting little rigor, with changes under ANLA receiving substantial attention. For instance, a 2014 decree reduced the state's window of time to evaluate environmental license applications from ninety to thirty days (SPDA 2016, 88

n. 8).[11] In a 2017 report on environmental licensing in Colombia since 1993, the Comptroller General (Contraloría General) depicted ANLA as overly lenient in approving EIAs[12] and noted the absence of a licensing process for many activities. The report found that ANLA required an excessively small scale for images in the "terms of reference," an early submission in the development of the EIA, and that environmental authorities managed insufficient information to know whether a potential project site overlapped with protected areas. The Contraloría also remarked that the CARs operated with limited oversight. Overall, as summarized in the report, during 2005–16 the state issued 1,182 national environmental licenses and rejected 80. At the regional level during that same period, 2,798 environmental licenses were granted and 452 denied (Contraloría General de la República 2017, 43–44, 73; *Semana* 5/20/2017).

Local EIA Hearings

Colombian environmental licensing included EIA hearings. Law 99 introduced the hearing to give local communities and other interested parties the opportunity to learn about and discuss proposed activities that could impact the environment. Although hearings date to 1994, they were not regulated until 2007, with Decree 330 (Rodríguez and Gómez Rey 2013, 94–95).

Per the 2007 regulations, hearings were not mandatory (SPDA 2016, 88–89). A hearing could be requested by the attorney general or their delegate; the Defensoría del Pueblo; the environment ministry; directors of the other state environmental authorities (e.g., CARs); governors; mayors; or, by petition, a group of at least one hundred individuals or three nonprofit organizations (Decree 330, Article 5). The environment authority had fifteen days to review requests and decide whether to allow a hearing (Article 6). If more than one actor or group solicited a hearing for the same EIA, the state would authorize a single event, unless the project traversed large areas, in which case it could permit two (Articles 5, 7.8, 11).

ANLA almost always held hearings for the licensing of large-scale mining and hydrocarbon projects,[13] but more generally, public hearings were uncommon. From 1993 through 2012, the Colombian state issued 2,331 environmental licenses and led only sixty hearings, many of which were in extractives—fourteen in hydrocarbons and eleven in mining (Rodríguez and Gómez Rey 2013, 95–97).

11. Time spent on a public hearing process did not count toward the EIA review period (Decree 2820, Article 25, Paragraph 3; and Decree 2041, Article 25, Paragraph 3).
12. On criticisms of ANLA's leniency, see also Rodríguez 2011.
13. Interview with two ANLA officials—one with extensive knowledge of mining and the other, hydrocarbons; Bogotá, July 7, 2016 (Interview C1).

In terms of EIA hearing procedures, before the hearing, the event's date, time, and location were advertised, and the project owner made available the draft EIA (Decree 330, Articles 7, 8). Members of the public could attend, and, through advance registration, speak (Articles 10, 12). An informational meeting (*reunión informativa*, commonly referred to as a *preaudiencia*) was held to review hearing procedures, at least ten days before the hearing (Article 9).

While the state did not mandate the EIA hearing for environmental licenses, it did compel "socialization" (*socialización*), a process similar to Peru's workshops. To fulfill the socialization requirement, the company led meetings with the communities—or at least community leaders—in a project's area of direct influence, within the larger area of influence.[14] Companies tended to conduct several socialization meetings, each in a different rural precinct (*vereda*) of the municipality. Several conflict experts interviewed for this study saw this practice as a tactic to divide, and in that way weaken, communities.

Bolivia: No State-Led EIA Hearing

Bolivia's government created new environmental institutions after the Rio Summit, as in the Colombian and Peruvian cases. However, the Bolivian norms did not provide for EIA hearings led by state officials.

Two institutional developments in Bolivia, both in 1992, were the creation of the Ministry of Sustainable Development (Ministerio de Desarrollo Sostenible) and the passage of an environmental law, Law 1333 (Rodríguez-Becerra and Espinoza 2002, 49, 72). Law 1333 and its 1995 regulations required an Environmental Impact Evaluation Study (Estudio de Evaluación de Impacto Ambiental, EEIA) for Category 1 and 2 development projects, which caused the greatest impacts (Regulations, Law 1333, Article 15). While it was crafting the EEIA, the company hosted a "public consultation" (*consulta pública*) to "take into account observations, suggestions and recommendations" of people impacted by the project (Article 162). To fulfill the public consultation component of licensing, extractive firms met with subnational political officials and at times civil-society leaders.[15] Because the company and not the state directed these events, they resembled socialization and EIA workshops in Colombia and Peru, respectively.

14. During ANLA's standard visit to the project area before issuing an environmental license, the agency met with the local mayor and asked them a set list of questions, one of which was whether socialization had taken place. Interview C1.

15. Interview with an attorney and an engineer who specialized in mining, a técnico in hydrocarbons, and the head of the hydrocarbon group within the Vice Ministry of Environment, Biodiversity, Climate Change, and Forest Management and Development, Ministry of Environment and Water; La Paz, June 13, 2017 (Interview B4).

PRIOR CONSULTATION

Alongside the EIA hearing, another participatory institution built into state approvals for new hydrocarbon and mining activities is prior consultation, which applies to Native communities in Bolivia, Colombia, and Peru.

The development of prior consultation norms varied across the three countries. CIDOB and the APG helped write the law and regulations governing consultations in Bolivian hydrocarbons. In contrast, the governments of Colombia and Peru created prior consultation institutions through top-down processes, though initially Indigenous organizations participated in writing the Peruvian regulations.

This cross-national variation permits an assessment of a leading perspective on prior consultation institutions: that Indigenous participation in designing prior consultation frameworks contributes to greater institutional legitimacy (see Chapter 1). In fact, despite the stark variation in how formal prior consultation institutions were installed, those rules were legitimate in Bolivia, Colombia, and Peru. Indigenous populations in the three countries criticized the institutions for not granting communities greater influence over development. And yet, overall, communities—as well as companies and the state—recognized and acted in accordance with the formal prior consultation procedures.

The national prior consultation structures were rooted in ILO 169, which was ratified in all three countries in the 1990s. The binding convention marked an international move away from the integrationist approach to Indigeneity that the 1959 ILO Convention No. 107 had upheld. In contrast, ILO 169 emphasized respect for the traditions and rights of Indigenous communities (Rodríguez-Piñero 2005), acknowledging "the aspirations of [Indigenous and tribal peoples] to exercise control over their own institutions, ways of life and economic development and to maintain and develop their identities, languages and religions, within the framework of the States in which they live" (ILO 1989, "Preamble"). With regard to development and Indigenous lands, ILO 169 detailed that Native peoples

> shall have the right to decide their own priorities for the process of development as it affects their lives, beliefs, institutions and spiritual well-being and the lands they occupy or otherwise use, and to exercise control, to the extent possible, over their own economic, social and cultural development. In addition, they shall participate in the formulation, implementation and evaluation of plans and programmes for national and regional development which may affect them directly. (Article 7.1)

In prioritizing Native communities' rights to their lands and ways of life, the convention stressed the right to prior consultation; signatories had to "consult the peoples concerned, through appropriate procedures and in particular through their representative institutions," about legislative or administrative measures that could affect them (Article 6.1). The consultation prerequisite applied to the exploration and extraction of subsoil resources owned by the state (Article 15.2).

Related to prior consultation is the concept of consent, or, commonly, "free, prior, and informed consent" (FPIC; Szablowski 2010; Rodríguez Garavito 2011). ILO 169 mandated that prior consultation be conducted with the "*objective* of achieving agreement or consent of the proposed measures" (Article 6.2, emphasis added). States were to *obtain* consent for a Native community's relocation:

> Where the relocation of these peoples is considered necessary as an exceptional measure, such relocation shall take place only with their free and informed consent. When their consent cannot be obtained, such relocation shall take place only following appropriate procedures established by national laws and regulations. (Article 16.2)

Relative to ILO 169, the nonbinding 2007 UN Declaration on the Rights of Indigenous Peoples (UNDRIP)—for which the Bolivian and Peruvian governments voted and on which Colombia's government abstained—placed greater emphasis on consent (United Nations 2007, n.d.).

Indigenous organizations in Bolivia, Colombia, and Peru advocated for community consent as the standard, and certain high-level court decisions on prior consultation referenced a consent requirement in certain situations. For example, in 2009, Colombia's Constitutional Court found that the state should obtain consent from communities of the Embera nation before approving the Mandé Norte mine, due to the severity of the project's impacts on Embera communities (see Chapter 6). A Peruvian superior court ruled in 2018 that the state needed consent from communities impacted by development in an oil block before the project could move forward (see analysis of Block 116 in Chapter 5). In its decision on a case involving the Itika Guasu capitanía, Bolivia's Constitutional Tribunal identified several scenarios that would require consent (see analysis of the San Antonio conflict, in Chapter 6).

Prior Consultation in Peru: Top-Down Institutional Development

Peru's government ratified ILO 169 in 1993 but did not embark on developing a prior consultation law until much later, in response to a 2009 Indigenous mobilization, the Baguazo. After the government passed the prior consultation law, Indigenous groups participated in an early stage of writing its regulations. However, they soon became disillusioned with the project and abandoned it.

The Baguazo as a Catalyst for the Prior Consultation Law and Regulations

The violent Baguazo took place outside the city of Bagua in Peru's northern region of Amazonas, on June 5, 2009. It marked the peak of Indigenous opposition to the García government's aggressive policies to open the Peruvian Amazon to resource extraction (Schilling-Vacaflor and Flemmer 2015, 819).

The uprising was prompted by decrees that threatened Indigenous lands. A December 2007 law granted the executive branch the authority to legislate for a period of 180 days, to help implement the FTA. The government used that temporary mechanism in August 2008 to pass ninety-nine legislative decrees that facilitated development in protected and communal lands (Stetson 2012, 78). Eleven of the decrees especially perturbed Indigenous communities, for directly affecting their livelihoods (Schilling-Vacaflor and Flemmer 2015, 819). Still in August 2008, Amazonian Indigenous organizations responded to the measures by blocking major waterways, pipelines, and roads, causing the legislature to retract two decrees (Decrees 1015 and 1073) that would have encouraged the partition and sale of communal landholdings (Schilling-Vacaflor and Flemmer 2015, 819; de Jong and Humphreys 2016, 558). The Indigenous Permanent Special Commission of the Awajún and Wampis Peoples (Comisión Especial Permanente de los Pueblos Awajún y Wampis, CEPPAW) organized the mobilization (Castillo Fernández 2016, 14–15).

Protest broke out again when the government did not revisit the remaining controversial decrees. On April 8, 2009, 1,350 Amazonian community leaders announced an "indefinite strike" throughout Peru's Amazon, to begin the next day. The strike was led by the Inter-Ethnic Association for the Development of the Peruvian Amazon (Asociación Interétnica de Desarrollo de la Selva Peruana, AIDESEP), a national lowland Indigenous organization that consistently fought for Indigenous lands and self-determination. The mobilization began on April 9, as planned, and culminated in the Baguazo.[16]

Three thousand activists participated in the Baguazo, the most violent of all social conflicts tracked by Peru's Defensoría del Pueblo at least through 2011. The uprising resulted in thirty-three deaths—with twenty-three of the deceased police personnel, killed by protesters—and injuries to another

16. United Nations Human Rights Council 2009, 5–8; Schilling-Vacaflor and Flemmer 2015, 819; and Castillo Fernández 2016, 14–16. On AIDESEP's commitment to Indigenous territorial rights and autonomy, see Yashar 2005, 264.

two hundred people. The police made eighty-three arrests in the conflict (Defensoría 2012b, 42, 54; Schilling-Vacaflor and Flemmer 2015, 819–20).

The national government responded to the violence by disparaging the Indigenous organizing, causing fear within and fragmenting Amazonian Indigenous communities (Castillo Fernández 2016, 18). García accused activists of representing manipulative NGOs and "leftist powers" (Schilling-Vacaflor and Flemmer 2015, 819). The regional police chief (of Peru's national police) portrayed the participating Indigenous groups as having ties to drug trafficking and Sendero Luminoso (Arce 2014, 113).

Yet the Baguazo also encouraged alliances between Indigenous organizations and other activist groups, including unions and environmental organizations, in a movement for Indigenous rights. Days after the Baguazo, more than ten thousand protesters took to the streets in Lima in support of Amazonian Indigenous peoples. The government faced other pressures to address Indigenous demands, as well. The UN special rapporteur on the rights of Indigenous peoples watched the events closely, as did the US government, which retained its focus on the FTA (a chief cause of the Baguazo). For their part, members of the financial and business sectors, adversely impacted by blockades, wanted the government to resolve the conflict (Schilling-Vacaflor and Flemmer 2015, 820).

In this context, the Defensoría del Pueblo presented to the national congress a proposed prior consultation law project in July 2009, in the interest of avoiding more violence (Schilling-Vacaflor and Flemmer 2015, 821; Defensoría del Pueblo 2017, 80). The National Coordinating Group for the Development of Amazonian Peoples (Grupo Nacional de Coordinación para el Desarrollo de los Pueblos Amazónicos, GNCDPA)—which the government established to address development priorities for the Amazon—built on the Defensoría's project. The GNCDPA produced, in the working group "Mesa 3," a detailed draft law. Congress passed a revised, simplified version, as Law 29785, on May 19, 2010 (Schilling-Vacaflor and Flemmer 2015, 820, 821).

Indigenous groups backed the new law but disagreed with several of its features, including that it did not allow communities to veto development. García also found faults with Law 29785. He wanted it to prioritize "national interests" and grant the right to prior consultation only to communities with titled land. He vetoed the law, but President Humala signed it in September 2011, shortly after taking office (Schilling-Vacaflor and Flemmer 2015, 821–22).

In the hope that effective regulations might address the new law's shortcomings, Indigenous organizations joined the effort to write its regulations (Schilling-Vacaflor and Flemmer 2015, 823). They would be disappointed.

To create the regulating decree, the Humala government carried out a process involving "internal deliberation" among Indigenous and peasant organizations at the regional and national levels, followed by a "multisectoral commission" (Schilling-Vacaflor and Flemmer 2015, 823). Indigenous groups characterized the endeavor as hurried and overly technical, and they objected to the fact that the commission included only six Indigenous organizations, alongside sixteen vice ministries. Four of the participating national Indigenous and peasant groups—AIDESEP, the National Agrarian Confederation (Confederación Nacional Agraria, CAN), the National Confederation of Peruvian Communities Affected by Mining (Confederación Nacional de Comunidades del Perú Afectadas por la Minería, CONACAMI), and the National Organization of Amazonian and Andean Indigenous Women of Peru (Organización Nacional de Mujeres Indígenas Andinas y Amazónicas del Perú, ONAMIAP)—left the commission after losing hope that regulations could address the inadequacies of Law 29785. The two organizations that stayed on were the Confederation of Amazonian Nationalities of Peru (Confederación de Nacionalidades Amazónicas del Perú, CONAP), a national Indigenous umbrella organization amenable to oil development; and the Peasant Confederation of Peru (Confederación Campesina del Perú, CCP), which historically had mobilized around class rather than ethnic identity (Schilling-Vacaflor and Flemmer 2015, 823–25). The regulations were implemented by decree in April 2012, with DS 001-2012-MC (Defensoría del Pueblo 2017, 81).

Prior Consultation Procedures

Peru's prior consultation law and regulations described several steps in prior consultation, including the identification of impacted communities; the provision of information to communities about the proposed measure, its impacts, and the prior consultation process (thirty to sixty days); discussion within the communities of the measure (up to thirty days); dialogue between the state and community representatives (up to thirty days with possible extensions); and the signing of a final document that identified any agreements and/or disputes between the state and communities. The agreed-upon portions of the document were binding, but the state could take actions of which communities disapproved.[17]

Consultations were directed by a state authority in the relevant sector. Until 2015, hydrocarbon consultations were led by Perupetro, the state entity responsible for licensing hydrocarbon blocks to private companies. Starting in 2015—the year of the first mining consultation—DGAA took on prior consultation in hydrocarbons and mining (Sanborn et al. 2016, 12; Leyva 2018, 16).

17. Information in this paragraph about the steps in Peruvian prior consultations is drawn from Lanegra Quispe 2014, 106–8; and Defensoría del Pueblo 2017, 84–87.

The Ministry of Culture and the Defensoría del Pueblo also had obligations in prior consultation. The culture ministry was responsible for imparting technical advice and guidance (Defensoría del Pueblo 2017, 82–83). According to a legal coordinator in the ministry in August 2018, for each completed prior consultation, a ministry representative had participated in all consultation stages, with the exception of internal community discussions.[18] The Defensoría del Pueblo served as an observer in some consultations, as part of its responsibility to protect communal rights and oversee the fulfillment of state administrative duties and public service provision (Defensoría del Pueblo 2017, 92–93). The Defensoría only participated in consultations that it regarded as "problematic," based on its research. It had participated in two consultations in mining and four in hydrocarbons as of mid-2018.[19] That limited involvement was due to a resource shortage; in 2018, the Defensoría's office specializing in Indigenous themes—only one of which was prior consultation—was staffed by three full-time employees and three consultants.[20]

The approval of EIAs in extractives did not hinge on the completion of prior consultations. In hydrocarbons, prior consultation took place for block contracts, before a company submitted a project design to the state for review, and for block transfers.[21] In contrast, prior consultation in mining occurred after the state approved the EIA (or for exploration, the DIA or EIA-sd), but before it issued permissions for project development.[22] Perhaps because prior consultations in mining began only in 2015, there had not been a mining operation for which impacted communities had been consulted for both exploration and extraction when research for this study was underway.[23]

The culture ministry and the Defensoría del Pueblo promoted making environmental licensing in extractives conditional on the completion of prior consultation.[24] Certain judicial decisions also supported this coupling: court rulings in 2018 and 2019, in the Block 116 and Afrodita conflicts, respectively,

18. Interview with Omar Livia, Legal Coordinator, General Directorate of Indigenous Peoples' Rights, Ministry of Culture; Lima, August 1, 2018 (Interview P4).

19. Community complaints to the Defensoría about prior consultation procedures would prompt a Defensoría investigation and possible Defensoría participation. However, community initiative was not necessary. In the two mining cases in which the Defensoría had participated, local communities had not communicated concerns to the Defensoría. Interview with Nelly Aedo, Head of the Indigenous Peoples Program, Defensoría del Pueblo; Lima, July 31, 2018 (Interview P5).

20. Interview P5.

21. Leyva 2018, 16–17; and Interviews P4 and P5. On the well-known case of prior consultation for the transfer of Block 192, see Sanborn et al. 2016, 39–43; and Guzmán-Gallegos 2017.

22. Lanegra Quispe 2014, 109; Leyva 2018, 27–31; and Interviews P4 and P5.

23. Interview P5.

24. Defensoría del Pueblo 2017, 100; Leyva 2018, 16–17; and Interviews P4 and P5.

required prior consultation before the granting of environmental licenses (*Servindi* 8/23/2018, 5/18/2019; see also Chapter 5).

Legitimate Prior Consultation Norms

Law 29785 and its regulations led to the institutionalization of prior consultation in Peru. Between 1995 when ILO 169 took effect,[25] and the 2011 passage of Law 29785, Indigenous participation in approvals for new hydrocarbon and mining activities consisted of communications between communities and private companies. Those meetings, which were directed by firms, promoted extraction and offered little information about projects or their impacts (Schilling-Vacaflor and Flemmer 2015, 817–18).

The law and regulations made prior consultation legitimate within government, civil society, and the private sector (Sanborn et al. 2016, 9). Peru's Indigenous organizations generally agreed to participate in prior consultations (Schilling-Vacaflor and Flemmer 2015, 817 n. 22). As of June 2016, the twenty-four consultations that had begun since the implementation of the regulations—in eight of Peru's twenty-five regions—had concluded (Sanborn et al. 2016, 10–11). Thirty-eight prior consultations had been completed by 2018, including thirteen in hydrocarbons and twelve in mining (Levya 2018, 11–12).

The legitimacy of the prior consultation structures is further evident in conflicts over prior consultation; in those cases, communities usually protested to insist on being consulted in accordance with the regulations (Sanborn et al. 2016, 9). By 2016, impacted communities not consulted in nine mining and hydrocarbon conflicts had contested their exclusion by using the *amparo*—a judicial process available to people claiming harm to their fundamental rights (CAAAP 2016, 34, 42–43).[26]

While Indigenous groups respected the 2011–12 norms, they also insisted that their right to prior consultation dated to 1995, attaching it to ILO 169 (Sanborn et al. 2016, 34–35). Indigenous groups made headway in their effort to gain recognition of the earlier date, through the courts (see analysis of Afrodita and Block 116, in Chapter 5).

25. The Peruvian government ratified ILO 169 in 1993 (with Legislative Resolution 26253). The decision was submitted to the International Labour Organization in February 1994, and the convention went into effect one year later (Defensoría del Pueblo 2017, 80).

26. The exclusion of communities largely was due to competing definitions of Indigenous and of Indigenous land rights, as analyzed in this chapter, in the section "Contested Boundaries in Extractive Zones."

Prior Consultation in Colombia: Top-Down Institutional Development with Adjustments by the Constitutional Court

Colombia's government instituted prior consultation in response to intense Indigenous mobilizing against extraction, as in Peru. However, unlike the Peruvian case, Indigenous organizations in Colombia were notably absent from the entire institutional design process. In 1998, the Colombian government regulated prior consultation with Decree 1320, during a standoff between the U'wa nation, on one hand, and the state and Occidental Petroleum, on the other, over an oil exploration project (Orduz Salinas 2014, 13–14, 33; see analysis of the Samoré conflict in Chapter 6).

Decree 1320 was layered on top of norms installed in the early 1990s. In 1991, the Colombian government ratified ILO 169 and the new constitution, which stated (in Article 330) that Indigenous communities would participate in decisions about natural resource extraction in their territories. Two years later, Law 99 recognized the right to prior consultation, referencing Article 330 (Rodríguez et al. 2010, 177; Orduz Salinas 2014, 8–9).

While Indigenous groups did not help write the 1998 regulations, they did influence the implementation of those rules, using the judicial system. The Constitutional Court's activist role in defending Indigenous rights in prior consultation is discussed here, in the section "Contested Boundaries in Extractive Zones" in this chapter, and in analysis of Colombian Indigenous conflicts in Chapters 5 and 6.

Prior Consultation Procedures

Three categories of Colombians had the right to prior consultation: Indigenous nations, Afro-Colombian groups, and the nomadic Roma population (Orduz Salinas 2014, 3, 5, 6). The Ministry of Interior was charged with overseeing consultations.

Decree 1320 outlined a rapid consultation process on measures that impacted communities, in a single meeting (Rodríguez et al. 2010, 183; Orduz Salinas 2014, 13). New regulations implemented in 2010 contained greater detail and partitioned prior consultation into several steps. The "preconsultation" (*preconsulta*) produced a meeting schedule; participants then discussed the project and its anticipated impacts; community representatives acknowledged the components of the measure and their impacts through the "preagreement" (*preacuerdo*); and, lastly, participants signed off on the consultation as a whole (Orduz Salinas 2014, 14; Presidential Directive 01, Section 4a).[27] For development that necessitated both an

27. The stages of Colombian prior consultations also were detailed by a coordinator in the Advisory and Technical Assistance Area, Directorate of Prior Consultation, Ministry of Interior (interview, Bogotá, August 1, 2016; Interview C2).

environmental license and prior consultation, ANLA could grant the license only after the consultation.[28] Consultations did not always address a project's EIA, as articulated by an official in the interior ministry's Office of Prior Consultation:

> *Is a draft of the EIA discussed and reviewed at these meetings?*
> Not necessarily. We as an office are more concerned with the social and cultural effects than the environmental impacts, though of course the environmental impacts are connected to social and cultural effects. The prior consultation results—findings and adjustments [to the project] based on the prior consultation—are incorporated into the EIA.[29]

Legitimate Prior Consultation Norms

Colombian ethnic rights organizations denounced the prior consultation regulations for not meeting ILO 169's standards and for not having undergone prior consultation (e.g., Baquero Díaz 2014, 108). Nonetheless, prior consultations overall were orderly and expeditious, evincing the legitimacy of the regulations. The vast majority of the approximately nine hundred consultations carried out in mining and hydrocarbons during 2010–13 had concluded by mid-2014 (Orduz Salinas 2014, 16).

Tensions that did arise over prior consultation could be formidable and were another indication that Indigenous groups valued the participatory institution. A legal expert of the Colombian NGO Dejusticia who specialized in prior consultation conflicts identified three main types of conflict. In most conflicts, communities that did not hold title to impacted land decried not being consulted. When the Constitutional Court ruled on such cases in favor of communities, it usually mandated remediation for the impacts of development that had taken place during the lengthy legal process. Communities also questioned the quality of consultation processes and challenged laws passed without consultations.[30]

The Role of the Constitutional Court

The Constitutional Court shaped prior consultation, especially by ensuring communities' access to consultation processes. The court's progressive stance in prior consultation was part of its broader role in defending social and communal, including Indigenous, rights (Van Cott

28. Interview C2.
29. Interview C2.
30. Interview with legal expert, Dejusticia; Bogotá, June 29, 2016 (Interview C3).

2000, 213–23; Nunes 2010, 82–88; Sandoval Rojas 2013, 195–96; Gómez Isa 2014).[31]

The court protected communities' right to prior consultation through the *tutela*, known elsewhere in Latin America as the amparo (Nunes 2010, 73). The Constitutional Court deemed the right to prior consultation a "fundamental right" and hence eligible for protection through the tutela process (Rodríguez et al. 2010, especially 178–79, 182).[32]

Initial tutela filings were processed quickly. Decisions by lower courts could be appealed and overruled at higher levels (Nunes 2010, 73). A Defensoría del Pueblo attorney who specialized in constitutional questions said that a first and then also a second court almost always rejected tutela requests ("you have lower courts that don't want to be the ones to hold up a huge development project").[33] The Constitutional Court, the final decider, had a strong record of safeguarding rights through the tutela process, in general and relative to the Council of State, or High Administrative Tribunal (Consejo de Estado; Nunes 2010, 80, 83).

Activism was crucial for gaining the Constitutional Court's interest in a prior consultation tutela. The court received thousands of tutela filings each month and might select only twenty or thirty to review. Communities reached out to NGOs to elicit the court's attention; sometimes a brief from an NGO with legal knowledge convinced the court to take a tutela.[34] Involvement by the Defensoría del Pueblo also could be pivotal, according to the Defensoría attorney: "[Communities] reach out to NGOs, for instance, and the NGOs contact the Defensoría. . . . The Defensoría then can ask the Constitutional Court to take a case."[35]

Consistent with the Constitutional Court's progressive tutela record in general, the court's decisions on prior consultation tutelas frequently backed communities. In total, twenty-eight major Constitutional Court decisions upheld communities' right to prior consultation (Defensoría del Pueblo 2017, 41–48). The interior ministry directly applied Constitutional Court case law when interpreting prior consultation regulations (see discussion under "Contested Boundaries in Extractive Zones"), though Indigenous rights advocates interviewed believed that the ministry could have done much more in that regard.

31. This progressivism has been traced to the court's genesis: the 1991 constituent assembly and constitution (Nunes 2010).

32. See also Nunes 2010 on the Constitutional Court's interpretation of fundamental rights in its application of the tutela.

33. Interview with Jorge Parra Norato, attorney, Constitutional and Legal Matters, Defensoría del Pueblo; Bogotá, July 25, 2016 (Interview C4).

34. Interview C3.

35. Interview C4.

There were limits to the Constitutional Court's influence in prior consultation. The court found Decree 1320 to be illegitimate for not affording true prior consultations as defined in ILO 169, and because the regulations had not been subject to a consultation process. Still, the decree remained on the books and continued being applied, somewhat ironically because it was not fixed to a law; the court could declare laws but not decrees unconstitutional (Orduz Salinas 2014, 14).

Prior Consultation in Bolivia: Bottom-Up Institutional Development

Similar to the Colombian and Peruvian experiences, Bolivian prior consultation norms were a consequence of Indigenous organizing. Bolivia's government ratified ILO 169 in 1991 (with Law 1257) in response to the 1990 March for Territory and Dignity (Falleti and Riofrancos 2018, 100). However, in contrast to the other cases, Bolivia is a conspicuous case of bottom-up institutional creation: Indigenous communities participated directly in designing the Bolivian prior consultation framework.

Also different from the cases of Colombia and Peru, Bolivian prior consultation was sectoral, with regulations implemented in hydrocarbons and mining in 2007 and 2015, respectively.[36] This section focuses on hydrocarbons, the first sector in which prior consultation was introduced and the sector of interest for the Bolivian conflicts analyzed in this book.

The Creation of Prior Consultation Structures

Prior consultation was institutionalized in Bolivian hydrocarbons with the 2005 hydrocarbon law (Law 3058, discussed in Chapter 2) and associated regulations. Previously, Law 1257 had ratified ILO 169, and 1995 revisions to the constitution had incorporated into the charter reference to social, economic, and cultural rights of Indigenous communities, including communal land rights (Bascopé 2010, 32).[37]

36. Prior consultation was instituted in Bolivian mining through the 2014 mining code (Law 535, especially Title VI) and regulated in 2015 (with the Ministry of Mining's RM 023-2015). Interview with a member of the Public Consultation and Community Participation Unit, General Directorate for the Environment and Public Consultation, Vice Ministry of Metallurgical Productive Development, Ministry of Mining; La Paz, June 12, 2017 (Interview B5).

37. Law 1257 and the 1995 constitutional revision have been identified as benchmarks in the evolution of Bolivian prior consultation, by the secondary literature (e.g., Bascopé Sanjinés 2010, 32) and by Indigenous activists, NGO officials, and other experts interviewed by the author in Bolivia, in 2012.

Lowland Indigenous groups were committed to prior consultation in hydrocarbons. In fact, their reason for joining the Unity Pact in 2004 was to secure a role in crafting Law 3058; they wanted the law to address prior consultation and other Indigenous rights (D. H. Bebbington 2012b, 142–43). CIDOB and the APG helped write both Law 3058, which treated at length prior consultation procedures, and the 2007 regulations on prior consultation (DS 29033) that were attached to the law (Schilling-Vacaflor 2017a, 662; Falleti and Riofrancos 2018, 101–2). Although Law 3058 devoted detail to prior consultation, formal consultations in Bolivian hydrocarbons began with the 2007 regulations; before 2007, consultations about Bolivian hydrocarbon development were "rudimentary" and mostly took place between extractive companies and communities.[38]

Prior Consultation Procedures

DS 29033 required that the state consult Bolivian peasant, Indigenous, and Native communities (*los pueblos campesinos, indígenas, y originarios*) impacted by any Category 1 hydrocarbon project, for the approval of the project's EEIA.[39] A prior consultation was initiated when a representative of the hydrocarbon ministry—which oversaw consultations—submitted a written proposal to the impacted communities for an informational meeting about the project at hand, copying the communities' regional, departmental, and national representatives (DS 29033, Articles 2, 10). The communities (through their local leaders) were to respond with a date and location for the preliminary event. At the meeting, a ministry representative described the project and furnished all public documents about the planned development (Article 10). The communities then proposed the time frame, locations, structure, and cost of consultation meetings, and identified any community consultant that would participate (Article 11). The hydrocarbon ministry and communities had thirty-four days to plan and hold both the informational meeting and a gathering to design the prior consultation. They committed to the plan by signing a "memorandum of understanding" (*acta de entendimiento*; Articles 10, 11). The consultation was to be completed within three months (Article 12). It concluded with an agreement (*convenio*) signed by the communities and ministerial representatives that listed any community comments about the hydrocarbon project (Article 13). The outcome of the consultation process was integrated into the project's EEIA, and only then could the environment

38. Schilling-Vacaflor 2013a, 207. See also Jaskoski 2012, 42–43; Falleti and Riofrancos 2018, 100; and the case of the Percheles and El Dorado fields, in Chapter 5.

39. DS 29033, Article 15; Law 3058, Article 115; and Regulations, Law 1333, Article 15.

ministry issue the environmental license for the project (Article 15; Schilling-Vacaflor 2017b, 1063).

The completion of a prior consultation formally marked the point at which compensation discussions between firms and communities were to commence. Yet the compensation question often arose during the consultation, when a list of mitigable and nonmitigable project impacts was produced. Firms tried to minimize the list of nonmitigable project impacts, for which communities would be compensated; while communities aimed to define impacts as nonmitigable (Schilling-Vacaflor 2013b, 19–20; 2017a, 662).

With the 2007 regulations in place, two subsequent decrees constrained Indigenous communities in prior consultations. The 2014 decree DS 2195 set ceilings on the amount of compensation impacted communities could receive, based on project type; and the 2015 decree DS 2298 limited the length of the consultation to forty-five days (Schilling-Vacaflor 2017b, 1065). In many cases, the new time restriction was not enforced. An official in the hydrocarbon ministry who specialized in prior consultation and who had twelve years of experience working in hydrocarbons—for YPFB and for the environment and hydrocarbon ministries—explained the situation as follows: "Communities go back to their traditions and customs [*usos y costumbres*]. They say they just need two weeks to set the schedule, that they need more meetings, et cetera. And there's nothing we can do. So these cases still take time."[40] A consultation for a project in the lowland department of Beni ("Exploración Sísmica Area Río Beni Fase 2") lasted from April to October 2016.[41]

Legitimate Prior Consultation Norms

Prior consultation was legitimate in Bolivia.

Community dissatisfaction about project impacts was generally contained within consultations. Schilling-Vacaflor and Kuhn (2015) analyze all forty-two Bolivian gas cases in which an environmental license was granted and prior consultation completed, during 2007–13. In most cases, conflict was low or very low (2015, 134).

Communities accepted prior consultation outcomes, even though the consultation process did not afford them influence over projects. A glance at consultations with the Guaraní is telling, as they participated in forty-two

40. Interview with Alexandra Lora Velasco, Head of the Socio-Environmental Prevention and Control Unit, Ministry of Hydrocarbons and Energy; La Paz, June 13, 2017 (Interview B7).

41. Interview with an environment ministry official who previously had worked for the hydrocarbon ministry as a consultant, leading prior consultation processes. In that capacity, he had directed the prior consultation for the Beni project (interview, La Paz, June 13, 2017; Interview B6).

of the fifty-eight prior consultations concluded in Bolivia between 2007 and 2015 (Schilling-Vacaflor 2017b, 1059). In her analysis of more than thirty final agreements from Guaraní consultations, Schilling-Vacaflor finds that only two agreements referenced noteworthy project changes, which might include an increase in the distance between project activities and community water sources, restrictions on a project's local water use, or the relocation of seismic lines used for gas exploration. In no case in the sample did the participating community reject a project (Schilling-Vacaflor 2017b, 1067–68).

There were exceptions to the overall trend of low-conflict prior consultations. Where conflict occurred, it was often because communities demanded the implementation of the prior consultation regulations—serving as more evidence of their legitimacy. In five of the six Bolivian hydrocarbon conflicts analyzed in this book, communities mobilized to insist on being consulted (see Chapter 5). More broadly, the Guaraní mobilized a great deal to achieve prior consultations:

> The Guaraní have organized several blockades and marches over the past few years to demand compliance regarding their right to prior consultation. The responses from the state to these contentious performances have taken the following forms: negative media campaigns against the protest leaders, repression by security forces, non-response, and the signing of agreements that have often been disregarded afterwards. The state representatives have justified the repression of Guaraní mobilizations by declaring the necessity of enhancing the state's neo-extractivist development model. (Schilling-Vacaflor 2017a, 668)

In addition to taking direct action, the Guaraní have issued public statements and engaged the executive directly. For example, in a July 2010 letter to President Morales, the APG Itika Guasu objected to the state's issuance of twenty environmental licenses for hydrocarbon activities on the capitanía's lands without prior consultation (Anthias 2018, 194). The APG published statements opposing the 2014 and 2015 decrees (DS 2195 and DS 2298, respectively) that limited Indigenous communities in prior consultations (Schilling-Vacaflor 2017b, 1065).

TIPNIS and the Prior Consultation Law Project

The Guaraní helped create prior consultation norms in Bolivia not only by contributing to Law 3058 and DS 29033 but also through their participation in a project to develop a national prior consultation law that would have applied across sectors.

The project was framed by an ethnoenvironmental conflict over the construction of a major highway through TIPNIS. The conflict caused CIDOB and CONAMAQ to defect from the Unity Pact, in 2011. Although the highway project was not in hydrocarbons, thereby disqualifying the TIPNIS case from inclusion in this book's conflict sample, it would have been a step toward creating access to large, remote natural gas fields in the park (McNeish 2013, 225–26).

A momentous event in the TIPNIS conflict was a 2011 march led by CIDOB, CONAMAQ, and environmental and human rights NGOs to protest the highway and its anticipated environmental and social impacts. In August 2011, two thousand people departed from Trinidad, the capital of Beni. The six-hundred-kilometer march concluded in La Paz on October 19, 2011, after interruptions at the forty-day mark by counterprotesting cocaleros (McNeish 2013, 224–27).

After the march, the government held a prior consultation process for the highway, though only after it ruled out, briefly, all development in TIPNIS. Reacting to the march and subsequent meetings with activists, Morales issued an October 24, 2011, decree that halted the highway plan and declared TIPNIS "intangible." The government later pointed to different interests across affected communities—some of which wanted development in the park—to justify a prior consultation for the highway. A February 2012 law structured the TIPNIS consultation (McNeish 2013, 225, 228, 230–31).

The state completed the prior consultation process, which consisted of consultations with sixty-nine communities, in December 2012. The government reported that 80 percent of the consulted communities welcomed the highway. An independent commission that visited thirty-six of the communities arrived at different results: thirty communities rejected the road, three accepted it, and three wanted project changes and/or more information about the project (McNeish 2013, 231).

The TIPNIS case generated plans to create a prior consultation law. The law was to combine two independent proposals—one of a government commission, and a second of the APG (Schilling-Vacaflor 2017b, 1063). An executive team was immersed in early work on the initiative in August 2012. At the time, the topic of a prior consultation law was tense, due to criticisms of the highway consultation process.[42] Members of the NGO and Indigenous activist communities viewed the law project as a government effort to support large-scale development rather than to protect Indigenous rights.[43]

Disagreement over the question of community consent hindered collaboration between the government commission and the APG. The APG wanted

42. Interview with two members of the executive prior consultation law project team; La Paz, August 29, 2012 (Interview B8); see also Fontana and Gruber 2016, especially 254.

43. For example, a representative of the NGO Fundación Tierra held this view (interview, Santa Cruz, September 5, 2012; Interview B9). See also Fontana and Gruber 2016, 254–56.

development to depend on FPIC, and prior consultation outcomes to be binding; in contrast, the commission insisted that the state have the last word on extraction. A discouraged APG ended its collaboration with the government in March 2013. Several months later, in August, the APG refused to participate in a meeting organized by the government commission for Indigenous and peasant groups. The commission did not alter the draft consultation law significantly during that gathering (Schilling-Vacaflor 2017b, 1063–65). The law was with the legislature in 2018 (*La Razón* 4/30/2018). No law had been passed as of June 2019 (Fundación Tierra 6/11/2019).

THE POPULAR CONSULTATION IN COLOMBIAN EXTRACTIVES

The third participatory institution of interest in this book is the popular consultation, which operated formally in extractives in Colombia (and not in Bolivia or Peru). This section reviews the Colombian popular consultation to provide a foundation for the analysis in Chapter 4 of several conflicts in which Colombian communities tried to hold municipal popular consultations, sometimes with success. It then presents the contrasting experience of Peru, where communities organized *informal* popular consultations that served to avert mining.

Formal Local Popular Consultation Norms, Applied to Hydrocarbons and Mining

The popular consultation in Colombia permitted voters at the national and subnational levels to vote yes or no on matters that affected them. Municipal popular consultations were regulated in the late 1980s and then by a new framework established through the 1991 constitution (especially Articles 103 through 106), the 1994 Law 134, and a 2015 statutory law (Ramírez Cleves and Padrón Pardo 2016, 419, 425). Political authorities, or regular citizens using signature drives, could request popular consultations. For a citizen proposal, members of the public had to collect signatures from a minimum of 10 percent of eligible voters, according to Articles 3 and 9 of the statutory law (Ramírez Cleves and Padrón Pardo 2016, 425–26). For subnational popular consultations, proposed consultation questions were reviewed by the departmental tribunal (Tribunal Contencioso Administrativo), which decided on their constitutionality (Ramírez Cleves and Padrón Pardo 2016, 423–24).

Once carried out, a popular consultation at any level was binding when at least one-third of eligible voters participated, according to both Law 134 (Articles 55, 56) and the constitution (Ramírez Cleves and Padrón Pardo 2016, 420, 424–25). The constitution further specified that (departmental) governors and (municipal) mayors could use popular consultations "to decide about matters of the respective department or municipality within their jurisdiction" and that, for national consultations, "the decision of the people will be binding" (Ramírez Cleves and Padrón Pardo 2016, 420, quoting Articles 105 and 104, respectively).

Municipalities first applied the popular consultation to extractives in 2013. That year, the Piedras municipality in the department of Tolima held a mining consultation, and the municipality of Tauramena, in Casanare, voted on hydrocarbon development.[44]

Hosting municipal popular consultations in hydrocarbons and mining was contentious. Companies and the national government maintained that only the central state could decide on the use of subsoil resources (as elaborated in the section "Contested Boundaries in Extractive Zones" in this chapter). Indeed, during 2013–18, there were 102 efforts in ninety-five municipalities to organize popular consultations on extraction, and most failed (Shenk forthcoming). The municipalities that succeeded overwhelmingly voted against development; more than 90 percent of participants rejected it in each case (*Semana sostenible* 10/12/2018).

Contrast: Informal Popular Consultations in Peru

Different from the Colombian experience, in Peru local popular consultations in extractives were informal. Consequently, this book sorts Peruvian conflicts based not on how communities used the popular consultation but, rather, on their employment of prior consultation and the EIA public hearing. The study likewise does not categorize as a case of popular consultation one Colombian conflict that included an informal vote on extraction (see analysis of the Mandé Norte conflict in Chapter 6).

That the Peruvian popular consultation was informal did not detract from its power to stop extraction in some cases. Chapter 6 analyzes the best-known use of the popular consultation in Peru: a vote against the Tambo Grande mine in the northern region of Piura that led to the project's cancellation. The 2002 consultation served as a model for mining consultations across Latin America

44. The La Colosa and Odisea 3D case studies in Chapter 4 include analysis of the Piedras and Tauramena consultations, respectively.

(Walter and Urkidi 2017), including the informal popular consultation on the Peruvian Río Blanco mine project, also in Piura and decisive (see Chapter 6).[45]

CONTESTED BOUNDARIES IN EXTRACTIVE ZONES

The first part of this chapter examined the evolution and procedures of EIA hearings, prior consultations, and popular consultations, highlighting cross-national variation: While Peruvian regulations mandated the EIA hearing, in Colombia, political officials or members of civil society had to request it. In terms of prior consultation, Indigenous groups actively helped create prior consultation norms in Bolivia but not in Peru, where they dropped out of the government-led project to regulate prior consultation; or in Colombia, where they were excluded altogether. Only in Colombia did communities have on hand, in extractives, the formal local popular consultation.

This part of the chapter addresses the boundaries that define access to the three participatory institutions, and especially the contested nature of those borders. It first analyzes the separation between subnational and central state spheres of power, and primarily the heated question of whether municipalities can have authority in extractives. The discussion then turns to the geographic border around communities affected by hydrocarbons and mining and how communities often take exception to physical boundaries recognized by the state. The last section introduces the frequently unclear line that delineates representatives of impacted communities.

This review of boundary struggles builds toward the analysis in Chapters 4–6, which will show how boundary contestation affected communities' uses of participatory institutions in thirty extractive conflicts.

Which Level of Government Has Jurisdiction in Extractives?

One boundary that helps to determine who has a voice during approvals for new extraction separates municipal and central state jurisdictions. Contestation over that boundary exacerbates for local communities the *event initiation challenge*, or the task of prompting a participatory process.

As discussed in previous sections of this chapter, in Colombia, the EIA hearing and popular consultation were convoked by request. This institutional design feature meant that communities faced the challenge of initiating the

45. On the political power of informal popular consultations in Peru, see also Szablowski 2010; and Fulmer 2014.

participatory processes. The question of whether a municipality *could* host either participatory event—or whether the matter at hand should be handled by the central state—arose in several Colombian conflicts. Contestation over jurisdictional boundaries served as an additional hurdle to secure a participatory process. In other words, it added to the event initiation challenge. The jurisdictional issue appeared in several conflicts in the research sample. In one case, groups pressed for an EIA hearing outside of the area of influence (in the Bucaramanga municipality, for the Angostura mine). In another conflict, communities wanted a hearing on a component of an oil project after the project had been approved (in the municipality of Guamal, in the Lorito 1 case).

Disagreement over policy jurisdictions was most intense where groups tried to organize municipal popular consultations. Activists contended that a municipality's right to decide on its development trajectory extended to extractives. Countering that position, the Colombian government and extractive firms insisted that the central state owned and controlled the subsoil. Each side in the debate was supported by law and/or the constitution. A 1994 law on the use of municipal lands (Law 136) called for a local popular consultation where development—including mining—could change a municipality's traditional activities, in its Article 33. Yet according to Articles 332 and 334 of the 1991 constitution, the state owned nonrenewable resources and the subsoil, and controlled both land use and the extraction of natural resources (Ramírez Cleves and Padrón Pardo 2016, 427, 433). Reasserting the state's authority in extractives, Article 37 of the 2001 mining code prohibited all subnational authorities from blocking mining (Ramírez Cleves and Padrón Pardo 2016, 434).

The jurisdictional question made organizing municipal consultations in extractives difficult. Beginning with a 2011 case, departmental tribunals denied a number of requests for such consultations, mainly by determining that municipalities could not decide about extraction; and that proposed questions were overly technical or biased. The mining and energy ministry and the attorney general tried to prevent consultations and punish responsible subnational officials that organized them (Ramírez Cleves and Padrón Pardo 2016, 450–59). In the days leading up to an important 2014 Constitutional Court decision on popular consultations in extractives, the Santos administration declared that the 2013 Piedras and Tauramena popular consultations had been illegal, citing national ownership of subsoil resources (Gálvez Aldana 2014).

For a period, the Constitutional Court seemed to champion municipal consultations on extraction. It found in its previously noted 2014 decision (Constitutional Court Sentence C-123-14) that Article 37 of the mining code excessively restricted local autonomy and land use (Ramírez Cleves and Padrón Pardo 2016, 434–35). In the decision, the court also identified a need to include subnational populations in decisions about mining projects that affected them; it pronounced that municipal and district entities could participate in authorizing mining exploration and extraction, "through agreements about the protection of watersheds and the health of the population, as well as the economic, social, and cultural development of communities" (Ramírez Cleves and Padrón Pardo 2016, 437, quoting Constitutional Court Sentence C-123-14).

The Consejo de Estado responded to the 2014 Constitutional Court decision by suspending the regulations for Article 37. To fill the regulatory gap, a December 2014 decree (Decree 2691) affirmed that the state owned subsoil resources while also emphasizing that municipal and district councils would participate in establishing environmental, social, cultural, and economic protections against possible impacts of extraction. The new regulations did not mention popular consultations (Ramírez Cleves and Padrón Pardo 2016, 437–41).

Another Constitutional Court decision, in 2016 (Constitutional Court Sentence T-445-16), also defended municipal autonomy. In that case, the court ruled that subnational entities could regulate land use and guarantee environmental protections, including by preventing mining, and it allowed the municipality of Pijao, in the Quindío department, to vote on large-scale mining (pending a revision to the proposed consultation question; Dejusticia 10/20/2016).

The Constitutional Court reversed course with its October 2018 decision (Constitutional Court Sentence SU-095-18) on a tutela filed by an oil company. The case concerned a popular consultation on hydrocarbon activities in the municipality of Cumaral, in Meta. The court concluded that municipalities lacked the authority to convene popular consultations about projects that modified soil use (Dejusticia 12/5/2018; see also Shenk forthcoming). The decision halted the use of the local popular consultation in extractives and served as a reference for the overturning of the Tauramena consultation (*Semana sostenible* 10/12/2018; Chapter 4).

Who Is Impacted by Extractive Development?

Added to the line between national and municipal jurisdictions, a second contested boundary in producing regions that determines community access to participatory institutions is geographic: the physical border around communities that are impacted by extraction and therefore that have the right to engage in participatory processes. In Bolivia, Colombia, and Peru, communities that the state defined as not impacted ("outsiders"), disagreed with this classification and, on those grounds, sought access to participatory institutions. That is, contestation over the boundary that defined impacted communities created the *inclusion challenge*, for outsiders.

Ascertaining whether a community is impacted entails identifying the reach of a community and of the area affected by planned development. In this study's conflict sample, a project's EIA-defined areas of influence and direct influence were fiercely disputed in the mining cases of Conga and Santa Ana, respectively: outsider communities in each conflict claimed that they were impacted sufficiently by a project to warrant their inclusion in the EIA hearing.

When identifying whether an area impacted by a project overlaps with a community, borders around communities also matter. The boundaries of non-Indigenous communities and other subnational units, such as municipalities, tend to be documented by the state and widely accepted. There can be less agreement about the placement of geographic lines demarcating Indigenous communities, which may claim lands that the state does not recognize as theirs.

This section identifies heated contestation over Indigenous communal boundaries in all three countries. It also discusses variation in the "rigidity" of state-drawn lines around Indigenous lands. In Bolivia, Indigenous rights to prior consultation depended on title to impacted lands—a rigid border. In Peru and Colombia, the boundaries of recognized Indigenous lands were nonrigid for prior consultation purposes, in that land rights did not depend entirely on title holdings; rather, they could be based on other community relationships to territory. Chapter 5 will reveal how boundary contestation and rigidity affected the strategies of outsider communities, in their fight to be included in participatory processes.

Bolivia: Rigid Indigenous Communal Boundaries and a Weak Land Regime

Bolivian Indigenous communities were consulted about extraction only if they held title to affected land (Schilling-Vacaflor 2017a, 664). In most of the Bolivian hydrocarbon conflicts analyzed in this book, Guaraní communities claimed rights to impacted land to which they did not have title. That discord arose in a particular context: the country's weak land regime impeded Indigenous communal land titling in the hydrocarbon areas of Bolivia's eastern lowlands.

Indigenous Land Rights

During the years under study in Bolivia, a 1996 land reform governed Indigenous land rights in the country. That system had replaced an earlier one that had distributed land through two agencies: the National Agrarian Reform Service (Servicio Nacional de Reforma Agraria, SNRA), created in 1953, after Bolivia's 1952 revolution; and the National Colonization Institute (Instituto Nacional de Colonización, INC), which was established in 1966 and supported "colonization," especially in parts of the Cochabamba and Santa Cruz departments and in the northern part of the La Paz department. Overall, the system led to substantial land redistribution to smallholders in the highlands while encouraging large landholdings in the lowlands (Yashar 2005, 157–58, 193–95; Assies 2006, 582–85). In 1992, a corruption scandal effected a judicial audit of SNRA and INC that revealed rampant corruption and poor practices. For instance, overlapping titles had been issued for 30–60 percent of Bolivia's national territory (Assies 2006, 53–84, 590).

The scandal and audit prompted the state to propose a new land law. Indigenous and peasant organizations responded with a counterproposal, and as of 1995 a commission of business, government, and Indigenous representatives was negotiating the law's content. Uncertainty in the trajectory of the law project led Indigenous and peasant groups to stage, in August 1996, a national march for territory, after which the law project talks resumed. When CIDOB gained meaningful concessions through its participation, highland Indigenous and peasant organizations pulled out of the negotiations, leaving CIDOB the main participating civil-society actor. The project produced the October 1996 agrarian reform law (Ley del Servicio Nacional de Reforma Agraria, or "Ley INRA"), which created the National Agrarian Reform Institute (Instituto Nacional de Reforma Agraria, INRA; Assies 2006, 590–91).[46]

Ley INRA bestowed on Indigenous communities the right to communal lands, to be titled as Indigenous communal land plots (Tierras Comunitarias de Orígen, TCOs; Assies 2006, 591; Schilling-Vacaflor 2017b, 1062). INRA, under the Ministry of Sustainable Development and the Environment, administered the new system (Assies 2006, 592).

The agrarian reform appeared to threaten interests of powerful agribusiness elites and large landowners, who feared losing land. Ley INRA required that medium and large properties meet a "social-economic function": "agricultural production, forestry, research, ecotourism, or biodiversity protection." (TCOs, community properties, and small plots owned by individuals or families had to fulfill a "social function" by benefiting their owners directly.) Holdings that failed to perform their social-economic function could be returned to the state through "reversion" (Assies 2006, 591–93). On its face, the reversion process benefited Indigenous and peasant communities, which could "demand land from the state, where and when it was available," with land transfers free of charge to communities (Assies 2006, 606 n. 60). The law also mandated

46. On Ley INRA, see also Yashar 2005, especially 216–18.

the clarification of land rights (*saneamiento*), in cases of overlapping claims. The clarification of TCO land involved identifying any land rights of non-Indigenous actors ("third parties," or *terceros*) within the TCO-claimed area. Clarification was to be completed within one decade (Assies 2006, 592).

The Weak Implementation of Ley INRA in Gas-Rich Areas of the Eastern Lowlands

Although on paper Ley INRA may have threatened elite interests in the lowlands, the reality was more complicated. The implementation of Ley INRA was slow, limited, and seemingly biased toward private landowners.

Delays in clarification were due in part to resource challenges. Clarification entailed considerable manpower to assess land use. In the Guaraní Itika Guasu's claimed TCO in Tarija, INRA agents took part in the "rounding up, marking, and counting of cattle, a time-consuming process" (Anthias 2012, 136). Speaking on the Guaraní's experience overall, a former general director of TCOs in the Vice Ministry of Lands (within the Ministry of Rural Development and Lands) depicted the titling process for TCOs as lengthy, because a team of a lawyer, a sociologist, and a topographer surveyed the land before it could be reclaimed from large landholders. During the former director's term (2006–9), the Danish government financed those processes. Yet even with that assistance, the state had insufficient resources to perform clarification work in a timely fashion.[47]

INRA's weak capacity did not manifest neutrally. Under Morales, the government allocated a substantial amount of land to Indigenous and peasant communities, including in the lowlands, but Indigenous land titling in areas of gas deposits stalled from the 2000s to the 2010s (Hinojosa et al. 2015, 111). By 2010, the Guaraní had achieved rights to only 1.45 million hectares, which was less than one-third of the total lands they had claimed (Schilling-Vacaflor 2017b, 1062). In contrast to the experience of Indigenous communities in gas regions,

> Private lands which overlapped with proposed gas infrastructure and gas exploration/production have been titled more quickly, leading to the often heard complaint from indigenous leaders that the land titling process has done more

47. Interview with Bienvenido Zaco Mborobainchi, former general director of TCOs, Vice Ministry of Lands, Ministry of Rural Development and Lands; Santa Cruz, June 16, 2017 (Interview B10). For details on the high cost and complexity of the TCO delineation and titling process, and the role of international support in clarification, see also Assies 2006, 593–95.

> to secure the land rights of third parties within their TCOs than secure the territorial integrity of indigenous groups. The suspicion has been that the gas companies have preferred to deal with private land owners and not indigenous groups to negotiate surface rights. (Hinojosa et al. 2015, 111)[48]

One way that INRA apparently assisted with hydrocarbon development was through reversion. Administratively, once land was reverted to the state as public land (*tierra fiscal*), it was open not only to Indigenous claims but also to private owners, and to "intercultural communities"—often settlers from outside the area, identified by many lowland Indigenous organizations as being campesino and not Indigenous. Indigenous communities and their advocates widely criticized INRA for classifying land as public. They maintained that the agency used this practice to transfer land to non-Indigenous people, bypass prior consultation, and encourage extraction. This system began in 2009, according to the director of CEJIS, a Bolivian NGO that supported Guaraní land titling.[49] Apart from INRA's actions, YPFB also played a role in making lands public and available for extraction, without prior consultation. The state company tried to avoid prior consultation processes by claiming rights to land (and also by classifying development as Category 2 projects).[50]

Experiences of Itika Guasu offer evidence of INRA's biased approach to titling. After the state granted Repsol YPF permission to operate in the Margarita Gas Field (one of Bolivia's megacampos), the company entered TCO Itika Guasu, in 1997. At that time, the state recognized the TCO, but private titles within it had not been clarified. Repsol negotiated access to nonclarified lands with cattle ranchers and did not also meet with Itika Guasu. INRA respected Repsol's agreements with the ranchers even after the agency's own fieldwork (in 2000) found that some of the ranchers could not demonstrate productive use of the land. As of 2012, none of that land had been awarded to Itika Guasu (Anthias 2012, 135–36).

INRA's bias has been attributed to the direct influence of non-Indigenous elites. INRA officials had family members who sought title to land within Itika Guasu's claimed territory; and they were part of elite networks in other ways, as well. Ranchers rented livestock to feign productive land use during INRA inspections. They also encouraged INRA officials to "lose" records after inspections (Anthias 2018, 99–100). In 2004, Tarija ranchers and landowner

48. For views among the Guaraní about how gas companies, as well as the state, impeded Indigenous titling in hydrocarbon regions intentionally, to facilitate extraction, see also Anthias 2018, 198–99.

49. Interview with Hernán Ávila, Director, CEJIS; Santa Cruz, June 20, 2017 (Interview B11).

50. Interview with a YPFB Chaco S.A. employee who previously had worked for (private) Chaco S.A.; Santa Cruz, Bolivia, September 6, 2012 (Interview B12).

groups in other departments organized for an increase in the expanse of land allocated per animal, for purposes of calculating whether land met its social-economic function. The effort failed, but it slowed TCO titling (Anthias 2018, 108–9).

Peru: Nonrigid Indigenous Communal Boundaries

Similar to the case of Bolivia, Peruvian Indigenous land rights have been tenuous. Indigenous titling in Peru expanded in the 1970s, due to both land reform and government efforts to organize highland communities into cooperatives and formalize communal lands in the Amazon. Yet from the 1970s to the 1990s, the tide turned again, with the weakening of communal land rights (Yashar 2005, 230–38, 252–58). Since then, as conflicts in this book illustrate, Indigenous communities have pursued title to their claimed lands.

Despite the importance of formal landownership for Peruvian Indigenous communities, those without title to impacted lands still could enjoy the right to prior consultation. Different from the Bolivian case, then, Indigenous communal boundaries in Peru were nonrigid—though, as discussed here, still contested.

Rights Based on Ties to Land

Peruvian Indigenous communities could gain recognition of land rights for prior consultation eligibility based on their cultural connections to land. A culture ministry guide and directive for determining Indigeneity during the identification phase of prior consultation listed criteria that included spiritual and historical ties to a territory, as well as a community's descendance from "original" populations, unique cultural and institutional practices, and collective Indigenous or Native identity (Directive 001-2014-VMI-MC, Article 7.1.1–2; Defensoría del Pueblo 2017, 85). Apart from guidelines for implementing Peru's prior consultation regulations, Peru's Constitutional Tribunal determined that ancestral lands of Native communities had the same status as formally titled property (Jima Chamiquit et al. 8/24/2016).

Most consequential in the identification process was a national database of Indigenous and Native communities (Base de Datos de Pueblos Indígenas u Originarios), which the culture ministry constructed in accordance with the prior consultation law (Defensoría del Pueblo 2017, 85). Legally a community did not need to be in the database to participate in prior consultations. However, the state resisted consulting unlisted communities (Sanborn et al. 2016, 21). The database grew as the ministry collected new information on communities. In 2018, the database identified fifty-five Indigenous peoples, 2,675 Native communities, and 3,041 campesino communities—mainly Quechua and Aymara—but still was not complete (Leyva 2018, 39).

Although Peruvian Indigenous communities did not need title to impacted land to participate in prior consultations, title still mattered. A culture ministry lawyer said that title to impacted land was "vital, because in the field visit, if a community has a recognized territory or area, then it is easy: we can see where the community lines are drawn and if there is overlap with the [project's] area of influence." He also explained that communities with titles automatically were placed in the culture ministry's database.[51] In addition, the environmental paquetazos—specifically, Article 6 of DS 054-2013-PCM, supported by Law 30230—weakened Indigenous vis-à-vis extractive firms' land rights; Article 6 did not differentiate between nontitled Indigenous lands, and "abandoned lands" (*terrenos eriazos*), and streamlined the issuance of easements on the latter. Article 6 was thrown out in March 2015 (by the Cuarto Sala Civil de la Corte Superior de Justicia de Lima; Leyva 6/6/2013, *Servindi* 3/20/2015). In June 2020, the Constitutional Tribunal ruled that Law 30230 did not apply to Indigenous communities, because they had not been consulted about it.[52]

The Contentious Identification Stage

The Peruvian state's failure to consult Indigenous communities about extraction caused conflict, as discussed in the section "Prior Consultation" in this chapter. Conflict often stemmed from the state's inadequate fieldwork to identify impacted communities, as part of prior consultation.

By late 2014, the Defensoría del Pueblo knew of sixteen cases in which MINEM had authorized mining exploration without consulting impacted Indigenous communities (Defensoría del Pueblo 2017, 98). When in 2015 it became public that MINEM had contracted out the identification fieldwork for fifteen mining projects, and that for at least one of those projects the ministry had authorized new exploration without consulting an affected community, MINEM revisited the mining cases in question, and DGAA assumed mining fieldwork (Leyva 2018, 40). Starting in 2016, contractors overseen by culture ministry officials performed the task, financed by MINEM. In hydrocarbons, a culture ministry representative accompanied

51. Interview P4.

52. In 2015, approximately ten thousand people, of several national Indigenous organizations, filed the case about the lack of prior consultation for Law 30230 (Ruiz Molleda 6/11/2020).

the field visits, which were carried out by Perupetro and then, beginning in 2015, by DGAA.[53]

The most contested aspect of identification was whether to list highland Indigenous communities in the culture ministry's database. Leaving them out would have meant that, generally, communities would not have been consulted about mining development, because Peru's hard-rock minerals were concentrated in the highlands. The debate took place within a historical context in which the Peruvian state had classified highland populations as peasants and not Indigenous, as part of state- and nation-building efforts (Yashar 2005, 229–35; Leyva 2018, 38).

When it was first released, the database did not include highland Indigenous communities. As per the prior consultation law, the culture ministry was to publish the database in 2012. In December of that year, the ministry created a version in which 60 percent of the listed Indigenous peoples were of the highlands. However, Peru's national mining, oil, and energy association (Sociedad Nacional de Minería, Petróleo y Energía, SNMPE) objected to the inclusion of highland communities—and, more fundamentally, to prior consultations in mining. The registry, which omitted highland communities, was made public in late 2013 (Sanborn et al. 2016, 21–22; Leyva 2018, 38–39).

The database did not inventory highland communities until July 2015 (Sanborn et al. 2016, 22; Leyva 2018, 38–39). Mining consultations commenced that year (Sanborn et al. 2016, 10).[54]

Colombia: Nonrigid Indigenous Communal Boundaries Backed by the Constitutional Court

As in the Peruvian case, Indigenous communities in Colombia strived to formalize their lands but could participate in prior consultations if areas outside of their titled lands were impacted by planned extraction. Yet Colombia is distinct, due to the Constitutional Court's central role in defining Indigenous rights to nontitled lands, and the relative strength of Indigenous territorial rights.

Resguardos

Indigenous communal landholdings in Colombia came out of an integrationist effort. A 1958 law, Law 81, was designed to impart credit, technical assistance,

53. Interview P4. On the introduction of the culture ministry's role in the identification stage in mining, see also Leyva 2018, 40.

54. The first mining consultation was carried out in 2015 for an exploration project in the Cusco region ("Proyecto de Exploración Minera Aurora"; Defensoría del Pueblo 2017, 98).

and land to Indigenous communities, using the terms "indigenous" and "campesino" interchangeably. Agrarian reform laws in the 1960s provided for *resguardos* as Indigenous communal landholdings but, like Law 81, emphasized social justice rather than Indigenous rights (Rodríguez-Franco 2017, 130–31).

Indigenous activists appropriated the resguardo concept to protect Indigenous autonomy and communal landownership, and in 1988 resguardos became the only legal form of Indigenous lands (Rodríguez-Franco 2017, 131–33). Article 63 of the 1991 constitution made resguardo lands permanent and specifically protected them from sale and seizure (Rodríguez-Franco 2017, 112–13, 134). Resguardos constituted 31.5 percent of national territory and 47.9 percent of the Colombian Amazon by 2013 (Rodríguez-Franco 2017, 123).

Nonrigid Indigenous Territorial Boundaries

If resguardos established strong communal land rights, they did not create uncontested borders. Indigenous communities often considered non-resguardo lands to be their territories. Depending on a community's relationship to those areas, it could secure the right to prior consultation about extractive development that impacted the lands, due to the Constitutional Court's interpretation of land rights: that Indigenous presence alone in an area impacted by extraction warranted prior consultation. The court adopted this interpretation in its 1997 decision on the Samoré case, the court's first ruling on prior consultation (Orduz Salinas 2014, 33; on Samoré, see Chapter 6).

Constitutional Court decisions tempered assessments that the interior ministry made when identifying impacted Indigenous communities. In that work, an interior ministry employee visited the project area, with a company representative and a contracted team that generally comprised an anthropologist and at least one other expert.[55] With its relatively narrow definition of Indigenous presence, the ministry often skipped prior consultation, which could give rise to legal battles, many of which reached the Constitutional Court. Court rulings would then serve as guidance for future identification trips. For instance, based on Constitutional Court decisions on tutela filings, the interior ministry considered a community to be impacted by a project if a river that was the community's only water source flowed through the project's area of direct influence; if a road that crossed into the area of direct influence was the only route connecting an Indigenous community to the nearest city;

55. Cartographers, engineers, lawyers, and/or sociologists were also contracted for these teams. Interviews C2 and C4.

or if a space considered sacred to a community overlapped with the area of direct influence.[56]

Who Speaks for Impacted Communities?

Unlike outsider communities, insider communities enjoy access to participatory processes in project approvals. Yet insiders, too, confront boundary contestation—over the line delineating their legitimate representatives, relative to the rest of the community. Debate over this boundary emerges where groups within a community have competing views about planned extraction.

That competition intensifies a challenge that is present for insider communities: the challenge of expressing views about the new extractive activity, or the *articulation challenge*. That is, insiders encounter the task of voicing their opinions about mining or hydrocarbons. The articulation challenge is greater where communities are fractured, because insiders cannot advance a unified position. As analyzed in Chapter 6, this situation limited activists' options for using participatory institutions in cases from Colombia and Peru.

In contrast, in the one Bolivian conflict in this study in which insiders mobilized, the impacted community was cohesive (see analysis of the San Antonio conflict in Chapter 6). Yet two Bolivian cases that are not in this study's sample have received attention precisely because they illuminate the divisiveness of extraction for insider communities, including at the prior consultation stage. More precisely, Indigenous leaders jockeyed for signing authority in prior consultations and, in doing so, advanced the consultations, and extraction.

In one conflict, communities responded to a plan by the Bolivian and Venezuelan YPFB Petroandina S.A.M. consortium to conduct oil exploration in the Lliquimuni oil block. Lliquimuni was located in the north of the La Paz department, an area relatively new to hydrocarbon development. The eight communities in TCO Mosetén, which was affected by the project, were represented by the Organization of the Mosetén Indigenous People (Organización del Pueblo Indígena Mosetén, OPIM), under the larger La Paz Indigenous People's Council (Central de Pueblos Indígenas de La Paz, CPILAP), of CIDOB (Pellegrini and Ribera Arismendi 2012, 105, 110–11).

When the hydrocarbon ministry learned of CPILAP's demands—which included a large compensation package, the completion of Mosetén land registration, and a role for the Mosetén in monitoring seismic tests—the ministry chose not to consult OPIM or CPILAP and instead met with the leaders of the individual communities (Pellegrini and Ribera Arismendi 2012, 111). The

56. Interview C2.

state's direct negotiations with the communities weakened the Mosetén organizationally. As a result of the conflict, four of the eight Mosetén communities claimed not to be represented by CPILAP or OPIM, and the two organizations underwent a legitimacy crisis (Pellegrini and Ribera Arismendi 2012, 111; Schilling-Vacaflor 2013a, 212–13).[57]

The second case involved a 2008–9 prior consultation for British Gas (BG) Bolivia's Palo Marcado project. BG Bolivia had operated on lands of the Weenhayek Indigenous nation in the Chaco since the late 1990s, when the company took over gas operations that had begun in the 1970s. For Palo Marcado, the firm would extract from three existing wells, drill a fourth well, and construct gas lines and a pumping station (D. H. Bebbington 2012a, 58–59).

In 2008, the hydrocarbon ministry began the Palo Marcado prior consultation with the Weenhayek, represented by the Organization of Weenhayek Captains (Organización de Capitanes Weenhayek, ORCAWETA), of CIDOB (D. H. Bebbington 2012a, 53, 59). At first, ORCAWETA leader Moisés Sapiranda used his signature authority to create delays in the consultation. He called for breaks during one of the consultation meetings to confer with capitanes. He then suspended the consultation process when "disagreements arose over how to proceed with complaints that BG-Bolivia had conducted other activities in the past year . . . without consulting ORCAWETA" (D. H. Bebbington 2012a, 61).

Prior consultation later advanced amid competition between Sapiranda and his rival, Pablo Rivera. Uninvited, Rivera and his followers attended a November 2008 meeting that marked the relaunching of the consultation process. In discord between the two groups, there was shouting and pushing. Rivera and his supporters refused to leave, causing Sapiranda to call YPFB and the local military unit to remove them. Rivera then claimed to be ORCAWETA's leader in a letter that he sent via facsimile to YPFB, BG Bolivia, and CIDOB. In December 2008, Sapiranda negotiated compensation for the ongoing BG operation. Afterward, the Palo Marcado consultation moved forward efficiently. A compensation agreement for the new project ensued (D. H. Bebbington 2012a, 61–63).

SUMMARY

This chapter presented an overview of participatory institutions that have formed part of state approval processes for new extraction in Bolivia, Colombia, and Peru. It also introduced the contested boundaries in extractive

57. On the Lluiqumuni case, see also Bascopé Sanjinés 2010, 57–93. The case was discussed at length by Wilma Mendoza, an Indigenous leader and a key activist in the conflict (interview, Santa Cruz, June 19, 2017; Interview B13).

zones that determine access to these institutions. The boundaries define (1) the policy jurisdiction of municipalities relative to the central state, (2) the communities affected by development, and (3) the representatives of impacted communities. Through analysis of thirty major mining and hydrocarbon conflicts in the three countries, Chapters 4–6 will show how tensions over the three boundaries contributed to and even spawned challenges for community participation; and how those challenges affected community uses of participatory institutions.

PART III

The Conflicts

CHAPTER 4

The Event Initiation Challenge and Contested Policy Jurisdictions

In the six conflicts examined in this chapter, from Colombia, communities used the EIA hearing and/or the popular consultation in their mobilizing. Colombian communities impacted by extractive development gained access to these participatory opportunities only by petition. That requirement created for communities the *event initiation challenge*, or the challenge of securing a participatory process. The event initiation challenge limited communities to a single use of the institutions: asking for participatory events and then taking part in them. That is, communities organized through the participatory institutions, by acting in accordance with formal procedures.

In four of the conflicts analyzed in the chapter, communities and central state actors disagreed about whether the local municipality had jurisdiction in extractives. This boundary contestation added to the event initiation challenge; the lack of clear municipal authority to host a popular consultation or public hearing was yet another obstacle for groups seeking the participatory process. Disputes over the boundary between municipal and central state jurisdictions took place in two cases in which the EIA hearing helped organize conflict. In each of those conflicts, the state environmental authority allowed the hearing, but only due to substantial community mobilizing.

The popular consultation brought exceptionally intense jurisdictional battles. Municipalities claimed that they could hold binding votes on mining and hydrocarbons, while extractive firms and the national government insisted that only the central state could make determinations about subsoil resources. The Constitutional Court's October 2018 Cumaral ruling against municipal popular consultations (discussed in Chapter 3) resolved

The Politics of Extraction. Maiah Jaskoski, Oxford University Press. © Oxford University Press 2022.
DOI: 10.1093/oso/9780197568927.003.0004

Figure 4.1 Event Initiation Challenge Heightened by Contested Jurisdictions

the matter, in Colombia in general and in three conflicts in this chapter—by encouraging the overturning of one municipal popular consultation (in the Odisea 3D case) and ruling out others (in the cases of Nogal and San Martín).

Figure 4.1 summarizes the causal logic by which the event initiation challenge arose and was exacerbated by contested policy jurisdictions; and how the challenge led communities to request and engage in formal participatory processes.

This chapter proceeds in three parts. The first section focuses on cases in which popular consultation was the most salient participatory institution, La Colosa and Odisea 3D. In these conflicts, communities held consultations before the companies would have submitted an EIA for review. The chapter then takes up community participation in EIA hearings, in the Angostura and Lorito 1 cases. In the final two conflicts, over development in the Nogal block and fracking in San Martín, groups solicited hearings and also organized signature drives to request popular consultations.

Table 4.1 summarizes the six cases. As shown in the table and analyzed here, in one conflict, over the proposed Angostura mine, activists participated in but also organized around the EIA hearing; they attached the concept of the "public hearing" to a march. As an additional use of participatory institutions, communities engaged in socialization meetings in the Odisea 3D case.

POPULAR CONSULTATIONS

This section examines two particularly well-known municipal popular consultations: the referendum carried out by the municipality of Tauramena that stalled development in the Odisea 3D oil block, and the Piedras consultation that voted down the La Colosa gold mine. Together, the two consultations—both held in 2013—established a precedent for the use of the local popular consultation to prevent extraction in Colombia (Ramírez Cleves and Padrón Pardo 2015, 449; see also Chapter 3 of this volume).

Table 4.1 THE EVENT INITIATION CHALLENGE: CASES

Conflict	Goal of mobilizing	Dominant participatory institution			Other uses of participatory institutions
		Institution	Contested municipal jurisdiction vis-à-vis central state	Use of institution	
La Colosa (Colombia; mining; 2010–17)	Block mine	Popular consultation	Control of subsoil resources	Mobilizing for and participation in consultations	n/a
Odisea 3D (Colombia; hydrocarbons; 2013–19)	Block oil exploration	Popular consultation	Control of subsoil resources	Mobilizing for and participation in consultation	Participation in socialization meetings
Lorito 1 (Colombia; hydrocarbons; 2012–17)	Block oil exploration	EIA hearing	Authority to host hearing on project element after project approval	Mobilizing for and participation in hearings	n/a
Angostura (Colombia; mining; 2010–11)	Block mine	EIA hearing	Authority to host second EIA hearing, outside of area of influence	Mobilizing for and participation in hearing	Application of "EIA hearing" concept to a march
Nogal (Colombia; hydrocarbons; 2014–18)	Block oil exploration	EIA hearing	n/a	Request for and active participation in hearing	Mobilizing for popular consultation
Fracking in San Martín (Colombia; hydrocarbons; 2016–18)	Block fracking exploration	EIA hearing; popular consultation	n/a	Request for hearing; mobilizing for popular consultation	n/a

La Colosa

AngloGold Ashanti's La Colosa open-pit mine project was in hills near the town of Cajamarca, in the municipality of the same name, in the Tolima department. The project had the estimated capacity to produce thirty-five million ounces of gold across twenty years (Cuevas Guarnizo 1/2/2014; McNeish 2017, 1130). AngloGold Ashanti chose the rural village (*corregimiento*) of Doima, in the Piedras municipality, as the site for a leaching pool and a tailings pond for the mine. It also planned to conduct exploration, in the municipality of Ibagué.[1] All three Tolima municipalities attempted to hold popular consultations on mining, and Cajamarca and Piedras succeeded. The Cajamarca vote led AngloGold Ashanti to suspend the project.

Cajamarca was AngloGold Ashanti's first exploration site in Colombia. In 2007, the company arrived and began holding socialization meetings and investing in local development, including agricultural projects and wireless Internet services.[2]

Opposition to La Colosa and its associated infrastructure was strong in Tolima, which depended on agriculture; communities worried about the mine's impact on water (McNeish 2017, 1130). Furthermore, AngloGold Ashanti titles overlapped with a páramo, generating concern for that fragile ecosystem (Cuevas Guarnizo 1/2/2014). The Environmental Committee in Defense of Life (Comité Ambiental en Defensa de la Vida), which was founded in 2010, headed the antimine effort (McNeish 2017, 1131–32). Several marches were staged in the La Colosa conflict. Ten thousand people participated in the eighth march, in June 2016.[3]

The Piedras Popular Consultation

Organizing in Piedras began in 2012. Late that year, representatives of the Comité Ambiental learned from a local teacher that AngloGold Ashanti had held meetings at a high school about recycling, without addressing in those gatherings the mine or the related planned development in Piedras. Comité members responded to the news by traveling to the municipality to speak with company personnel and Piedras residents about La Colosa and its potential environmental impacts.[4] Consternation grew in Piedras about the mine, especially its impacts on a local river and, in turn, rice crops and fishing (McNeish 2017, 1130). Nearly

1. Interview with the Manager of Human Rights and Strategic Projects, AngloGold Ashanti; Bogotá, July 28, 2016 (Interview C5).
2. Interview C5.
3. Interview with Renzo García, member of the Comité Ambiental en Defensa de la Vida in Tolima; by phone from Bogotá, August 1, 2016 (Interview C6).
4. This description of the high-school meetings and Comité response is based on McNeish 2017, 1130, 1132; and Interview C6.

three hundred people participated in Piedras's first mobilization, in Doima, in December 2012.[5] Local protests in Piedras interrupted the movement of company vehicles throughout the first half of 2013 (McNeish 2017, 1130).

Alongside activism in the street, department-level discussions took place about legal options for stopping the mine. Those conversations brought together the Comité Ambiental, the Tolima CAR, the regional human rights ombudsman, agricultural producers' associations, environmental organizations, and other members of civil society. The unusually broad coalition helped bring about the Piedras consultation (McNeish 2017, 1132, 1136), Colombia's first popular consultation on extractives.

In May 2013, Piedras's mayor submitted to the municipal council proposed language for the referendum. He emphasized in his submission the municipality's reliance on agriculture and the mine's anticipated impacts on the environment and on economic and social life. The Piedras municipal council approved the consultation plan, and in June 2013 the Tolima tribunal followed suit (Ramírez Cleves and Padrón Pardo 2016, 443–44).

AngloGold Ashanti sought the nullification of the tribunal's decision.[6] Company allies also tried to thwart the referendum. On July 25, 2013, just three days before the vote, the hydrocarbon group within the attorney general's office sent a formal notice to the Piedras mayor stating that municipal authorities could not interfere with mining, referencing Article 37 of the 2001 mining code.[7] The notice also underscored that public servants who violated the constitution and the law could be investigated (Ramírez Cleves and Padrón Pardo 2016, 445).

The Piedras consultation took place on July 28, 2013. Residents were asked the following:

> Do you agree, as a resident of Piedras, Tolima that in our jurisdiction, the following activities are carried out: exploration, exploitation, treatment, transformation, transportation, washing of materials that originate from large scale gold mining; or that materials that are harmful to health and the environment are stored or used, specifically cyanide and/or any other substances or hazardous materials associated with these activities; furthermore, that surface and ground water is used from our town in such operations or any other similar operations that may affect and/or limit the supply of potable water for human consumption, and for agriculture, the traditional productive vocation of our municipality? (McNeish 2017, 1141 n. 27)

Of the 2,975 votes cast (by 58 percent of registered voters), only 24 supported mining (McNeish 2017, 1141 n. 28).

5. Interview C6.

6. In the coming months, the Tolima tribunal denied the company's request. The case reached the Consejo de Estado, which ruled against the firm in 2014 (Ramírez Cleves and Padrón Pardo 2016, 445).

7. On Article 37 of the mining code, see Chapter 3.

After the popular consultation, the attorney general's office investigated the Piedras mayor and municipal council for violating national law with the consultation, and made threats of disciplinary actions against all Tolima municipal officials that might consider organizing future popular consultations on the mine (McNeish 2017, 1134).

AngloGold Ashanti reacted to the Piedras vote by ruling out Doima as a possible site for the leaching pool and tailings pond.[8]

The Cajamarca Consultation and AngloGold Ashanti's Departure

Communities in Ibagué and Cajamarca also pursued popular consultations. Gaining the Tolima tribunal's permission for the Ibagué consultation proved an obstacle, due to alleged bias in the phrasing of the consultation question.[9] With the consultation process stalled, Ibagué's municipal council used a local instrument ("Acuerdo 012") to prohibit medium- and large-scale metal mining in the municipality. The Tolima tribunal overturned that measure in late 2017, asserting that the council could not prohibit mining. Municipal leaders responded to the tribunal's decision by resuming the popular consultation project (*El Tiempo* 12/5/2017; Jáuregui Sarmiento 12/7/2017).

During the Ibagué struggle, Cajamarca's popular consultation blocked La Colosa. The Cajamarca referendum was delayed, as the attorney general's warning to municipal officials (see under "The Piedras Popular Consultation") had had a chilling effect. In early 2015, the Cajamarca municipal council voted against holding a popular consultation. The council referenced the attorney general's notice and pressures from AngloGold, which had threatened to halt its investment in local development should the municipality hold a consultation (McNeish 2017, 1134). The prospect of a popular consultation in Cajamarca, the location of the mine, was exceptionally problematic for the company, as summarized by an AngloGold Ashanti community relations manager in July 2016, when the mine still seemed viable:

> There is the possibility of a popular consultation in Ibagué and another consultation in Cajamarca. The one in Cajamarca is riskier, because the mine is there—it would look very bad for the company if there were a popular consultation in Cajamarca and if the vote were more opposed to the mine than for it. In Ibagué, it's not as worrisome if there is a consultation.[10]

8. Interview C5.

9. The proposed question as of 2017 was, "Are you in agreement YES or NO with mining projects and activities in the Ibagúe municipality that involve the contamination of land, the loss or contamination of waters, or impacts on the municipality's agricultural and tourism sectors?" (*Portafolio* 2/20/2017).

10. Interview C5.

Ultimately, Cajamarca held its consultation, in March 2017. Ninety-eight percent of participants (6,165 residents) voted against mining (Hernández Bonilla 3/26/2017). The state claimed that the consultation was illegitimate. The mining and energy minister issued a statement that the vote had no impact on AngloGold Ashanti's right to develop its project, basing his argument on central state ownership of the subsoil (*El Espectador* 3/27/2017). AngloGold Ashanti nonetheless suspended La Colosa, in response to the Cajamarca consultation (Cobb 4/27/2017).

Odisea 3D

As in the La Colosa case, activists used the municipal popular consultation in a conflict over an Ecopetrol exploration project in the Odisea 3D oil block, in the department of Casanare. A December 2013 consultation in the Tauramena municipality successfully halted the project, though that victory was reversed in 2019, as detailed here.

Local Apprehensions about Water, and the Popular Consultation Initiative

Casanare, with Arauca and Meta, made up Colombia's large, oil-producing eastern plains (the Llanos Orientales; Rettberg and Prieto 2018, 148–49). At the time of the Odisea 3D conflict, 90 percent of Tauramena was "concessioned" to the oil industry, according to Tauramena's mayor (*El Tiempo* 12/16/2013). Communities in the municipality were accustomed to oil extraction, but they regarded the Odisea 3D exploration as hazardous. The project, which entailed drilling, seismic exploration, production, and transport, was expected to affect a crucial water recharge area for Tauramena and four other Casanare municipalities (Molano Jimeno 12/15/2013; *El Tiempo* 12/16/2013). The project overlapped with nearly one-half of Tauramena and would have impacted eleven Tauramena veredas (Molano Jimeno 12/15/2013).

To stop the Odisea 3D development, Tauramena's mayor submitted a popular consultation proposal to the municipal council, which authorized the vote in September 2013. The Casanare tribunal issued its approval of the consultation the next month (Ramírez Cleves and Padrón Pardo 2016, 446–47).

State Attempts to Prevent the Consultation

With the consultation project underway, the national government and Ecopetrol made multiple attempts in 2013 to move forward with the Odisea 3D development. Ecopetrol held twelve socialization meetings in four municipalities during the second half of the year, to seek public backing for the exploration. When that strategy proved futile, the company suspended the project, hoping to de-escalate conflict and reduce interest in a popular consultation (*Prensa libre Casanare* 9/4/2013, 12/11/2013). Knowing the temporary nature of the suspension, the consultation team sustained its momentum.[11]

Ecopetrol, with the mining and energy ministry, shifted to a negotiation strategy. Eight days before the scheduled vote, the mining and energy minister and Ecopetrol's president invited twelve members of the Tauramena consultation organizing committee to Bogotá, to pressure them to call off the event.[12] The meetings filled two days. Attendees included government attorneys from ANLA, Ecopetrol, the mining and energy ministry, and the National Hydrocarbon Agency (Agencia Nacional de Hidrocarburos, ANH). The popular consultation organizers were not swayed.

The day after the Bogotá meetings concluded, Ecopetrol's president and the environment, interior, and mining and energy ministers traveled to Tauramena to discuss the Odisea 3D project with the local population. Between four thousand and five thousand Tauramena residents attended that meeting, which lasted from 9:00 a.m. to 5:00 p.m. The many interjections by members of the public confirmed that there was overwhelming local enthusiasm for the popular consultation. As a last, desperate, measure to thwart the referendum, the visiting officials offered multiple high-level government and Ecopetrol posts to at least one member of the consultation planning committee.

The Consultation and its Aftermath

In the December 15, 2013, Tauramena popular consultation, 96 percent of the 4,612 participants rejected hydrocarbon exploration, production, and transport in the eleven impacted veredas (Ramírez Cleves and Padrón Pardo 2016, 446, 448).[13]

The Tauramena consultation motivated the other four municipalities affected by the Odisea 3D exploration to organize their own popular

11. Interview with Luis Arturo Ramírez Roa, an attorney who was pivotal in organizing the Tauramena consultation; by phone from Bogotá, July 30, 2016 (Interview C7).

12. This paragraph and the following one are based on Interview C7. The visit by Ecopetrol and the various ministers to Tauramena to stop the consultation is also referenced in Molano Jimeno 12/15/2013.

13. The question for the consultation was as follows: "Do you support hydrocarbon seismic exploration, exploratory drilling, production, and transport in the veredas of San José, Monserrate Alto, Monserrate la Vega, Guafal del Caja, Bendiciones, Visinaca, Lagunitas, Aguamaca, Zambo, Oso, and Jaguito, where the Tauramena municipality's water recharge area is located?" (Ramírez Cleves and Padrón Pardo 2016, 446).

consultations (Molano Jimeno 12/15/2013). The municipality of Monterrey progressed furthest. Monterrey's mayor joined with local residents to request a consultation. The Casanare tribunal approved the proposal, but Ecopetrol challenged that decision with a tutela action against the tribunal. The case reached the Consejo de Estado, which ruled for the company. The Consejo's decision was based on due process, but it also stated that the central state and not municipalities had jurisdiction over the subsoil (Ramírez Cleves and Padrón Pardo 2016, 455–56).

The jurisdictional issue made Tauramena's victory temporary. Ecopetrol went to the courts in 2014 to have the municipality's consultation deemed invalid (Comité por la Defensa del Agua del Municipio de Tauramena–Casanare 4/4/2018). The lower court and the Casanare tribunal ruled that municipalities did not have the authority to make decisions about subsoil resources, referencing the constitution. Tauramena residents filed a tutela with the Consejo de Estado. The Consejo denied the tutela in 2019 on the grounds that the Tauramena petitioners had not shown direct impact on fundamental rights. It also referenced the state's authority over subsoil resources, pointing to the Constitutional Court's October 2018 Cumaral decision (*El Espectador* 10/18/2019).

EIA PUBLIC HEARINGS

This section analyzes two more cases in which communities asked for and participated in formal participatory processes that were held in their municipalities, despite contestation over municipal jurisdiction. However, unlike in the previous section, the participatory institution pertinent to this second pair of conflicts was the EIA public hearing, and not popular consultation. Specifically, after an oil exploration project was approved, people protested for the right to debate the location of one of the project's wells, Lorito 1, in a public hearing. In a conflict over the planned Angostura mine, at issue was whether residents outside of Angostura's area of influence had sufficient interest in the mine's impacts to warrant a second EIA hearing, in their municipality.

Lorito 1

The Lorito 1 oil well was a component of an exploration project in the CPO-9 block, in Meta. The sixty-four-thousand-hectare project overlapped with sixty-four veredas, in five Meta municipalities—Acacías, Castilla La

Nueva, Cubarral, Guamal, and San Martín (*El Tiempo* 10/2/2013). Although Meta was a major producer of oil, the sector's impact on water sources meant that hydrocarbon expansion in the department still could be politically sensitive (*El Tiempo* 7/24/2013). Of the planned wells for the CPO-9 project, Lorito 1 was the most promising and, due to the water question, the most controversial (Rubiano 9/4/2017).

Communities participated in two public hearings in the Lorito 1 conflict—one for the CPO-9 project and a second for Lorito 1. The separate well hearing was authorized only after communities protested for it, as elaborated in this case study. Residents participated in the Lorito 1 hearing itself, and also in the preparatory informational meeting, to help establish hearing procedures. That planning work further evinced community organizing through the hearing, as it showed activists' commitment to meaningful participation at the event.

Mobilizing over Lorito 1 stalled the well's development for several years.

Participation in the CPO-9 EIA Hearing

During the environmental licensing process for the CPO-9 project ("Área de Perforación Exploratoria CPO9"), 216 members of the civil-society organization Communal Association of Councils (Asociación Comunal de Juntas, "Asojuntas") of Acacías requested a public hearing. ANLA led the hearing on April 12, 2012, in Acacías (Resolution 0331, 3).

Hearing participants addressed the project's impacts, especially on water, and altered the project through their involvement in the meeting. The hearing discussions pushed ANLA to establish 575 meters above sea level as the uppermost limit for exploration, thereby forestalling development in approximately twenty veredas beyond that limit. Environmentalists saw public participation in the hearing as having been essential in bringing about the revision, which they considered significant (*El Tiempo* 7/26/2012; La Liga Contra el Silencio 1/16/2019).

Despite the project change, apprehension about the exploration mounted, primarily over impacts on water and the possibility that seismic testing would destabilize terrain; Guamal residents attributed a recent landslide in a rural Guamal vereda to early seismic testing for the project. Protest erupted in Guamal in early May 2012 (*El Tiempo* 5/13/2012).

On May 15, 2012, ANLA granted a license to Ecopetrol for exploration and extraction in CPO-9.[14] The locations of the project's well platforms had yet to be determined (*El Tiempo* 7/26/2012).

14. Resolution 0331; Rubiano 9/4/2017; and La Liga Contra Silencio 1/16/2019.

A Second Hearing

Organizing for a second hearing, on Lorito 1, took place after ANLA authorized, in late February 2013, Ecopetrol's chosen Lorito 1 site. It was in Guamal, which relied on ranching and agriculture, not oil (*El Tiempo* 2/26/2013; Rubiano 9/4/2017). Lorito 1 would be close to the water intakes that channeled water from the Humadea River to two aqueducts—one serving Castilla La Nueva, and the other, the Humadea vereda, in Guamal (*El Tiempo* 2/26/2013, 3/21/2013).

In response to the siting of Lorito 1, activists held several marches, in Acacías, Guamal, and four other Meta municipalities—Cumaral, Puerto Gaitán, Restrepo, and Villavicencio. Protesters rejected the planned exploration and especially Lorito 1, again focusing on water, as well as on residents' fundamental rights to health and life. July 24, 2013, marked the 152nd day of protest in Guamal over the well (*El Tiempo* 3/19/2013, 7/24/2013).

One impetus behind the mobilizing was to convince ANLA to hold another public hearing, on Lorito 1. The regional water board (Mesa Hídrica Ambiental del Meta), an environmental NGO (Tierra Mágica), a national senator, Meta's governor, and the Castilla La Nueva mayor, requested a hearing on the well. Their goal was to relocate it. ANLA did not respond at least through July 2013, but, in the midst of a blockade of the project (discussed under "The Blockade and Administrative Challenge"), it scheduled a Lorito 1 hearing for early October of that year, in Guamal (*El Tiempo* 7/24/2013, 9/20/2013).

In September 2013, civil-society leaders in the struggle against Lorito 1 attended the informational meeting for the October hearing (*El Tiempo* 9/20/2013). They considered the meeting an opportunity to help set the "rules of the game" for the hearing. Among their accomplishments at the meeting, participants ensured that each resident listed on the hearing agenda would have up to ten minutes to speak.[15]

Participants used the October 2013 hearing as a forum in which to vent disquiet over the CPO-9 project and to lament shortcomings in the EIA participatory process. Local mayors discussed the concept of sustainable development in oil-affected zones and said the exploration project's environmental impacts on local communities were unacceptable. They also contended that Lorito 1 was too close to the Humadea River, making water contamination probable. The national senator who had solicited the hearing

15. Interview with two NGO leaders, each of whom represented an NGO that had been active in the Lorito 1 conflict—including Edgar Humberto Cruz Aya, the legal representative of the Environmental and Tourism Corporation of the Humadea River (Corporación Ambiental y Turística del Río Humadea, CORPOHUMADEA)—and both of whom had attended the September 2013 planning session for the Lorito 1 hearing; phone interview from Bogotá, August 5, 2016 (Interview C8).

was in attendance; she asked that ANLA expedite future petitions for public hearings (*El Tiempo* 10/5/2013).

Protest continued after the hearing. For instance, an April 2014 mobilization broke out when ANLA failed to respond to a request for a public presentation on the details of Lorito 1 (*El Tiempo* 4/24/2014).

The Blockade and Administrative Challenge

Perhaps communities protested Lorito 1 most powerfully with a blockade. Immediately after ANLA approved the well platform location in February 2013, residents organized a roadblock to prevent the conveyance of company equipment to the Lorito 1 site. The blockade consisted of a rotating group of roughly thirty people (*El Tiempo* 3/19/2013). During the blockade, organizers submitted a complaint to the Meta tribunal in which they claimed that the Lorito 1 platform would put at risk the environment and the community's well-being. In August 2013, after access to Lorito 1 had been halted for 188 days, the tribunal ordered the suspension of all exploration in CPO-9 (*El Tiempo* 8/29/2013). Activists lifted the blockade in October 2013, the month of the Lorito 1 hearing (La Liga Contra el Silencio 1/16/2019).

The Tutela

In January 2014 the Consejo de Estado suspended the Meta tribunal's August 2013 decision on appeal (La Liga Contra el Silencio 1/16/2019), but a tutela process delayed Lorito 1 for three more years. An Humadea resident filed the tutela, claiming that the well threatened the health of her daughter and of other Humadea residents. The case reached the Constitutional Court, which granted the tutela in July 2014. The court ordered the suspension of Lorito 1 until ANLA had conducted a technical analysis to determine whether the platform complied with the standards established in the CPO-9 environmental license (*El Tiempo* 7/31/2014). Having met those requirements, Ecopetrol announced in August 2017 that it had recommenced work on Lorito 1.[16]

Angostura

Conflict over the proposed Angostura mine in the Santander department mirrored the Lorito 1 case, in that community members organized for and

16. Colectivo de Abogados "José Alvear Restrepo" and Corporación Ambiental y Turística del Río Humadea–CORPOHUMADEA 4/8/2016; and *Prensa libre Casanare* 8/14/2017.

participated in an EIA hearing, in a context in which their municipality's jurisdiction was in question.

People protested Angostura mainly to protect a páramo. The open-pit mine project overlapped with the Santurbán Páramo, which provided water to the larger region. Opposition to the mine produced a series of marches and led the state to deny the Angostura environmental license. Subsequently, national protections for páramos made nonviable the project owner's new, underground project.

Anti-Angostura mobilizing took place predominantly in Santander's capital, Bucaramanga, which was outside of the project's area of influence. The Bucaramanga movement attained a second EIA hearing, in the city, only after demonstrating extraordinary interest in participating, and after an unanticipated weather event barred access to the first hearing (which was held in Angostura's area of influence).

While activists participated in the Bucaramanga hearing, they also organized around the EIA participatory stage. They appropriated the term "public hearing" to describe one of the marches, to communicate the idea that residents could express their interests more effectively by marching than by speaking at a state-led meeting about the EIA.

Grievances about the Greystar Project

Angostura would have produced an estimated 2.3 million ounces of gold and silver annually for fifteen years (*Portafolio* 2/22/2011). The project was in the Santander municipalities of Vetas and California, which bordered the department of Norte de Santander. The National Institute of Geological-Mining Research (Instituto Nacional de Investigaciones Geológico-Mineras, Ingeominas), the Colombian state agency that assigned mining titles, granted the Canadian firm Greystar Resources Limited exploration rights in Vetas and California in 1995. Greystar began exploration but then left, due to insurgent violence that included the 1999 kidnapping of a company employee. The firm returned in 2003, after a Colombian military battalion had secured the area, and encouraged by the new 2001 mining code (Jiménez Jiménez 2016, 480–81).[17]

Greystar's renewed exploration sparked a powerful movement in Bucaramanga to avert Angostura's development. Residents of the capital worried about the environmental impacts of open-pit mining, chiefly on Santurbán, which spanned ninety thousand hectares in Santander and Norte de Santander (Flórez Flórez 2012, 465; Jiménez Jiménez 2016, 483, 490). More than one-half of the project area, eleven hundred hectares, overlapped with the páramo (*Portafolio* 2/22/2011). Santurbán was sixty-seven kilometers

17. On the 2001 mining code, see Chapter 2.

from Bucaramanga but was the city's main source of drinking water (Flórez Flórez 2012, 465–66). Added to their concern for the páramo, Bucaramanga groups believed Angostura's operations would increase the cost of water for communities in the region and cause negative sociocultural impacts—for example, competition for new, specialized jobs and the displacement of communities (Jiménez Jiménez 2016, 483–84, 493).

In contrast to the organizing in Bucaramanga, residents of California and Vetas did not associate with environmental groups and in fact supported Angostura. Given their long history of artisanal mining, the municipalities would not advocate for protecting Santurbán from mining. Moreover, they had positive relationships with Greystar, which had invested in local employment, health, education, and environmental monitoring and management in the two municipalities (*Portafolio* 2/22/2011; Jiménez Jiménez 2016, 40–82, 485, 500; Prieto 2/14/2016).

The Conflict Arc: Socialization, Escalation, Marches, and the Denial of the Environmental License

The EIA was a rallying point throughout the Angostura conflict.[18] In December 2009, Greystar submitted the Angostura EIA to MAVDT. Upon learning in 2010 that the EIA was under review, the manager of Bucaramanga's metropolitan aqueduct began speaking publicly about the project's anticipated harms to Santurbán and to Bucaramanga's drinking water. The media picked up that information (Flórez Flórez 2012, 466, 468–69). City residents at large became increasingly aware of the project from a Greystar socialization campaign.[19]

The Committee in Defense of Water and the Santurbán Páramo (Comité en Defensa del Agua y el Páramo de Santurbán) led the anti-Angostura movement. The organization enjoyed wide respect in Bucaramanga as a result of its horizontal structure and diverse composition; the Comité consisted of environmental groups, students, unions, and, as principal leaders, business-sector representatives (Jiménez Jiménez 2016, 485–86, 500–501). In their resistance to the mine, Bucaramanga groups benefited from their ties to international environmental organizations and actors at the national level

18. Consistent with the present analysis, Jiménez Jiménez (2016) emphasizes the importance of the EIA process for influencing the formation, evolution, and impact of the Bucaramanga movement.

19. Interview with Erwing Rodríguez-Salah, Executive Director, National Federation of Merchants (Federación Nacional de Comerciantes) Santander, and one of two official voices of the Committee in Defense of Water and the Santurbán Páramo (Comité en Defensa del Agua y el Páramo de Santurbán); by phone from Bogotá, July 30, 2016 (Interview C9).

that included senators, universities, and television personalities (Jiménez Jiménez 2016, 494).

Mobilizing against Angostura in Bucaramanga most visibly took the form of four marches held in 2010 and 2011. The first march, in June 2010, involved an estimated two hundred people and was followed by October and November 2010 marches of twenty-five hundred and five thousand people, respectively (Jiménez Jiménez 2016, 502). The February 2011 march drew an estimated thirty thousand to forty-five thousand people and was accompanied by simultaneous solidarity marches in Bogotá and Cúcuta, the capital of Norte de Santander (Jiménez Jiménez 2016, 503; Prieto 2/14/2016).

Amid outrage over the mine, MAVDT denied the Angostura environmental license at the end of May 2011. The ministry explained its decision by noting environmental impacts and social discontent.[20] Greystar responded to the MAVDT rejection by scrapping the open-pit plan, changing its name to Eco Oro, and embarking on designing a new, underground project (Ebus 3/23/2017).

Participation in EIA Hearings

During the Angostura conflict, activists organized through the EIA public hearing, by working to achieve and then participating in a hearing in Bucaramanga.

Civil-society organizations and 238 members of the public requested an EIA hearing on the project. Bucaramanga groups asked that the meeting be held in their city, on the basis of the project's impact on its water supply.[21] MAVDT approved one hearing, in California. Subnational and national government officials and eighty-nine other individuals spoke at the event, held in late November 2010 (Resolution 1015, 4–5; SPDA 2016, 92). Severe flooding prevented residents of Bucaramanga from traveling to the hearing.[22]

Shortly after the hearing, in early December 2010, the attorney general for environmental matters (Procurador Delegado para Asuntos Ambientales y Agrarios) asked for a second hearing. MAVDT authorized a Bucaramanga hearing. In its denial of Angostura's environmental license, MAVDT justified the second hearing and its location by quoting the attorney general's letter. The excerpt noted that the number of participants in the California hearing had been small relative to the number of registered speakers; and that the weather event had prevented attendance by Bucaramanga residents, including those who had requested the meeting (Resolution 1015, 6).

20. Resolution 1015, 114–27; and SPDA 2016, 93–94.

21. Interview C9; and Interview with Florentino Rodríguez, member of the Comité en Defensa del Agua y el Páramo de Santurbán; by phone from Bogotá, July 29, 2016 (Interview C10).

22. Jiménez Jiménez 2016, 505; and Interview C10.

The March 4, 2011, Bucaramanga hearing was attended by 480 people, 27 of whom spoke.[23] Participation was passionate and loud; attendees held up banners and shouted (Jiménez Jiménez 2016, 505). The disorder caused the environment ministry official leading the hearing to walk out, cutting the meeting short.[24] In its denial of the Angostura environmental license, MAVDT treated the Bucaramanga event as a second hearing, while also observing that it had suffered interruptions (Resolution 1015, especially 22).

Of note is that the hearing disruptions likely were part of attendees' enthusiastic participation in the meeting and not indicative of a plan by Bucaramanga groups to suspend it. Erwing Rodríguez-Salah, a leader in the Bucaramanga movement, had wanted to participate but was unable to do so because the hearing had adjourned early.[25]

Rhetorical use of the February 2011 March as a "Public Hearing"

In anticipation of the March 2011 hearing in Bucaramanga, civil-society leaders organized around that participatory process by branding the largest march in the Angostura conflict a "public hearing."

The week before the Bucaramanga hearing, Rodríguez-Salah described the recent February 2011 march as "a true public hearing. It demonstrated that the residents of Bucaramanga are openly in favor of preserving water and against large-scale mining" (*Vanguardia* 2/26/2011). In an interview for this research, Rodríguez-Salah elaborated on this characterization of the march, as follows:

> The big march [*gran marcha*] in defense of water was really a public hearing. Forty-five thousand people out expressing their views—that's a public hearing. I said publicly that this is really the public hearing.
>
> *Did you mean to refer to the "public hearing" in the environmental licensing process?* Yes, of course. Because here we have forty-five thousand people participating, expressing their voice. Everyone was there. . . . I would call it this [in my statements] to the press to emphasize that a real public hearing is when so many people come out and express themselves. [The march] was one week before the official public hearing, which was scheduled for March 4, 2011. So there was meaning in the march about what was coming up.[26]

23. Resolution 1015, 10; Jiménez Jiménez 2016, 505; and SPDA 2016, 92–93.
24. Resolution 1015, 9–10; Jiménez Jiménez 2016, 505; and Interviews C9 and C10.
25. Interview C9.
26. Interview C9.

National Páramo Protections and Eco Oro's Departure

Land status, and specifically the páramo question, definitively blocked the development of Angostura. In January 2013, the regional CAR (Corporación Autónoma Regional Para la Defensa de la Meseta de Bucaramanga, CDMB) classified 11,700 hectares of Santurbán as a natural park, which added environmental protections to the area. Subsequently, in April 2014, the environment ministry and a research institute (Instituto de Investigación de Recursos Biológicos Alexander Von Humboldt) established Santurbán's boundaries, making forty-four thousand hectares of the páramo off limits to mining (SPDA 2016, 94). A 2016 Constitutional Court decision that outlawed mining in páramos (see Chapter 2) was another serious setback for Eco Oro (Guidi 3/15/2016). In 2016, following the court decision and after páramo protections had cut in half Eco Oro's project, the firm sued the Colombian government for damages. During the legal battle, in March 2019, Eco Oro informed the government that it would be withdrawing from the Angostura concession (*Reuters* 6/28/2019).

TWO-PRONGED APPROACH: EIA HEARING AND POPULAR CONSULTATION

In the remaining two conflicts in this chapter—the Nogal and San Martín cases—communities fought extraction by conforming to the procedures built into participatory institutions, as in the conflicts previously discussed. However, Nogal and San Martín differ, because they involved communities that tried both the EIA hearing and popular consultation routes.

Nogal

Residents who objected to exploration in the Nogal oil block in southern Colombia requested a public hearing and participated in the hearing and its associated informational meeting. Communities also attempted to organize popular consultations, but without success.

The Nogal conflict began well before the EIA hearing was planned. In that early phase of mobilizing, local campesinos formed a blockade on a bridge to prevent the company from carrying out preliminary feasibility studies for the EIA. The blockade and the government's violent response to it incited a departmental movement against oil activities in Nogal.

Despite the organizing, the Nogal project advanced. Civil-society actors then participated in the EIA process. As part of that participation, they assembled their own EIA to rival the company's version and presented their document at the public hearing. In the end, the state granted the Nogal environmental license.

Grievances and Challenges to Organizing in Southern Caquetá

The 2012 Nogal exploration contract between Ecopetrol and Emerald Energy PLC Colombia, a subsidiary of the Chinese firm Sinochem, was part of the Caquetá department's expansion in hydrocarbons (Díaz 5/20/2016). Between 2002 and 2015, the state allocated 42 percent of Caquetá's habitable lands for oil projects (Koop 8/15/2015). As of 2016, exploration was underway in forty of the department's forty-three licensed blocks. Nogal, in southern Caquetá, was the largest of all awarded oil blocks in Colombia's Amazon region (Díaz 5/20/2016). Many communities impacted by exploration in Nogal relied on farming and ranching and worried that oil development would harm local water sources (Bermúdez Liévano 11/29/2017).

Leading up to the Nogal conflict, southern Caquetá was a center of violence in Colombia's civil war. Especially germane to this analysis is the experience of the Valparaíso municipality, where communities formed the bridge blockade. At the departmental level, Caquetá was a FARC stronghold in the armed conflict. Paramilitaries spread into the southern part of Caquetá in the 2000s, causing Valparaíso communities to flee. When the paramilitaries departed in the late 2000s, residents of Valparaíso returned.[27] Experts on the Nogal conflict have portrayed Valparaíso campesinos as exceptionally brave to have engaged in collective action, considering their recent displacement and suffering.[28]

Emerald Energy began holding socialization meetings about Nogal in early 2014. The municipalities impacted by the project—Belén de los Andaquíes, Florencia, Milán, Morelia, and Valparaíso—already had as a point of reference the negative environmental impacts that oil activities had caused in the nearby municipality of San José del Fragua. By the end of 2014, southern Caquetá communities had serious trepidations about the Nogal oil development. Members of the five impacted municipalities attended a December 2014 socialization meeting in Morelia for the exploration. Community participants expressed frustration about the project's environmental management plan,

27. Bermúdez Liévano 7/1/2015; Ciro et al. 2016, 421–22, 428–29, 432; and Interview with Natalia Orduz, researcher and codirector and producer of the *La vida es de los arriesgados* documentary about the Valparaíso conflict; Bogotá, August 1, 2016 (Interview C11).

28. Ciro et al. 2016, 428–29; and Interview C11.

which they found wanting in detail and inaccurate in its description of the local area. They called for an updated plan (Ciro et al. 2016, 418, 429–30; Díaz 5/20/2016).

The company pressed on in 2015, contracting residents of the impacted municipalities to obtain campesinos' support for the project—or at least their signatures, which the company then used as evidence that socialization had taken place. This strategy fractured communities (Ciro et al. 2016, 430).

Puente Resistencia and the Scaling Up of Organizing in Caquetá

The most intense period of the Nogal conflict spanned two months in 2015, when campesinos from Valparaíso and other Caquetá municipalities staged a blockade to prevent Emerald Energy from constructing the stratigraphic well A3 to study Nogal's promise for oil production (Neira 10/31/2016).[29]

The blockade went up in May 2015, when Valparaíso residents learned of Emerald Energy's imminent arrival, with exploration equipment. Community members met with the Southern Vicariate (Vicaría del Sur, of the Florencia diocese), which was well established in southern Caquetá. The meeting participants deliberated stopping the project through judicial routes, but with only days left before the exploration work was to begin, they settled on direct action.[30] Approximately one hundred local residents maintained the blockade during May and June 2015, on a small bridge that, because of the conflict, became known as "Resistance Bridge" ("Puente Resistencia"). Communities hoped not only to impede Emerald Energy's work on the well, but also to compel the state to cancel the Nogal contract (Flórez Góngora 7/2/2015; Koop 8/15/2015; Bermúdez Liévano 11/29/2017).

The national government responded to the blockade with a failed attempt at dialogue and then force. The vice minister of interior led a May 29, 2015, meeting at the Florencia diocese, attended by campesino leaders, Caquetá's governor, police and army commanders, and representatives of the company and of the Colombian Oil Association (Asociación Colombiana de Petróleo, ACP). The meeting gave rise to a plan for a dialogue table (*mesa de concertación*). The initiative collapsed after the first session. At that June 2 meeting, the government refused the campesinos' call for a one-week suspension of the exploration, to give them time to review the Emerald Energy contract (Bermúdez Liévano 7/1/2015; Flórez Góngora 7/2/2015).

Deadlock—both at the negotiating table and on the bridge—brought on a series of high-level communications about how the state might handle the

29. This initial exploration work did not require an environmental license (Koop 8/15/2015).

30. Ciro et al. 2016, 429; Orduz and Thiesing 2016; and Interview C11.

situation. The head of the ACP pressed for government intervention, claiming that Emerald Energy had positive relations with the local communities and that only a small group of people was holding up the project. The attorney general's office issued a warning that described the blockade as illegal and punishable under law. In reaction to that notice, the bishop of Florencia and a national senator asked for dialogue—the senator, in a letter to President Santos and three of his ministers. The environment ministry responded to the senator's letter by declaring the matter outside of its jurisdiction (Bermúdez Liévano 7/1/2015).

The government put an end to the bridge standoff unexpectedly, by deploying an estimated 150 riot police personnel, which arrived from Bogotá on June 30. The community members stationed on the bridge stood their ground, and clashes ensued. Thirteen campesinos were wounded, three badly. Within two hours, the police dismantled the encampment at the bridge, sequestered participating campesinos on a farm, and cleared the road to allow Emerald Energy vehicles to pass (Bermúdez Liévano 7/1/2015, 11/29/2017).

Exploration continued. Emerald Energy installed the stratigraphic well and carried out seismic testing using explosives, in Milán, Morelia, and Valparaíso (Neira 10/31/2016). Local community members staged intermittent blockades during the exploration work.[31]

Spurred by the Puente Resistencia events, organizing against the development of Nogal spread in Caquetá, importantly due to unease about deforestation. Caquetá had suffered more deforestation than any other department in the country, a reality that has been attributed to colonization, migration, and ranching (Ciro et al. 2016, 421, 428; Revelo-Rebolledo 2019, 177–200). United under the broad theme of protecting the Amazon, civil-society groups formed commissions for the life of water (comisiones por la vida del agua) in the southern Caquetá municipalities (Díaz 5/20/2016). The Departmental Committee for the Defense of Water and Territory (Mesa Departamental por la Defensa del Agua y el Territorio), based in Florencia, brought together campesino, academic, religious, private-sector, and policy leaders. Thousands of people participated in marches in defense of water, and local committees for the protection of water and against oil development emerged in most of the department's municipalities (Bermúdez Liévano 11/29/2017). At issue was not only the protection of the Colombian Amazon but also Caquetá's very status as Amazonian. President Santos's Plan Nacional de Desarrollo 2014–18 had placed Caquetá outside of the Amazon. Groups in Caquetá disputed the new classification, arguing that it facilitated oil development in the department (Ciro et al. 2016, 419).[32]

31. Interview C11.
32. On the Plan Nacional de Desarrollo 2014–18, see Chapter 2.

Increased Exploration and EIA Participation

After the bridge blockade, another important stage in the Nogal conflict began in 2016. At that time, Emerald Energy was looking ahead to submitting an EIA to commence more advanced exploration work (Bermúdez Liévano 11/29/2017). Emerald Energy representatives spoke at an October 2016 Caquetá departmental assembly meeting about the company's proposal to extract oil in Milán, Morelia, and Valparaíso. At the event, the Caquetá deputies disapproved of the plan. The meeting alarmed Caquetá environmental and peasant organizations, which worried that oil development could accelerate deforestation and jeopardize local livelihoods—especially agriculture and tourism (Neira 10/31/2016). Emerald Energy applied for an environmental license in April 2017 for an exploration project that involved the construction of ten oil platforms and, from each platform, the drilling of five wells (Bermúdez Liévano 11/29/2017).

Valparaíso campesinos asked for a public hearing on the EIA with a petition signed by seven hundred people (Bermúdez Liévano 11/29/2017). Six hundred community members assembled at the informational meeting—many more than the 200- to 250-person turnout that ANLA had anticipated. Attendees were mainly campesinos from twenty-one veredas in the three affected municipalities. They emphasized the project's medium- and long-term impacts on ecosystems, and its use of surface and underground water. They also raised material interests: compensation, social investment, job creation, and local service contracts with the company. The meeting lasted seven hours and was "cordial" throughout (ANLA 2/8/2018).

The actual public hearing took place in Morelia, in March 2018. Twelve hundred people attended, and more than two hundred spoke. Participants concentrated on the environmental impacts of development in the oil block, the apparent dearth of serious environmental studies for the project, human rights violations by public security in the face of project opposition, the company's failure to recognize Indigenous community presence in the project's area of influence, and, related, the omission of prior consultation for the project (Díaz Parra 3/20/2018).

One tactic communities used when organizing through the public hearing was to present an independent EIA to counter the official company document. The competing study—developed by the Colombian NGO Corporación Geoambiental Terrae—was financed by the NGO Caritas Alemana, which had ties to the Vicaría del Sur. Terrae's director presented the parallel document at the (official) EIA hearing, emphasizing the absence of information in the company's EIA about wetlands, flood zones, underground and above-ground water, and threats to native fauna and flora (Bermúdez Liévano 11/29/2017; Díaz Parra 3/20/2018).

While the EIA hearing was a space for groups to come together to protest the Nogal project, it also highlighted local divisions. Communities that rejected the project received support at the hearing from representatives of the Caquetá departmental assembly and the Morelia municipality and mayor's office. In contrast, the Milán and Valparaíso municipal governments were not represented, an absence that signaled their amenability to the project (ANLA 2/8/2018; Díaz Parra 3/20/2018).

ANLA approved the environmental license for exploration in Nogal in September, 2018 (Resolution 01606, Valencia 10/2/2018).

Popular Consultation Endeavors

In addition to working through the EIA participatory process to try to obstruct exploration in Nogal, communities in southern Caquetá tried to initiate popular consultations. As of late 2017, Morelia residents had collected 670 signatures, two-thirds the number needed to petition for a consultation. Valparaíso communities had suspended their popular consultation effort in 2016 when they saw they lacked mayoral support. They now were considering holding a signature drive but awaited the outcome of the EIA hearing (Bermúdez Liévano 11/29/2017). Weeks after the hearing, the Constitutional Court issued the October 2018 Cumaral ruling.

Fracking in San Martín

Like the Nogal case, activists who resisted unconventional natural gas production (hydraulic fracking) in San Martín—a municipality in the department of Cesar—worked through the EIA participatory process and toward a popular consultation.

Community activism in San Martín also was similar to the Caquetá organizing in that it focused on preliminary and, later, advanced exploration. As discussed in this analysis, when early exploration was underway, San Martín residents blocked company access to an exploration site, marched, and collected signatures for a popular consultation. Later, when communities learned of plans for more extensive exploration that required an environmental license, groups continued the popular consultation signature drive and solicited an EIA hearing.

Neither participatory event transpired. ANLA canceled the fracking project before it would have scheduled the hearing. The agency issued its decision shortly after the Constitutional Court's 2018 Cumaral ruling had foreclosed the possibility of a municipal consultation.

Preliminary Exploration Using Picoplata No. 1

Exploration for hydraulic fracking in San Martín was part of ConocoPhillips and Canacol Energy's exploration plans in the VMM3 oil block (Güesguán Serpa and Silva Numa 4/13/2016; *El Tiempo* 10/27/2016).[33] VMM3 was the first fracking endeavor in Colombia, which showed potential in fracking: as of 2018, there were unconventional reserves in at least forty-three of the country's hydrocarbon blocks (*Radio mundo real* 4/3/2018).

During the preliminary exploration, an environmental license already was in place for traditional oil extraction in VMM3 that allowed for testing to prepare an EIA for fracking. Picoplata No. 1, a well in the Cuatro Bocas corregimiento, was used for the testing (*El Tiempo* 4/28/2016; *Semana sostenible* 9/22/2016).[34]

San Martín communities learned about the Picoplata No. 1 exploration work in early March 2016, when ConocoPhillips began holding socialization meetings (Güesguán Serpa and Silva Numa 4/13/2016; *RPT noticias* 4/17/2016). The municipality had direct experience with the impacts of traditional oil production, but activists were skeptical of the new technologies that fracking entailed (Güesguán Serpa and Silva Numa 4/13/2016). Specifically, based on what they had read about fracking in the United States, movement leaders worried about the contamination of underground aquifers, the release of methane gas, the use of large volumes of water, quakes, and adverse public health impacts.[35]

San Martín residents took to the streets against fracking on three occasions in 2016. Three thousand people participated in the first, spontaneous march, on March 17 (Güesguán Serpa and Silva Numa 4/13/2016). Activism then became more organized. The Corporation for the Defense of Water, Territory, and Ecosystems (Corporación Defensora del Agua, Territorio y Ecosistemas, CORDATEC) formed and led the new movement against fracking in San Martín. Another march, of six thousand people, was held on April 17. The third mobilization lasted for three days in October and resulted in confrontations between protesters and the national police (*El Tiempo* 10/27/2016).[36]

33. For a description of this conflict phase, see also Hernández Marín 2018, 110–18.

34. According to 2015 EIA regulations (Decree 1076), companies did not need an environmental license for the extraction of nonconventional hydrocarbons if the work was part of existing extractive activities (Contraloría General de la República 2017, 73).

35. *El Tiempo* 4/28/2016; and Interview with Carlos Andrés Santiago, leader of the San Martín antifracking movement's main organization, the Corporation for the Defense of Water, Territory, and Ecosystems (Corporación Defensora del Agua, Territorio y Ecosistemas, CORDATEC); Bogotá, July 27, 2016 (Interview C12).

36. The three marches also were discussed during Interview C12.

As organizing against fracking progressed, divisions in San Martín deepened. The San Martín mayor was a fracking advocate, and the municipality allocated jobs and contracts according to applicants' positions on fracking. Those direct economic pressures hurt community cohesion and even caused rifts within the antifracking movement.[37]

Community members not only marched against fracking but also physically obstructed the Picoplata No. 1 tests.[38] On April 18, 2016—the day after the second march—Cuatro Bocas residents erected a blockade. The six-week roadblock interrupted exploration and prevented the company from holding several remaining socialization meetings.

The blockade gained the central government's attention. For two weeks, interior ministry officials held workshops in San Martín about hydraulic fracking to try to improve community relations. Representatives from ANH, ANLA, and the mining and energy ministry also were in attendance. Antifracking leaders criticized the gatherings for being unrepresentative, because the interior ministry had disallowed them from helping to structure the meetings and prohibited them from participating. (The only members of the public permitted to speak were residents of the small communities in which the workshops took place.)

For its part, ConocoPhillips changed its approach to socialization in response to the local opposition. Whereas the firm had devoted early socialization meetings to project details, in late July 2016, it began using the events to try to bribe residents, a strategy that fractured Cuatro Bocas. On one Sunday, July 24, 2016, company representatives brought to the corregimiento a musical group; a traditional, large pork dish; and other gifts. According to the head of CORDATEC, "This wasn't a socialization meeting. It was a party. [Company officials] were trying to buy off the community. They wanted to be able to persuade the community to allow them to pass, so that they could do the technical tests [*pruebas técnicas*] they need to do."[39] As of late July 2016, Cuatro Bocas was allowing the work.[40]

Communities near Picoplata 1 cut off project access again, during ten days in September 2016. As a result, ConocoPhillips paused its work and asked ANH to suspend temporarily its oil production contract (*Semana sostenible* 9/22/2016). The company later resumed its testing, which lasted until June 2017 (*Semana sostenible* 2/15/2018).

37. Hernández Marín 2018, 114–16; and Interview C12.
38. This paragraph and the following one are based on Interview C12.
39. Interview C12. On divisions that the company created by offering gifts to Cuatro Bocas residents, see Hernández Marín 2018, 116–17.
40. Interview C12.

Expanded Exploration and EIA Participation

The second phase of the San Martín conflict began in early 2018, during ANLA's review of the EIA for expanded exploration. The proposed work consisted of drilling wells, installing new infrastructure, and enlarging the exploration area. The project ("Area de Perforación Exploratoria—APE Planta") was in San Martín and the neighboring municipality of Aguachica, also in Cesar (*RCN radio* 2/7/2018).

A critical incident in the conflict was the February 2018 discovery of oil in a water well that served families in Pita Limón, a San Martín vereda less than four kilometers from Picoplata No. 1. Photographs and videos showing the contaminated well water were circulated on social media and raised suspicions about ConocoPhillips's work (*Semana sostenible* 2/15/2018).

In late August 2018, CORDATEC and four other civil-society organizations asked for a public hearing on the new exploration. ANLA responded to the groups within three weeks. The agency committed to holding a hearing, pending actions by ConocoPhillips; it had instructed the company to provide additional information about the project. ANLA found ConocoPhillips's submission deficient and denied the environmental license, on October 23, 2018 (Order [Auto] 06445, especially 4–5; *Censat Agua Viva noticias* 11/6/2018).

Popular Consultation Plan

Over the course of the San Martín conflict, organizers worked toward a popular consultation. They held a signature drive rather than appealing to the mayor, given the latter's support for fracking.[41] They began the initiative by April 2016; a main objective of the march that month was to collect signatures (Güesguán Serpa and Silva Numa 4/13/2016). In late March 2018, CORDATEC and the San Martín, Cesar, Pro-Popular Consultation Committee (Comité Pro Consulta Popular de San Martín Cesar) submitted to the municipal registry (Registraduría Municipal del Estado Civil) the thousands of signatures that had been collected (*Radio mundo real* 4/3/2018).

The popular consultation never took place, with the Constitutional Court's Cumaral decision proving important. As of April 2018, the court was reviewing the case (Observatorio de Conflictos Mineros de América Latina 7/31/2018), on which it ruled in October 2018, the same month that ANLA denied the environmental license for the San Martín exploration.

41. Interview C12.

SUMMARY

As demonstrated in this chapter, Colombia's popular consultation and EIA hearing channeled local community complaints about proposed extraction. The rules governing participation explain this active participation by communities in the participatory processes. Popular consultations and EIA hearings were triggered by request, creating for communities the event initiation challenge and providing them only one path: petitioning for and taking part in formal participatory events.

If institutional design features produced the challenge of securing a participatory process, contestation over the line that defined municipal vis-à-vis central state power amplified that challenge. This disagreement about jurisdictions left unresolved the question of whether a municipality had the right to decide on, or even discuss in a formal setting, extraction, and led communities to mobilize more intensively to achieve participatory opportunities. The jurisdictional issue arose in the La Colosa and Odisea 3D popular consultation cases, and in the Lorito 1 and Angostura conflicts, which involved EIA hearings.

To supplement its focus on how communities worked within participatory processes, this chapter also put forth one example of action around them. Movement leaders in Bucaramanga tethered the term "public hearing" to a march against Angostura that they claimed communicated Bucaramanga's interests more effectively than participation in a formal EIA hearing. That is, while the principal dynamic in the Angostura case was one of communities participating in the public hearing process, they also mobilized around it, to express their clear dissatisfaction with the quality of participation and representation offered by hearings.

Chapters 5 and 6 continue this analysis of popular organizing through and around participatory institutions. They show how communities in extractive regions confronted the two remaining challenges theorized in this book: the inclusion challenge, confronted by communities left out of the participatory stage of project approvals (Chapter 5); and the articulation challenge, encountered by communities that enjoyed the opportunity to participate and had to decide how to express their positions on new hydrocarbon and mining development (Chapter 6).

CHAPTER 5

The Inclusion Challenge and Contested Geographic Boundaries

In contrast to the Colombian EIA hearing and popular consultation, which were at work in the conflicts in Chapter 4, the relevant participatory institutions in the remaining conflicts in this study guaranteed participatory opportunities to communities impacted by extraction. These institutions were the Peruvian EIA hearing and prior consultation in Bolivia, Colombia, and Peru.

In cases in the present chapter, activist groups and the state disputed whether certain communities were affected by planned extraction. That is, there was contestation over the geographic boundaries that demarcated impacted communities. This disagreement generated the *inclusion challenge* for communities that claimed impact and, on that basis, the right to participate in the approval of new hydrocarbon and mining development; and yet that the state defined as not impacted and ineligible to participate. Outsider communities responded to the inclusion challenge by organizing around participatory institutions. They demanded the right to participate by questioning either state-recognized Indigenous territorial boundaries, or the EIA-defined lines that established the areas impacted by extractive projects.

The conflicts illustrate how differences in the rigidity of territorial boundaries—variation introduced in Chapter 3—affected the tactics of outsiders. In the Peruvian conflicts and in one Colombian case, outsider communities dealt with nonrigid geographic boundaries: boundary placement was somewhat flexible, based on formal rules governing participation. Communities could argue for certain borders around a project's disputable areas of influence and direct influence; and there was leeway to deliberate whether

The Politics of Extraction. Maiah Jaskoski, Oxford University Press. © Oxford University Press 2022.
DOI: 10.1093/oso/9780197568927.003.0005

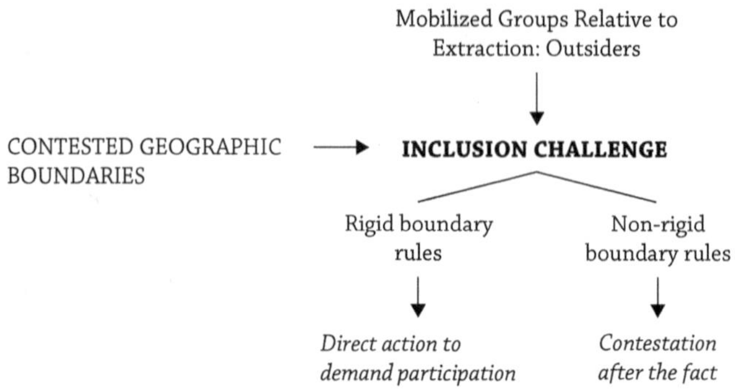

Figure 5.1 Inclusion Challenge Caused by Contested Geographic Boundaries

an Indigenous community had rights to lands defined as impacted and, consequently, to prior consultation. Due to ambiguities built into the boundary rules, communities advocated for their preferred boundaries after the participatory stage, often using legal-administrative arguments and procedures.

Bolivian Indigenous communities' right to prior consultation depended on whether communities held title to areas impacted by extraction, a rigid measure. Because of these rigid boundaries, outsider Indigenous communities in Bolivian gas conflicts in this chapter could not ensure prior consultation through legal or administrative processes. Instead, they physically blocked projects (or, in one case, threatened to do so) at the moment when prior consultation would have taken place or directly thereafter. Communities also relied on direct action in one Colombian case in which outsider Indigenous communities previously had secured an extension of their resguardo, and the state already had denied the communities the right to prior consultation beyond the new border.

Figure 5.1 depicts how contested geographic boundaries caused the inclusion challenge for outsiders and the effect of boundary rigidity on outsiders' responses to that challenge.

Table 5.1 summarizes the twelve outsider conflicts examined in this chapter. The discussion first treats the cases in which communities argued that they should have been included in project approvals, after the participatory stage had passed. The chapter then analyzes direct action by Indigenous communities that blocked projects as a tactic to force prior consultation or, if prior consultation proved elusive, negotiations with the state. A final section addresses an outlier case from Peru in which mobilized communities resided relatively far from the area of influence and did not question their outsider status.

To accompany the overriding logic of the outsider conflicts—that is, communities' insistence on inclusion in participatory processes—several cases

Table 5.1 THE INCLUSION CHALLENGE: CASES

Conflict	Goal of mobilizing	Dominant participatory institution			Other uses of participatory institutions
		Institution	Contested territorial boundary	Use of institution	
Conga (Peru; mining; 2010–17)	Block mine expansion	EIA hearing	Area of influence	Contestation of exclusion after the fact	n/a
Santa Ana (Peru; mining; 2008–2011)	Block mine	EIA hearing	Area of direct influence	Contestation of exclusion after the fact	Holding of alternative meetings in parallel with EIA workshops
Afrodita (Peru; mining; 2007–)	Block mine	Prior consultation	Indigenous territory	Contestation of exclusion after the fact	Contestation of disregard of prior consultation process for park
Block 116 (Peru; hydrocarbons; 2008–2019)	Block oil development	Prior consultation	Indigenous territory	Contestation of exclusion after the fact	Active participation in hearing for block licensing; interruption of EIA workshop; holding of meeting on EIA after EIA hearing
Putumayo fields (Colombia; hydrocarbons; 2014–18)	Alter oil expansion	Prior consultation	Indigenous territory	Contestation of exclusion after the fact	n/a
Percheles and El Dorado fields (Bolivia; hydrocarbons; 2007–8)	Compensation	Prior consultation	Indigenous territory	Demand for inclusion using direct action	n/a
Río Grande plant (Bolivia; hydrocarbons; 2011–12)	Compensation	Prior consultation	Indigenous territory	Demand for inclusion using direct action	n/a
El Dorado exploratory wells (Bolivia; hydrocarbons; 2015)	Compensation	Prior consultation	Indigenous territory	Demand for inclusion using direct action	n/a
Timboy X-2 (Bolivia; hydrocarbons; 2010)	Block gas exploration; mitigation	Prior consultation	Indigenous territory	Demand for inclusion using direct action	Challenge to legitimacy of completed prior consultation process for different project
Gran Chaco plant (Bolivia; hydrocarbons; 2010–13)	Compensation	Prior consultation	Indigenous territory	Demand for inclusion using direct action	n/a
Magallanes (Colombia; hydrocarbons; 2013–16)	Block gas exploration	Prior consultation	Indigenous territory	Demand for negotiation using direct action	n/a
Gasoducto del Sur (Peru; hydrocarbons; 2010–; *outlier*)	Alter gas pipeline	n/a	n/a	n/a	Postponement of EIA hearing by insiders

demonstrate additional uses of participatory institutions, as summarized in Table 5.1 and described in the individual case studies.

CONTESTING EXCLUSION AFTER THE FACT

In five conflicts from Colombia and Peru, outsiders rose up after a participatory process had concluded or after the state had bypassed it entirely. This section first presents the Peruvian Conga and Santa Ana mining conflicts, in which communities rejected the EIA's definition of a project's area of influence or direct influence. The communities in these cases viewed themselves as impacted by proposed mining and for that reason maintained that they should have been included in EIA participatory processes.

The section then turns to community mobilizing over the omission of prior consultation: protest against expanded oil production in the Colombian department of Putumayo, and against the Afrodita mine project and oil development in Block 116, in Peru. In each of the three cases, excluded communities pushed for state recognition of their lands, arguing that they had rights to areas impacted by extraction and should have been consulted.

In the Santa Ana, Afrodita, and Block 116 conflicts, communities not only insisted on their right to be invited to an EIA hearing (for Santa Ana) or to be consulted (for Afrodita and Block 116); they also employed participatory institutions in other ways. The lead organization in the movement against Santa Ana disparaged the project in meetings that coincided with the EIA workshops (which left out the mobilized communities). Communities pressed for state recognition of a completed prior consultation process that had established a protected park in the Afrodita mine area. Communities that opposed oil development in Block 116 organized around an exclusionary EIA participatory process by protesting an EIA workshop and reviewing the EIA at their own meeting; and at a block-licensing hearing, they competed with pro-development groups—akin to the use of EIA hearings by divided insiders, a pattern analyzed in Chapter 6.

Conga

The powerful movement against the Peruvian Conga mining project succeeded in bringing the project to an indefinite standstill. The Conga EIA contributed substantially to social tensions over the project (Arribasplata 2011; De Echave and Diez 2013; Gamu and Dauvergne 2018, 966). One issue pertained to participation: communities outside of Conga's area of influence were not invited to the EIA public hearing. They protested that exclusion and, therefore, the very legitimacy of the hearing.

The Fraught EIA

The $4.8 billion open-pit Conga project was in Peru's northern region of Cajamarca and, more precisely, in the districts of Encañada, in the province of Cajamarca; and Sorochuco and Huasmín, in the Celendín province. The project belonged to Minera Yanacocha, a joint venture of the Denver-based Newmont Mining Corporation and the Peruvian firm Buenaventura. Yanacocha owned Latin America's biggest gold mine. The Yanacocha mine, which began producing in 1993, transformed agriculture-based Cajamarca into the country's leading region in gold production and made the region second to Apurímac as a recipient of mining investment (De Echave and Diez 2013, 23–28, 71–72; SPDA 2016, 177). Conga was near Yanacocha and was considered an expansion of the mine.

According to the Conga EIA, the project's area of influence overlapped with thirty-two communities, in the Cajamarca and Celendín provinces (Prado 10/29/2011). Communities in the area of influence benefited from Yanacocha's local development projects, which included potable water provision, education, healthcare, and investment in agriculture and small businesses (Gamu and Dauvergne 2018, 966). Two December 2009 workshops were held for the EIA, and in March 2010, MINEM led the EIA public hearing, in the community of San Nicolás, in La Encañada (SPDA 2016, 179 n. 39, 180 n. 44). The hearing proceeded without difficulty; afterward, the regional vice president of Newmont's South America office said the communities had "approved" the Conga EIA (Prado 10/29/2011). MINEM approved the EIA in late October 2010 (with RM 351-2010-MEM/AAM; SPDA 2016, 177 n. 26).

Dissatisfaction about the EIA primarily came from Huasmín and Sorochuco communities outside of Conga's area of influence (Prado 10/29/2011). Groups found several deficiencies in the document. One set of concerns related to the representativeness of the public hearing. The Cajamarca-based Training and Intervention Group for Sustainable Development (Grupo de Formación e Intervención para el Desarrollo Sostenible, GRUFIDES), which was active in the movement against Conga, claimed that the state should have held hearings in Huasmín and Sorochuco, because the vast majority of Conga's area of extraction was in the two districts (*La República* 3/4/2012, 2–3).[1] GRUFIDES also averred that hearing participants had included Yanacocha workers and individuals whom the company had transported to the meeting and who may not have been local residents. Finally, due to the project's threat to basin

1. Media sources reported that 95 percent of the area of extraction for Conga was in Sorochuco and Huasmín and only 5 percent in La Encañada (SPDA 2016, 180 n. 44).

headwaters that were the sources of many rivers in Huasmín, La Encañada, and Sorochuco, GRUFIDES claimed that the true area of influence encompassed all communities in the three districts (*La República* 3/4/2012, 2–3).

Communities were most alarmed about the EIA's description of Conga and its impacts. The project threatened water sources, including four mountain lakes that received special attention in the conflict: Azul, Chica, Mala, and Perol. Communities doubted that Yanacocha's plan to create reservoirs by diverting water from the lakes would ensure sufficient water for surrounding populations (Arribasplata 2011; Loayza 11/20/2011; *La República* 3/4/2012, 2–3).

A historical basis for communities' distrust of Yanacocha was the company's dismal social and environmental record in Cajamarca. In the words of one mining consultant, Yanacocha's approach to community relations was the "old way" of extractive firms: neglect.[2] Newmont's CEO said in 2012 that Yanacocha's poor reputation in Cajamarca was the main impediment to the development of Conga (Álvarez Rodrich 8/23/2012).

Early on in the Conga conflict, it seemed that changes to the EIA could resolve tensions. In May 2010, Gregorio Santos—who would be elected Cajamarca's regional president months later—met with Yanacocha officials to advocate for EIA revisions that might appease communities. The company refused to alter the document (Romo Espinoza 1/3/2012). As of January 2011, there was not "generalized opposition" to Conga in Cajamarca. The conflict increased somewhat in early 2011, when several local mobilizations caused Cajamarca regional officials to travel to the area of Perol to assess possible project impacts (De Echave and Diez 2013, 93).

Escalation of Protest and Independent EIA Reviews

Mobilizing surged after Newmont announced in July 2011 the approval of Conga's financing and the company's plan to begin production by 2015. Lead activists included Gregorio Santos—now Cajamarca's president—and Wilfredo Saavedra, who headed the Cajamarca Environmental Defense Front (Frente de Defensa Ambiental de Cajamarca; Arribasplata 2011). Throughout 2011 and into 2012, organizing against Conga scaled up to the regional and national levels and caused two independent reviews of the EIA, government and company commitments to project revisions, and temporary suspensions of the project.

The "defense fronts" (*frentes de defensa*) of the Cajamarca, Celendín, and Chugur districts (in the provinces of Cajamarca, Celendín, and Hualgayoc, respectively) released their first joint declaration about Conga on August 1, 2011. The statement asked for a regional ordinance to protect the mountain

2. Interview with mining consultant; Lima, March 22, 2012 (Interview P6).

lakes and other water sources impacted by Conga. At another meeting later the same month, the fronts articulated several other requests that ranged from a regional review of the EIA, to regional restrictions on mining and protections for agriculture and water sources, to stronger national environmental regulations that included the protection of basin headwaters (De Echave and Diez 2013, 93–94).

A series of mobilizations followed. The first major protest erupted in the city of Cajamarca in September 2011, when Yanacocha refused to let a regional government commission visit the area of Perol. Thousands of people turned out for the protest, with noteworthy participation by local and regional public officials, Cajamarca district residents, and, from outside of the district, *ronderos*—members of *rondas campesinas*, or community self-defense and rule-of-law organizations (De Echave and Diez 2013, 94).

All thirteen of Cajamarca's provinces were represented at a late October 2011 assembly of the Cajamarca defense fronts. Following that meeting, more than two thousand people—including subnational officials and ronderos and other members of civil society—marched from Huasmín to the affected lakes. Participants gave Yanacocha eight days to remove all company equipment from the project site (Arribasplata 2011; De Echave and Diez 2013, 95).

With conflict spiraling, the central government intervened on October 28, 2011, by forming a national roundtable that included representatives of MINAM, MINEM, the PCM, Yanacocha, the national legislature, the Cajamarca provincial and regional governments, and the Chugar, Huasmín, La Encañada, and Sorochuco district governments (De Echave and Diez 2013, 95). As an outcome of the roundtable, on November 2, 2011, the environment, agriculture, and energy and mining ministers traveled to the project area, and MINAM planned to review the EIA (Arribasplata 2011; De Echave and Diez 2013, 95).

MINAM's report on the EIA, publicized in late November 2011, found, among other problems, inaccuracies in the EIA's definition of Conga's area of influence and description of anticipated harms to the mountain lakes. The report also underscored that Azul and Chica's only function for Conga was to store waste from the mining operations (Gorriti 11/25/2011).

A regional strike began days after MINAM completed its review of the EIA. The strike interfered with local businesses, caused school closures, and blocked various access roads to the Cajamarca province (De Echave and Diez 2013, 96). More than ten thousand people protested in the city of Cajamarca (Finlayson 1/19/2012). Three thousand people from the Cajamarca, Celendín, and Hualgayoc provinces marched to the vicinity of the lakes. Approximately fifteen hundred protesters—led by Gregorio Santos and Huasmín's mayor—entered the Conga project area and congregated around Perol. Near Azul, twenty people were wounded in clashes with the national police, two gravely (Arribasplata 2011; De Echave and Diez 2013, 96–97).

The Cajamarca defense fronts held a regional congress during the November 2011 strike. At the meeting, delegates from all thirteen provinces called for the immediate halting of work on Conga and the cancellation of the project's EIA (De Echave and Diez 2013, 96–97). Yanacocha suspended the project, on November 29, 2011 (Arribasplata 2011; *El Peruano* 11/30/2011).

Protest only became more violent. In early December 2011, the Humala government declared a state of emergency and sent a national delegation to Cajamarca. The dialogue effort failed, causing ten ministers to resign (Finlayson 1/19/2012). Also in December 2011, Cajamarca's government issued a regional ordinance (Ordenanza Regional 036-2011-GR-CAJ-CR) protecting all Cajamarca basin headwaters and declaring Conga unfeasible. (The attorney general swiftly challenged the ordinance, on constitutional grounds.)[3]

By 2012, the company had missed any opportunity it may have had to address concerns in Cajamarca about the project's design. As Santos said in a January 2012 interview,

> Now the Yanacocha problem has become a consent and social license [*licencia social*] issue. That is the fundamental problem. The company thinks that the issue is to convince the people about how it will address project criticisms [*observaciones*], but this is not the people's thinking. Residents do not want Yanacocha to expand. It doesn't matter anymore which experts come; whatever happens, they aren't going to want it. (Romo Espinoza 1/3/2012)

In the February 2012 Grand National March for the Right to Water and Life (Gran Marcha Nacional por el Derecho al Agua y la Vida), more than one thousand people walked for nine days from Cajamarca to downtown Lima, where they were joined by approximately one thousand Lima-based demonstrators. The march pursued several goals, including the protection of basin headwaters from mining, the declaration of water access as a human right, and community control over natural resources (Poole and Rénique 2012, 4–5; Castro and Prado 2/9/2012).

Humala tried to settle the Conga conflict through another review of the EIA, but to no avail. In February 2012, the government contracted three international consultants to conduct the evaluation (De Echave and Diez 2013, 99). The team finished its work that April, and Humala approved of its recommendations, including that Azul and Chica be preserved (*El Comercio* 4/19/2012, *La República* 5/9/2012). Later that month, movement leaders in

3. In April 2012, Peru's Constitutional Tribunal nullified the ordinance on the grounds that, with the measure, the regional government had exceeded its administrative powers (De Echave and Diez 2013, 100, 152).

Cajamarca threatened an indefinite regional strike if the national government did not cancel Conga by the end of May 2012 (De Echave and Diez 2013, 100).

The strike, which began on May 31, 2012, marked the start of another protest wave. The government responded by announcing in late June 2012 that in order for Conga to move forward, Yanacocha would need to guarantee water provision for residents and comply with the recommendations of the international EIA review team. Yanacocha accepted the terms. In a July 1, 2012, meeting with sixty-five district and provincial mayors from Cajamarca, Humala offered to fund several rural development infrastructure projects. Protest in Cajamarca continued, prompting the government to declare a state of emergency on July 3. Five protesters were killed and dozens wounded in the ensuing violence (De Echave and Diez 2013, 101). National hostility toward Conga increased, too, and in late July sympathizers of the Cajamarca movement carried out solidarity marches in Lima and in the southern city of Puno (De Echave and Diez 2013, 100–101).

Newmont company representatives and the prime minister announced in August 2012 the postponement of Conga due to the absence of "social conditions" for its development (De Echave and Diez 2013, 102).

Ongoing Conflict and Project Suspension: 2012–17

From late 2012 through Conga's indefinite suspension in 2016, conflict took the forms of direct action to block Yanacocha's work, marches, failed government dialogue efforts, and state repression (Defensoría del Pueblo, Adjuntía para la Prevención de Conflictos Sociales y la Gobernabilidad 2017a, 7–21). Also salient in the larger conflict, Yanacocha directly targeted movement leaders, a strategy that hurt Conga's reputation, including in the international arena.

The Indigenous Organizations of Peru Unity Pact (Pacto de Unidad de Organizaciones Indígenas del Perú) had submitted a petition to the Organization of American States (OAS) Inter-American Commission on Human Rights (IACHR) in December 2011, complaining about threats against activists. In May 2014, the IACHR issued a precautionary measure ordering the Peruvian state to guarantee the life and integrity of several people who were at risk due to their organizing against Conga: forty-six leaders of communities and rondas campesinas, a journalist, and a family of the name Chaupe (*Servindi* 5/9/2014).

Máxima Acuña Chaupe was the most well known of the threatened individuals. Acuña and her family refused to move to make way for Conga. In early August 2011, Minera Yanacocha security personnel, accompanied by one hundred members of the national police's special operations unit (Dirección Nacional de Operaciones Especiales, DINOES), arrived at the Acuña residence to remove the family from its land, without official documentation. Acuña and her daughter went to the courts, as did Yanacocha, which also claimed rights to the land (Asurza 2015).

The Acuña case concluded with a May 2017 Supreme Court decision in Acuña's favor (Asurza 2015; *El Comercio* 5/3/2017). Throughout the legal battle, Acuña and her family suffered ongoing threats and property destruction by Yanacocha employees, DINOES, and private security forces (Asurza 2015; Defensoría del Pueblo, Adjuntía para la Prevención de Conflictos Sociales y la Gobernabilidad 2017a, 23–24).

With organizing against Conga ongoing, in April 2016 Buenaventura's president declared Conga "nonviable" due to poor community relations (*El Comercio* 4/26/2016). Yanacocha announced in August of that year that it had given up on the project because Conga did not have a social license (*La República* 8/11/2016).

Santa Ana

Conflict over the Santa Ana mine project in Peru's southern Puno region approximated the Conga case, in that Santa Ana outsiders protested their exclusion from the EIA hearing. The most intense phase of the conflict occurred shortly after the hearing, when the movement against the mine joined with groups that pursued other causes, in the 2011 "Aymarazo." That mobilization began in southern Puno, where Santa Ana was located and which was populated by the Aymara Indigenous nation (Quiñones 2013, 18, 22), and spread throughout the region. The protests caused Santa Ana's cancellation and a moratorium on new mining in Puno.

Permissions for Foreign Mining in Borderland Reserves

Santa Ana belonged to Bear Creek Mining Company Sucursal del Perú, of the Canadian Bear Creek Mining Company. The open-pit mine was projected to produce 63.2 million ounces of silver. Four thousand people resided in the project's area of direct influence, which was primarily in the district of Huacullani, in the province of Chucuito (Quiñones 2013, 25–26, 29). Local communities did not have experience with open-pit mining.[4]

4. Southern Puno also had not been a traditional mining area, whereas unregulated small- and medium-scale mining had a long history in the region's north. The conferral of legal mining titles in Puno, including in Chucuito, surged starting in the early 2000s (Quiñones 2013, 32–34).

Jenny Villavicencio, who would become Bear Creek's legal representative in 2006, confronted two obstacles when pursuing title to the Santa Ana concessions. First, the concessions overlapped with the protected Aymara Lupaca Reserve, where mining was prohibited. To address that issue, Villavicencio sought local community support for the reduction of Aymara Lupaca so as to situate the mine outside of it. Communities in Huacullani had little enthusiasm for the reserve; they believed it could interfere with their livelihoods, including, for instance, animal grazing. In addition, they thought the mine would bring investment in local public infrastructure. In 2004 local leaders accepted the reserve modification (Quiñones 2013, 35, 37–39, 45–46). A January 2006 decree resized Aymara Lupaca, and Villavicencio obtained the Santa Ana concessions during April 2006–December 2007 (Quiñones 2013, 41–42).

The second titling barrier for Villavicencio was that the Santa Ana concessions were within fifty kilometers of the international border; Peru's 1993 constitution prohibited foreign entities and individuals from holding mining rights in borderlands, other than in cases of public necessity (Article 71). Villavicencio asked that an exception be made, given that Santa Ana titles already had been transferred. The Council of Ministers made the allowance by decreeing, in 2007 (with DS 083-2007-EM), that the mining would bring development to the border region (Quiñones 2013, 42–43).

Organizing against Santa Ana would occur outside of the mine's area of direct influence, in a context in which Bear Creek had caused rifts between the communities nearest to the project, and those that were more remote. Leaders from outside of the area of direct influence thought their communities should have been part of the Aymara Lupaca and titling discussions. Furthermore, during exploration, Bear Creek invested in health, rural development, and other programs in communities in the area of direct influence. Because of those investments, much of Huacullani wanted the mine, whereas neighboring districts, as well as the community of Yorocco—in Huacullani but not in Santa Ana's area of direct influence—did not (Quiñones 2013, 40, 47–49, 58–61).

The 2008 Taking of the Mine

The first of the two principal Santa Ana conflict episodes occurred in 2008, with the start of sustained exploration for the mine. The arrival of company personnel and equipment alerted Chucuito communities at large to the mine project and to the concessions transfers. In early 2008 consternation within communities grew, due to Santa Ana's potential environmental impacts, and especially contamination of the Callacame River (Quiñones 2013, 47–49, 60).

Bear Creek suspended its exploration work in response to an October 2008 mobilization that concluded with the taking of the mining camp and the destruction of company offices (Pinto Herrera 2013, 214; Quiñones 2013, 50,

61). The Southern Puno Natural Resources Defense Front (Frente de Defensa de los Recursos Naturales de la Zona Sur de Puno, FDRNZS) led the protest. The Frente, which had formed to obstruct Santa Ana, brought together political and civil-society leaders from Yorocco and four Chuquito districts. The organization adopted a discourse oriented around blocking the mine and protecting the environment, but it also made a list of material requests that included direct company investments premised on project development (Quiñones 2013, 60–61).

The Aymarazo

Conflict over Santa Ana arose again during the drafting, presentation, and potential approval of the EIA, a period in which the FDRNZS was "reactivated" (Quiñones 2013, 64). The EIA review process aggravated divisions over Santa Ana by including only communities within the mine's area of direct influence. Communities that were left out responded by organizing around the EIA participatory process. That activism contributed to the escalation of the mine conflict, which culminated in the Aymarazo (Pinto Herrera 2013, 213; Quiñones 2013, 61–62, 64–65).

Work on the EIA and the associated company-led workshops began in 2009. Bear Creek used the forty-eight workshops mainly to promote the project and promise jobs. Afterward, outsider community members resented that the company had held all of the workshops in the area of direct influence. While the EIA workshops were in progress, the FDRNZS led its own meetings, in Chucuito, to criticize the mine (Pinto Herrera 2013, 211–12; Quiñones 2013, 52–57).

Approximately one thousand Santa Ana supporters attended the EIA hearing, which transpired without incident in the city of Huacullani in late February 2011. Following the hearing, communities outside of the area of direct influence complained that they had not been included (Hualpa 3/23/2011; Pinto Herrera 2013, 213; Uceda 1/7/2014).

Mobilizing increased beginning in March 2011. Civil-society leaders, including the head of the FDRNZS, took issue with the mine due to its environmental impacts. They requested a regional ordinance prohibiting mining in Puno, on the basis of likely damage to the environment, agriculture, and land; the fact that mining would not benefit the local population; and the lack of prior consultation with impacted communities.[5] Puno's regional council issued the ordinance. The measure was only symbolic, given that the central state distributed mining concessions. Nevertheless, it encouraged organizers

5. Peru's executive did not sign the prior consultation law until September 2011, and the law was not applied in mining until 2015 (see Chapter 3).

from southern Puno to congregate later that month in Yorocco, where they insisted on Bear Creek's departure, the nullification of the EIA hearing, and the regional president's endorsement of the ordinance (Hualpa 3/23/2011; Cavero 2014, 26–27, 70).

When the president refused to sign the ordinance, two thousand people marched to the regional capital on March 30 (Cavero 2014, 70). In late April, the FDRNZS and other groups—including CONACAMI, rondas campesinas, cocaleros, and the National Union of Aymara Communities (Unión Nacional de Comunidades Aymara)—led a forty-eight-hour strike against the regional government and the mine, paralyzing southern Puno (Cavero 2014, 71; Defensoría del Pueblo, Adjuntía para la Prevención de Conflictos Sociales y la Gobernabilidad 2016, 4–5).

As protest increased, the national executive instated a roundtable to manage the conflict, but more strikes began on May 9, 2011, that would extend throughout Puno. In the Aymarazo, more than four thousand people blocked the highways that connected the Puno and Tacna regions, and Peru and Bolivia. The strike was continuous, with the exception of a one-week pause at the end of May, to accommodate an election. The mobilization peaked on June 24, 2011, when police personnel and army soldiers shot at protesters who were attempting to take control of the regional airport in the city of Juliaca, killing six (Pinto Herrera 2013, 214–17; Defensoría del Pueblo, Adjuntía para la Prevención de Conflictos Sociales y la Gobernabilidad 2016, 5).

The strike spread not only geographically but also in terms of the matters at stake. Activists seeking to prevent Santa Ana were joined by groups that protested other large-scale development plans in southern Puno, advocated for a prior consultation law, and opposed informal mining due to its environmental impacts (Pinto Herrera 2013, 210, 215–17; Quiñones 2013, 17).

Project Cancellation

The Aymarazo ended in late June 2011, when national authorities met most of the conditions of organizers. Among its actions, the government withdrew permission for the mining activities in the borderlands by revoking DS 083-2007-EM; required that any mining or hydrocarbon development in Puno undergo prior consultation; and suspended all new mining in Puno for three years (Pinto Herrera 2013, 217–18; Quiñones 2013, 18–19).

Peru's government faced consequences for appeasing the protesters. Bear Creek disputed the legality of the revocation of its mining rights, and the Peruvian state floundered in search of a procedural justification for the decision. It ultimately argued that Bear Creek had no authorization for Santa Ana, since the state had granted permissions to Villavicencio, as an individual, to mine near the international border (Uceda 1/7/2014). The World

Bank Group's International Centre for Settlement of Investment Disputes decided in favor of Bear Creek and ordered the Peruvian state to pay the company $30.2 million (Huanachín 12/4/2017).

Afrodita

In another Peruvian mine conflict, over the Afrodita project in the northern Amazon, again outsider communities protested their exclusion from the approval process for new mining development, which they opposed. However, different from the Santa Ana and Conga cases, the most relevant participatory institution in the Afrodita conflict was prior consultation rather than the EIA hearing. After the state sidestepped prior consultation for Afrodita's activities, Indigenous communities of the Awajún and Wampis nations turned to the judicial system to defend, successfully, their right to be consulted.

Communities also used prior consultation in a second way in their effort to block Afrodita: they fought for recognition of a completed consultation process that had created a protected national park that encompassed the Afrodita project area.

Much of the Afrodita conflict unfolded in a context of weak cohesion among Awajún and Wampis communities, due importantly to the Baguazo (see Chapter 3), in which the two nations had participated;[6] after the Baguazo, some Awajún and Wampis communities that wanted to avoid confrontation with the government accepted the Afrodita project (Castillo Fernández 2016, 19–20). By contrast, the Organization for the Development of the Border Communities of El Cenepa (Organización de Desarrollo de las Comunidades Fronterizas del Cenepa, ODECOFROC, of AIDESEP) consistently defended the outcome of the park consultation, demanded prior consultation for Afrodita's activities, and rejected extraction (Castillo Fernández 2016, 9–10).

Prior Consultation for a Park

In 1993, the Peruvian state granted the Afrodita mining concessions—which were in the Condor Mountain Range (Cordillera del Cóndor) and in Awajún and Wampis ancestral lands—to the exploration company Metalfin, of the British Hochschild Group. Metalfin later formed Compañía Minera Afrodita S.A. and transferred, in 1999, all 203,000 hectares of its Condor gold exploration properties to the new firm (*Business News Americas* 6/30/1999; Equipo de

6. Twenty-one of the twenty-two Indigenous people accused of serious crimes following the Baguazo were of the Awajún or Wampis (Castillo Fernández 2016, 31–32). On the role of the Awajún and Wampis in the Baguazo, see also Chapter 3.

Investigación de ODECOFROC 2009, 28, 41). In the early 2000s, the mine site became part of a protected national park, due to a collaboration between the state and the Awajún and Wampis. The park initiative had roots in the 1995 Peru-Ecuador Cenepa War in Condor, which broke out during the countries' long-standing border dispute. Peace accords signed in 1998 concluded the conflict and produced the Binational Development Plan of the Peru-Ecuador Border Region (Plan Binacional de Desarrollo de la Región Fronteriza Perú-Ecuador). The plan included a commitment by both governments to work with local Indigenous communities to institute protected ecological areas in the combat zone (Castillo Fernández 2016, 4).

In following with the Plan Binacional, negotiations between the state and the Awajún and Wampis created the Santiago Comaina Reserve (Zona Reservada Santiago Comaina, ZRSC) as a step toward establishing a park. Awajún and Wampis interests in the park endeavor were multiple. Communities of the two nations, which had struggled for decades for land titles, hoped to formalize their lands within the ZRSC (Castillo Fernández 2016, 5, 6–7). They also had cultural ties to the area and valued it as environmentally unique and as a water source for the region (Equipo de Investigación de ODECOFROC 2009, 12, 17–19).

The ZRSC was enlarged in 2000, with Indigenous participation. Subsequently, a prior consultation process with the Awajún and Wampis—Peru's first prior consultation—defined the boundaries of the Ichigkat-Muja Condor Mountain Range National Park (Parque Nacional Ichigkat Muja—Cordillera del Condor, PNIMCC), inside the expanded ZRSC. The consultation process concluded in November 2004 (Castillo Fernández 2016, 5–6, 11).

Contraction of the Park

Afrodita tried multiple avenues to secure permission to mine in Condor. At first, the company ignored the environmentally sensitive nature of the area and applied for mining exploration privileges through the Institute of Natural Resources (Instituto Nacional de Recursos Naturales, INRENA), the state agency that founded and oversaw protected areas. INRENA denied Afrodita's request in 2001, declaring mining to be incompatible with Condor's ecological and geological characteristics. The agency referenced the ongoing national park project; and the anticipated destruction of moisture-retaining vegetation and interference with water flows and quality, from mining (Equipo de Investigación de ODECOFROC 2009, 28–30).

Subsequently, in August 2004, the company turned to MINEM's General Directorate of Environmental Affairs in Mining (Dirección General de Asuntos Ambientales Mineros, DGAAM) for permission to explore in three of the Afrodita concessions. In its request, the company reasoned that, because the exploration was to take place near an international border, the project fell under the army's purview and not under ZRSC rules. DGAAM routed Afrodita's submission to INRENA, which refused to allow the exploration on the basis of the reserve's protected status (Equipo de Investigación de ODECOFROC 2009, 30).

Having been foiled by the ZRSC environmental protections, Afrodita utilized a different strategy: to reduce in size the PNIMCC so as to position the mine project outside of the park (similar to Villavicencio's approach to the Aymara Lupaca reserve, in the Santa Ana case). The owner of Afrodita, Jorge Bedoya Torrico, met several times in 2005 with state officials about redrawing the park's boundaries. He aimed to convince the defense and foreign affairs ministries that, relative to a national park, Afrodita's operations on the border would defend more effectively national sovereignty from ongoing informal Ecuadorian mining activities. A November 2005 meeting of Bedoya and representatives of INRENA, MINEM, the military joint command, and the defense and foreign affairs ministries resulted in a signed memorandum committing INRENA to resizing the park (Equipo de Investigación de ODECOFROC 2009, 30–32; Kayap Jempekit and Ruiz Molleda 8/29/2013). In January 2006, INRENA presented a new PNIMCC park project (Equipo de Investigación de ODECOFROC 2009, 31–33; Castillo Fernández 2016, 12). An August 2007 decree diminished the size of the ZRSC and formalized the PNIMCC, which was 58 percent smaller than the park dimensions defined in 2004 (Castillo Fernández 2016, 11).

With the 2007 decree in place, mining interest in Condor expanded. By 2008, there were a total of fifty-three granted Condor concessions, forty-six of which had been issued during 2007–8 (Castillo Fernández 2016, 12; see also Equipo de Investigación de ODECOFROC 2009, 31).

The Awajún and Wampis reacted to Afrodita's PNIMCC maneuver by defending the prior consultation process that had concluded in 2004, and by confronting the state for not having consulted them about mining development in their territories. In March 2007, representatives of ODECOFROC and two other organizations (Organización de Desarrollo de las Comunidades del Alto Comaina, ODECOAC, and Organización de Desarrollo de las Comunidades Indígenas Numpatkaim y Alto Comaina, ODECINAC) signed the "Awajún Wampis Cenepa Pronouncement" ("Pronunciamiento Awajún Wampis del Cenepa"), addressed to President García. In the document, the groups described contamination from Afrodita's preliminary exploration activities, and asked to meet with the president and for state recognition of the park's original dimensions. In a historic moment in Awajún-Wampis organizing, the main leaders of the nations—from five river basins in the provinces of Condorcanqui and Bagua (in the Amazonas region) and Datem del Marañón (in Loreto)—agreed to convoke, in August 2007, a special general assembly. The assembly produced the Special General Assembly of Leaders and Communities of the Ancestral Territory (Asamblea General de Líderes y Comunidades del

Territorio Ancestral), a sovereign decision-making body of the Awajún and Wampis (Castillo Fernández 2016, 13–14, 15).

Surface Rights

One dimension of the Afrodita conflict was the struggle over surface rights for exploration. It began in December 2009, when MINEM approved Afrodita's DIA for exploration in Condorcanqui (*Andina* 12/10/2009).

The Awajún and Wampis held up exploration for several years by threatening a massive strike. After the DIA approval and still in December 2009, ODECOFROC denounced mining in Condor in writing, to MINEM (Defensoría del Pueblo, Adjuntía para la Prevención de Conflictos Sociales y la Gobernabilidad 2017c, 2). In early February 2010 in the Cenepa district in Condorcanqui, Indigenous groups signed an agreement with INRENA's successor, the National Service for Natural Protected Areas of the State (Servicio Nacional de Áreas Naturales Protegidas del Estado, SERNANP), to pursue an expansion of the PNIMCC. Fifty-two communities were poised to hold a large mobilization later that month in the Peruvian Amazon to protest Afrodita's exploration work and its impacts, all without prior consultation. In response, MINEM suspended Afrodita's exploration privileges, finding that the company did not have communities' permission to access land for the exploration (*Servindi* 2/17/2010). Afrodita remained stalled until 2013 (Observatorio de Conflictos Mineros en el Perú 2015, 24).

The problematic DIA process drove Afrodita to the subnational level. Bedoya distributed the Afrodita titles across several companies of which he was the legal representative. The restructuring transitioned Afrodita to the small-scale mining sector, governed by regional environmental rules (SPDA n.d.b; Observatorio de Conflictos Mineros en el Perú 2015, 24; Castillo Fernández 2016, 31). That move meant for Bedoya less cumbersome requirements relative to those of the national environmental regime, including with regard to community participation.[7]

Bedoya and his firms—referred to here as Afrodita for the sake of simplicity—built strong relationships with Amazonas regional government officials and sympathetic communities.[8] In 2013, Afrodita requested from the Amazonas government access to fifty-six hectares, to extract from

7. Observatorio de Conflictos Mineros en el Perú (2015, 24); and Interview with Vanessa Schaeffer, a member of the CooperAcción team that worked on the Afrodita conflict; Lima, August 3, 2018 (Interview P7).

8. For example, support for Bedoya's mining plans from local communities and regional public officials produced, in 2014, the document, "Declaration of Regional Interest in the Condor Mountain Range Mining Project" ("Declaratoria de interés regional al proyecto minero en la Cordillera del Cóndor"; Observatorio de Conflictos Mineros en el Perú 2015, 25).

Comaina 1, one of the Condor concessions. The regional government then approached the state authority that granted easements on public lands, the National Superintendency of State Assets (Superintendencia Nacional de Bienes Nacionales, SBN). SBN classified the property as "abandoned land" and granted the easement, making it possible for the Amazonas government to approve the Afrodita operations, which it did, in June 2014.[9] That December, MINEM allowed the extraction on the basis of the abandoned land status. DREM-Amazonas issued the construction permissions for the project in early 2015 (Hurtado 12/16/2015; Observatorio de Conflictos Mineros en el Perú 2015, 24), and in April 2016, it authorized extraction (Jima Chamiquit et al. 8/24/2016).

The Awajún and Wampis achieved the reversal of the April 2016 permissions. In a context in which the 2013 easement had lapsed, and in line with an ODECOFROC request and advisement by the Defensoría del Pueblo, the Amazonas council unanimously recommended in August 2016 that the regional governor reverse the approval for extraction. The vice governor of Amazonas, Carlos Navas—who at the time was handling matters for the governor in the latter's absence—refused. Finally, in December 2016, the Amazonas governor withdrew the permission.[10] That reversal happened after the company had built encampments, and exploration had impacted the area significantly.[11]

Amparos

The surface-rights conflict overlapped temporally with the Awajún and Wampis's legal defense of their right to prior consultation, a right that they grounded in the national government's ratification of ILO 169 in the 1990s, long before the 2011 prior consultation law (Castillo Fernández 2016, 31).

ODECOFROC representative Zebelio Kayap Jempekit filed an amparo in 2013 against MINEM and the Geological, Mining, and Metallurgical Institute (Instituto Geológico, Minero y Metalúrgico, INGEMMET), the state agency responsible for granting titles to mining concessions. Kayap decried the issuance of titles and the approval of exploration without a prior consultation

9. As discussed in Chapter 3, Article 6 of the 2013 environmental paquetazo DS 054-2013-PCM facilitated development in nontitled Indigenous lands by defining them as abandoned.

10. Jima Chamiquit et al. 8/24/2016; and Defensoría del Pueblo, Adjuntía para la Prevención de Conflictos Sociales y la Gobernabilidad 2017c, 12. ODECOFROC leaders initially sought support from Amazonas's vice governor, with whom they had worked well in the past, to have the regional permissions overturned. When they saw that he was an advocate of the mine project, they turned to the governor and gained his backing. Interview with Zebelio Kayap, a former president of ODECOFROC; Lima, August 3, 2018 (Interview P8). See also Chamiquit et al. 8/24/2016.

11. Interview P7.

process. Following a negative outcome from a lower court, the communities proved victorious: in April 2019, a court ruling (by the Décimo Juzgado Constitucional de la Corte Superior de Lima) nullified 111 mining concessions in Awajún and Wampis territory for having been transferred without prior consultation. The decision also invalidated the administrative processes that had approved Afrodita's DIA for exploration, and the EIA-sd for an exploration project of a different mining firm.[12]

In another filing, in 2017, ODECOFROC defended the outcome of the 2004 prior consultation—that is, the original dimensions of the PNIMCC (Ruiz Molleda 6/6/2017). That case was pending in 2020 (Movimiento Ciudadano frente al Cambio Climático 2/27/2020).

Block 116

While the Awajún and Wampis were organizing against Afrodita, they also protested oil development in Block 116 and the state's failure to consult them about it.

In the Block 116 conflict, communities complemented their mobilizing around prior consultation with their use of other formal participatory institutions. Local groups that rejected oil development were included in a block-licensing hearing.[13] They participated in that gathering, to compete with pro-extraction organizations. Communities also mobilized in response to the EIA participatory process, from which they were excluded: they took action to interrupt an EIA workshop, and after the oil project's EIA hearings, they held a meeting where they discussed the content of the EIA.

Splits among and within communities in Block 116 over oil development were evident. The divisions were due not only to the Baguazo but also to the fact that the project owner concentrated its social investments in the area of influence, neglecting other communities. In addition, in Domingusa, one of the five basins of the Awajún and Wampis, the company financed the travel of select community leaders to the town of Santa María de Nieva, in the district of Nieva, in Condorcanqui; and to other towns in the province; so that those leaders could solicit subnational government investment in basic services for their communities (CAAAP and CooperAcción 2015, 72–75).

12. Defensoría del Pueblo, Adjuntía para la Prevención de Conflictos Sociales y la Gobernabilidad 2017c, 8; Resolution Twenty (Resolución veinte); and *Servindi* 5/18/2019.

13. The Peruvian government introduced participation into block licensing with February 2008 regulations that governed citizen participation in hydrocarbons (see Chapter 3).

Overview of Block 116 and the Local Communities

In December 2006, Perupetro and Hocol Perú S.A.C. signed a licensing contract for Block 116, most of which was in Condorcanqui but which also overlapped with Bagua and Datem del Marañón. The rights were then transferred again, to Maurel Et Prom Colombia, in May 2010. In June 2013, Pacific Stratus Energy S.A. Sucursal del Perú, a subsidiary of Pacific Rubiales Energy Corporation, became the operator of the project, with a 50 percent stake in it (CAAAP and CooperAcción 2015, 28, 33, 36).

Block 116 extended into the territory of seventy-three Awajún and Wampis communities, in the five river basins. It covered just under 37 percent of the ZRSC; and 48.5 percent of another reserve, the Tuntanain Communal Reserve (Reserva Comunal Tuntanain; CAAAP and CooperAcción 2015, 28). The Native communities that organized in the Block 116 conflict had not experienced adverse environmental or social impacts from extraction.[14]

Participation in Block Licensing

The Awajún and Wampis participated in the March 29, 2008, public hearing on the licensing of Block 116. The hearing was preceded by a March 12, 2008, informational session (*encuentro informativo*). Immediately following that first meeting, the Awajún-Wampis Asamblea General convened to prepare for the actual hearing. The assembly produced a special commission, which developed a document condemning all oil activities in Block 116 for violating ILO 169, to be read at the hearing (Castillo Fernández 2016, 14–15).[15]

Competing groups participated in the Santa María de Nieva hearing on March 29. The special commission read its document. The Regional Organization of the Northern Amazonian Indigenous Peoples (Organización Regional de los Pueblos Indígenas de la Amazonía Norte, ORPIAN) also disapproved of exploration and extraction in Block 116; at the meeting, both the commission and ORPIAN ignored a presentation by a representative of CONAP, which accepted development in Block 116 (Castillo Fernández 2016, 14, 15). Perupetro remarked in its report on the hearing that participants had

14. From 1968 to 1998, several hydrocarbon firms conducted exploration in the block—which at the time was Block 50—including some drilling. That work resulted in discoveries of gas and oil (CAAAP and CooperAcción 2015, 34–35). However, in the exploration area for the Block 116 project analyzed here, there were no environmental liabilities (*pasivos ambientales*) from previous oil activities. CAAAP and CooperAcción 2015, 40; and Interview with Vanessa Schaeffer, a member of the CooperAcción team that worked on the Block 116 conflict; via Skype from Arizona, May 16, 2017 (Interview P9).

15. The commission would be renamed CEPPAW, which organized the August 2008 mobilization prior to the Baguazo (see Chapter 3).

opposed oil activities and had characterized the state as not in compliance with ILO 169 (CAAAP and CooperAcción 2015, 36).

On March 30, 2008, the day after the public hearing, Hocol submitted to MINEM the terms of reference for its exploration project (CAAAP and CooperAcción 2015, 37).

EIA Public Hearings

Whereas they had been included in the licensing hearing, antiproject communities, which resided beyond the project's area of influence, were left out of the EIA participatory stage. Those outsider communities mobilized around the participatory process by protesting their exclusion and by examining the EIA at their own meeting, after the EIA hearings.

Maurel Et Prom Perú reduced the Block 116 project's scope while it was developing the EIA, due to community resistance. The company had planned to drill four exploratory wells from two platforms, PUT-1X and DOM-1. However, in an August 2009 opinion that SERNANP issued to Maurel Et Prom Perú, the agency noted that PUT-1X was in the Tuntanain reserve. For their part, company representatives were disturbed that local communities had blocked the company from evaluating the PUT-1X site and believed social conflict threatened company employees' physical well-being. In September 2010, the firm scaled back the project to two wells, from platform DOM-1 (CAAAP and CooperAcción 2015, 30, 37).

The state convened three EIA hearings, during March 8–10, 2011, in Nieva. Two were in communities in the EIA-defined area of direct influence: Kashap, in which exploratory drilling was planned, and Ciro Alegría, the location of the planned oil base camp. The third hearing was in Santa María de Nieva, in the project's "area of indirect influence." The hearings were carried out efficiently (*Inforegión* 3/17/2011; CAAAP and CooperAcción 2015, 56–57). Participants expressed some apprehension about environmental impacts from extraction, but they also articulated hopes that the project would generate jobs and company investments in local development, including potable water (*Inforegión* 3/17/2011). A member of the team from the Peruvian NGO CooperAcción that worked on the Block 116 conflict described the hearings as "a formality" (*un trámite*).[16] The state approved the EIA for the exploration project in October 2011 (CAAAP and CooperAcción 2015, 37).

Outsider communities organized around the EIA participatory process. When describing the overall Block 116 conflict trajectory, Awajún leader Zebelio Kayap said that by leaving out communities, the EIA participatory process had produced consternation. He recounted that members of outsider

16. Interview P9.

communities had attended one EIA workshop in 2010 in Kashap to which they had not been invited, to protest. They succeeded in causing the meeting's adjournment. More generally, he described frustration within communities excluded from EIA participation; he said the communities had been defined as not residing in the area of influence, but that they were impacted by the project and saw themselves as such.[17]

The March 19–21, 2010, Special Assembly of 110 Representatives (Asamblea Extraordinaria de 110 Representantes) is striking evidence of outsider activism around the EIA hearings. That Santa María de Nieva gathering, held shortly after the hearings, included community leaders and intellectuals from the five river basins. The consultants who had drafted the EIA also attended, by invitation, to discuss the document and the project. After the meeting, the assembly produced a statement admonishing the oil company for not having engaged with all of the communities impacted by the Block 116 development.[18]

The Amparo

Outsider communities' primary use of participatory institutions in the Block 116 case was to challenge, through the courts, the lack of prior consultation for activities in the oil block. The Awajún and Wampis began their legal struggle in 2013, in response to exploration work.[19] As they had done in the case of Afrodita, communities dated their right to prior consultation to the Peruvian government's ratification of ILO 169.

In 2014, ODECOFROC and CEPPAW filed an amparo against MINEM and Perupetro for not consulting Native communities before either licensing Block 116 or approving exploration in it. In a March 2017 decision, the Fourth Constitutional Court of Lima (Cuarto Juzgado Constitucional de Lima) ruled for the communities, requiring prior consultation with and also consent from them, for the oil development. The court nullified the contract for exploration and extraction and ordered the cessation of all exploration work in Block 116 until communities had been consulted, and the departure from the block of Maurel Et Prom Perú and Pacific Stratus Energy Perú (*Servindi* 3/31/2017).[20] MINEM appealed the decision, which was upheld in 2018 by the Superior Court of Justice of Lima (Corte Superior de Justicia de Lima). The 2018 ruling

17. Interview P8.

18. Estrada 4/25/2013; CAAAP and CooperAcción 2015, 54; and Castillo Fernández 2016, 18–19.

19. Interview P8.

20. The legal team working on the amparo filed the case in Lima, hoping that a decision made in the capital would carry more weight in future cases involving other oil blocks. The oil company wanted to have the case tried locally. Interview P7.

also required prior consultation for any new EIAs for future exploration or extraction in Block 116 (*El Comercio* 4/4/2017; *Servindi* 8/23/2018). The following year, the Cuarto Juzgado Constitucional de Lima ordered the enforcement of the 2018 decision (Instituto de Defensa Legal 8/8/2019).

Putumayo Fields

Indigenous mobilizing in the oil-producing department of Putumayo in southern Colombia serves as one more example of outsider communities protesting their exclusion from project approvals after having been denied prior consultation. The project in question, which the state authorized in 2014, expanded production in the Cohembi, Quillacinga, and Quinde oil fields. It affected the Nasa Indigenous nation, known for its organizational capacity, including in challenging extraction and engaging in prior consultations.[21] In the conflict, the Nasa and another impacted Indigenous nation, the Awá, used the tutela to win partial victories: the Constitutional Court rulings on the cases mandated prior consultation but did not suspend the oil project.

Extraction, Conflict, and Negotiation in Putumayo

Cohembi, Quillacinga, and Quinde were in the municipality of Puerto Asís, a major contributor to Putumayo's overall oil output (Silva Montealegre 2015, 42; Martínez and Delgado 2017, 49, 125, 128). In addition to oil, Putumayo—including Puerto Asís—produced coca for the cocaine trade and had seen substantial violence tied to Colombia's civil war (Martínez and Delgado 2017, 106–11, 116–19).

There were important precursors to the outbreak of conflict over the 2014 expansion project. In 2006 the state and local communities in Puerto Asís first engaged in conversations about oil development. In those negotiations, the state promised to cap the number of wells at thirty-nine and to invest in the region to limit the environmental and social impacts of oil extraction (Pulido 8/29/2014).

The state did not consult Indigenous communities about oil development in Cohembí, Quillacinga, and Quinde, because of the interior ministry's 2008 determination, based on a 2006 field visit, that there was no Indigenous presence in the project area. In 2009, MAVDT granted an

21. Interview C4; Interview with Carlos Ariel Ruiz, a consultant working with the Ministry of Interior on Indigenous matters; Bogotá, July 14, 2016 (Interview C13); and Interview with an academic specializing in extractive conflict; Bogotá, July 26, 2016 (Interview C14).

environmental license for oil extraction in the fields, without prior consultation (with Resolution 0937, for the project "Desarrollo de Campos Quinde, Cohembí y Quillacinga"). The state approved an expansion project in 2010 (with MAVDT's Resolution 1930), also without consulting communities (Pulido 8/29/2014; Constitutional Court Sentence T-730/16, Section I.5).

Direct Action

The conflict of interest began in 2014 when ANLA allowed a modification to the 2010 project. Once again, communities were not consulted. By that time, they had experienced serious adverse environmental impacts from the 2010 expansion.[22] The 2014 modification (approved with Resolution 0551) involved extraction from one hundred additional wells by the Colombia Energy consortium, disregarding the thirty-nine-well limit.[23]

As of late August 2014, protests had been ongoing for more than one month, and approximately four hundred campesinos and Indigenous people were preventing Vetra, Colombia Energy's operator, from accessing the new expansion area. With the blockade, residents hoped to achieve a dialogue with the government (Pulido 8/29/2014).

Organizing against the 2014 expansion project merged with a strike in the nearby municipality of Villagarzón, an action motivated in part by harm to crops from aerial fumigations intended to target coca. The greatest violence in the mobilizations was between police personnel and the Nasa and Afro-Colombians, in Puerto Asís. By September 26, 2014, the oil conflict had lasted seventy-two days. Forty-eight people had been wounded, six gravely (Hidalgo y Costilla and Ramírez 9/26/2014).

Senior government officials met with the Nasa in Putumayo during three months in late 2014 to resolve the conflict. The meetings resulted in several agreements, one of which provided for two independent studies of the effects of the 2010 expansion—one by a government team and the second by members of civil society. The civil-society group conducted its research from late 2014 into early 2015. It found that the project had not met international standards for contamination and health, and that Colombian standards were

22. Interview with a Nasa anthropologist in Putumayo who had conducted research on the environmental impacts of the 2010 project; by phone from Bogotá, July 28, 2016 (Interview C15). In 2011, communities in Puerto Asís declared their situation a humanitarian crisis due to the impacts of oil activities on their water sources (*Semana sostenible* 10/24/2016).

23. Pulido 8/29/2014; and Interview C15.

lax. It also concluded that the state should have consulted the Indigenous communities in the project area.[24]

Defense of the Right to Prior Consultation: The Judicial Route

Added to the dialogue process, the Nasa and the Awá—which also were impacted by the 2009, 2010, and 2014 projects—filed tutelas. With their tutela filing in 2015, the Nasa wanted to be consulted so as to adjust the project to protect their lands, including sacred spaces.[25] The Constitutional Court decided on the Nasa's tutela in 2016. In its ruling, the court required prior consultation with the Nasa and compensation for environmental impacts. It stopped short of interrupting oil activities, characterizing Putumayo's oil production as crucial for national development (Constitutional Court Sentence T-730/16, Sections III.8, IV).

As for the Awá, a representative of the Awá community of La Cabaña (in Puerto Asís) also submitted a tutela action in 2015. La Cabaña maintained that the state should have consulted the community about exploration or extraction in the oil fields and asked for the suspension of twenty-seven local, operating wells. Two courts denied the tutela. In November 2018 the Constitutional Court found that the oil operations directly impacted the community by contaminating its water sources and air, killing local fauna on which it relied for food, adversely impacting medicinal plants, and in general harming the community's health. The court ruled that the state should have consulted the Awá for the 2009, 2010, and 2014 projects; required a prior consultation to identify the environmental, spiritual, cultural, and social impacts of extraction on the Awá; and mandated preventative, mitigation, and restoration measures as needed. The Court again chose not to pause oil work, taking into consideration, among other factors, the importance of production in the oil fields for the national and regional economies.[26]

DIRECT ACTION TO DEMAND PARTICIPATION

In the conflicts addressed in the first part of this chapter, outsider communities protested being left out of approval processes for new extraction, after the state had denied them participation. Outsiders in this section used blockades

24. Interview C15. On the studies and resulting reports, see also *Semana sostenible* 10/24/2016.
25. Interview C15.
26. *El Tiempo* 2/18/2016; Constitutional Court Sentence SU123/18, I.2, II.25.2, III.25.5, V; and *Semana* 11/19/2018.

and occupations, or the threat thereof, to hold up development at or immediately following the participatory stage, to force prior consultation or at least meaningful discussions with the state. The form and relatively early timing of community activism were due to rigid Indigenous land boundaries; communities could not achieve prior consultation based on administrative or legal arguments. Instead, they turned to direct action.

Five of the conflicts examined here involved the Guaraní in Bolivia, where prior consultation was sanctioned only for communities with title to impacted land. In the last conflict in this section, Colombian communities protested the Magallanes gas project. As discussed in Chapter 3 and illustrated by the Putumayo case analyzed earlier in this chapter, Colombia's prior consultation framework was based on nonrigid boundaries, in that it determined Indigenous communal land rights using a range of dimensions, the measurement of which could be debated by communities and the state. However, the Magallanes case exemplifies limits to the expanse of territory that Colombian Indigenous communities could claim when seeking access to prior consultation. The communities in question, of the U'wa nation, previously had tested that limit and therefore protested the Magallanes project with a blockade.

Alongside the employment of direct action to be consulted (or at least to spur negotiations), in one of the conflicts, over the Timboy X-2 well, Guaraní communities mobilized around prior consultation in a second way: they conditioned the development of Timboy X-2 on the completion of prior consultation for a separate hydrocarbon project.

Percheles and El Dorado Fields

The Takovo Mora capitanía, which consisted of eleven Bolivian Guaraní communities in Santa Cruz's Cordillera province (Candela, September 2015), secured for the first time its right to prior consultation in hydrocarbons through the Percheles and El Dorado gas fields conflict.[27] Experts in Bolivia interviewed for this study described the Percheles and El Dorado case as one of significant conflict, because it included an extended blockade and a long, meeting-intensive prior consultation process (see also Schilling-Vacaflor and Kuhn 2015, 136–37).

The conflict took place in 2007–8, shortly after the implementation of the 2007 prior consultation regulations (DS 29033), when many actors had little or no knowledge of the new prior consultation procedures, according to an

27. This case study is based on Interview B2. The interviewee spoke based on her recollection of conflict details and also referred to specific documents in a thick binder in her possession.

APG specialist (*técnico*) in themes of prior consultation.[28] Similarly, a former employee of Chaco S.A., the private company that had led the Percheles and El Dorado projects, said that the conflict had marked the beginning of a state—rather than solely company—role in community relations in Bolivian hydrocarbons. She said that throughout the conflict, Indigenous groups had exhibited deep knowledge of the regulations and had ensured the prior consultation process.[29]

Takovo Mora acted independently of the APG in this case. Due to its allegiance to the Morales administration, which was an advocate of the Percheles and El Dorado projects, the APG did not support, and in fact broke with, Takovo Mora during the conflict. At the time, the APG stated publicly that it would resolve the matter through talks with the national government.

Blocking of the Plant

Chaco's plans for the Percheles and El Dorado fields consisted of three projects. Two of them—seismic studies and the construction of gas lines—were in TCO Takovo Mora, and the third—the drilling of wells and the construction of the Percheles Plant—was outside of but bordered the TCO.

The Takovo Mora capitanía learned of the projects in August 2007, when Chaco employees entered the TCO without permission, to gather sand for the Percheles plant construction. Chaco also failed to communicate with the Cabezas municipal government before crossing into a part of the municipality (on lands that did not overlap with TCO Takovo Mora) for sand. In response to the trespassing, Takovo Mora community members, with non-Indigenous campesinos and Cabezas municipal representatives, physically blocked the plant site. They held their position for several months.

Takovo Mora and the municipality also reported the invasion to the environment ministry. The ministry affirmed that there should have been a prior consultation process and communication with the municipality, for the planned development. On September 8, 2007, Takovo Mora community leaders met with the company, which acknowledged that two of its projects were on Indigenous land.

Consultation and Compensation

A prior consultation ensued that extended from December 2007 into February 2008, with some meetings lasting forty-eight hours. After the final

28. Interview B2.
29. Interview B12.

consultation agreement was signed, the state issued Chaco an environmental license, and discussions about compensation began. The company promised social investments amounting to $300,000 annually for five years, to be apportioned among Takovo Mora, the municipality, and local campesinos. The company also committed to funding Indigenous monitoring of the Percheles and El Dorado development.

Río Grande Plant

In 2012 Takovo Mora staged another blockade, to demand to be consulted about YPFB's $160 million Río Grande Liquid Separation Plant (Planta de Separación de Líquidos de Río Grande), in the Río Grande field (Schilling-Vacaflor and Kuhn 2015, 140–41).[30] The capitanía was anxious about the gas plant's environmental impacts, given that two Takovo Mora communities resided within two kilometers of the project. The APG Takovo Mora also feared that the project would contaminate the Río Grande river, on which Takovo Mora relied for drinking water (*Servindi* 1/27/2012). Through its mobilizing, the capitanía ensured the completion of an interrupted prior consultation process for the gas plant. The consultation lasted thirty weeks, including the interludes (Schilling-Vacaflor and Kuhn 2015, 140–41).

Different from the Percheles and El Dorado case analyzed previously in this section, Takovo Mora did not have state-recognized rights to areas impacted by the Río Grande plant, in a context of Takovo Mora's ongoing land-titling difficulties. In 1996, the capitanía petitioned the state for collective ownership of more than 272,000 hectares. As of May 2013, it held title to only 8,514 hectares of that land (Schilling-Vacaflor 2017a, 667). By contrast, wealthy third parties acquired with relative ease titles to many parcels dispersed throughout the claimed TCO (*ERBOL* 8/24/2015).

Interrupted Prior Consultation

At first, the Bolivian state recognized Takovo Mora's rights to land impacted by the Río Grande plant. In mid-2011, YPFB asked for a meeting with the capitanía, to structure a prior consultation for the project. However, the legal status of the affected land then changed. In August 2011, INRA declared the lands public and slated for YPFB's plant project.[31] In September 2011, before

30. This analysis of the Río Grande case is based on Interview B2 and the other referenced sources. The interviewee spoke based on her recollection of conflict details and also referred to specific documents in a thick binder in her possession.

31. Centro de Estudios para el Desarrollo Laboral y Agrario 6/2/2011; Instituto Nacional de Reforma Agraria (INRA) 1/13/2012; and *Bolivia.com* 1/18/2012.

the date of the first scheduled prior consultation meeting, YPFB forged ahead, clearing eleven hectares of land to construct Río Grande, under the watch of military personnel.

Takovo Mora revived the consultation process, though only temporarily. The capitanía challenged INRA's August 2011 lands decision by filing a complaint with the National Agrarian Tribunal, the highest court in Bolivia's agrarian judiciary (Assies 2006, 592; INRA 1/13/2012). In early October 2011, with the complaint still under review, the hydrocarbon minister traveled to the plant location and signed a memorandum to commence prior consultation, which began three days later. At that time, participants planned to conclude the consultation on November 11. Instead, at that November meeting, Takovo Mora introduced a new proposal, that project land revert to Takovo Mora upon the plant's completion.

With the prior consultation still in progress, in early December 2011, the National Agrarian Tribunal upheld INRA's August 2011 determination, and the environment ministry issued the Río Grande environmental license (INRA 1/13/2012; *Bolivia.com* 1/18/2012; Vásquez 1/19/2012).

Occupation of the Plant, Prior Consultation, and Community Divisions

Takovo Mora responded to the licensing by occupying the plant site on January 16, 2012. The community wanted prior consultation, the nullification of the Río Grande environmental license, and $37 million for the community, paid across twenty years. The money would have been for compensation, right-of-way fees for the use of TCO lands, and investment in social development and in socioenvironmental monitoring of the plant. YPFB's president responded to the request with a statement that the $37 million sum would "practically make inviable" the development of Río Grande (*Bolivia.com* 1/18/2012). On January 18, 2012, officials from the environment, hydrocarbon, and rural development and lands ministries met with the APG Takovo Mora and tried, unsuccessfully, to convince that body that no prior consultation was needed (Vásquez 1/19/2012).

After nearly three weeks of the blockade, the state folded. The environment and hydrocarbon ministries wrote an addendum to the Río Grande environmental license to justify a prior consultation process (YPFB 4/10/2012). The consultation concluded in February 2012. On April 10, 2012, YPFB and the APG Takovo Mora reached a compensation agreement for seven million *bolivianos*, or approximately $1 million (YPFB 4/10/2012; Schilling-Vacaflor 2017a, 669).

The Río Grande case stands out for causing friction within Takovo Mora. One sector of the capitanía strongly preferred not to resume the consultation in January 2012, claiming that doing so would ascribe false validity to incorrect procedure: the state had issued an environmental license without first consulting the community, and only afterward had led a consultation, with the license still in place. Disagreement within Takovo Mora over this sequencing question continued through the conclusion of the prior consultation.

The Río Grande conflict also weakened Takovo Mora's ties to the APG. The APG leader (new since the Percheles and El Dorado conflict), was a MAS supporter who allegedly enjoyed employment opportunities through his party ties. He distanced himself from Takovo Mora during the mobilizing over Río Grande, in exchange for government promises of social investment in Guaraní communities (Schilling-Vacaflor 2017a, 669).

As a closing comment on Río Grande, the concurrent TIPNIS struggle, discussed in Chapter 3, partly explains the protracted nature of the plant conflict. CIDOB made a strategic decision to suspend all prior consultations until the TIPNIS issue was resolved. That moratorium lasted approximately six months.[32] YPFB attributed at least two months of the Río Grande project delays to the TIPNIS-induced pause on prior consultations (YPFB 4/10/2012).

El Dorado Exploratory Wells

In another conflict involving Takovo Mora, the capitanía set up blockades in its effort to be consulted about the drilling of four exploratory wells in the El Dorado field. The YPFB project was on private property. The level of police force used to clear the blockades made the conflict a case of unusually harsh state repression against the Guaraní.[33] The state finally consulted Takovo Mora about the wells in a rapid prior consultation that included an illegitimate community leader.

State Repression

YPFB planned to construct the four wells in Chivatos and San Juan de El Dorado, private landholdings that together spanned thirty-five hundred hectares within the claimed TCO Takovo Mora. In contrast to the capitanía's lengthy, incomplete land-titling experience, the two plots were transferred to their private owner through a five-year process (*ERBOL* 8/24/2015).[34]

32. Interview with Silvana Méndez, a former técnico for the APG Charagua Norte who had worked in a prior consultation during the TIPNIS conflict; Charagua, June 22, 2017 (Interview B14). On CIDOB's moratorium on prior consultations, see also Schilling-Vacaflor 2013b, 8.

33. Interview B3.

34. The leader in natural resources matters within the Council of Guaraní Captains of Santa Cruz (Consejo de Capitanes Guaraní del Departamento de Santa Cruz) pointed to the Chivatos and San Juan de El Dorado titles to illustrate his view on why third

Takovo Mora initially expected to be consulted about the wells, based on previous communications with YPFB Chaco. Instead, without prior consultation, the company obtained an environmental license for the project. YPFB then entered a Takovo Mora community in late July 2015 to initiate its work (*ERBOL* 7/31/2015).

Feeling deceived, Takovo Mora organized (*ERBOL* 7/31/2015). The capitanía asked INRA's Santa Cruz office to revoke the Chivatos and San Juan de El Dorado land titles in early August 2015, arguing that the owner had not fulfilled two titling requirements: physical presence on and productive use of the properties (*ERBOL* 8/24/2015). Takovo Mora's leaders also asked to meet with representatives of multiple state ministries about the matter on three occasions but received no response (Schilling-Vacaflor 2017a, 670).

The state's silence caused the capitanía to obstruct physically the gas project (Schilling-Vacaflor 2017a, 670). Beginning on August 10, Takovo Mora community members blocked the entrance to the El Dorado field. On August 13, the national police cleared the blockade with tear gas. That night, residents returned, and the next day more people joined them; on August 14, protesters totaled at least five hundred (*Página siete digital* 8/14/2015).

Police personnel took control of the El Dorado entrance, but the protesters then cut off the main highway that connected Santa Cruz with Argentina, early on August 18. Later that day, more than three hundred national police personnel arrived at the scene. They unsuccessfully tried to persuade the residents to lift the roadblock and then resorted to using tear gas. The Takovo Mora residents fled and repositioned themselves in trees, from which they threw rocks at the police (*ERBOL* 8/18/2015; *Oxígeno* 8/18/2015). The police then entered the closest community, Yatirenda—comprising seventy-seven families—in pursuit of activists (Candela, September 2015). The police "opened thirty-five doors" of Yatirenda homes[35] and detained twenty-seven people, including two minors (Candela, September 2015). Takovo Mora's elected leader was among the people arrested.[36]

Community Divisions

Relations between Takovo Mora and the state remained tense after the violence. They worsened in September 2015 when Vice President Álvaro García Linera visited as part of an unrelated government social investment project

parties so expeditiously obtained title to land claimed by Takovo Mora; he believed that, by conferring land rights to third parties and not to Takovo Mora, the state intentionally facilitated YPFB operations (*ERBOL* 8/24/2015).

35. Interview B3.
36. Interview B3.

(Schilling-Vacaflor 2017a, 670).[37] While in Yatirenda, García Linera explained to residents why the state had not consulted Takovo Mora about the gas wells (Candela, September 2015; Vicepresidencia del Estado Plurinacional de Bolivia 9/26/2015).

The visit contributed to discord within Takovo Mora, and a new leadership was installed that supported the MAS. It lasted only weeks before the capitanía decided to hold elections for another replacement (Schilling-Vacaflor 2017a, 670–71). In the meantime, the pro-MAS capitán grande engaged in a brief, twenty-five-day prior consultation for the wells project. He participated "with fear," given the recent state repression.[38]

Timboy X-2

In a conflict over the Timboy X-2 well project, another Guaraní capitanía pressed to be consulted about development on lands it claimed but to which it did not hold title. Timboy X-2 was in a national park. In the conflict, the Yaku Igua capitanía—of Tarija's Gran Chaco province—hoped to block the project, protect the park from new hydrocarbon exploration and extraction more generally, and secure mitigation of the impacts of previous hydrocarbon development in the park. Yaku Igua attained some mitigation but was not consulted about Timboy X-2, which advanced, as did other gas development in the park.

In trying to achieve prior consultation for Timboy X-2, Yaku Igua threatened to form a blockade to hold up a different hydrocarbon project, as leverage. The capitanía justified the maneuver by rejecting as inadequate the completed prior consultation for that project.

Yaku Igua and Aguaragüe National Park

Timboy X-2 would be constructed in the long, narrow Aguaragüe National Park, which stretched through Tarija from north to south. In 2000, the state created the Aguaragüe National Park and Integrated Management Area (Parque Nacional y Área de Manejo Integrado Aguaragüe), encompassing a park and a buffer zone (Campanini et al. 2014, 81, 89–90).

More than ten thousand people, most of whom belonged to the Guaraní and Weenhayek nations, resided in Aguaragüe (Seas Yelma 1/23/2013).

37. Shortly following the violence over the wells project, the central government constructed 125 homes in Takovo Mora communities as compensation for homes lost in an October 2013 earthquake (Candela, September 2015; Vicepresidencia del Estado Plurinacional de Bolivia 9/26/2015).

38. Interview B3.

The park provided 70 percent of Gran Chaco's water and all of Yaku Igua's (Campanini et al. 2014, 100). Although the Guaraní and Weenhayek regarded Aguaragüe as their ancestral territory, they failed to gain title to parkland (Campanini et al. 2014, 78, 105). In the case of Yaku Igua, under Ley INRA the capitanía requested title to three hundred thousand hectares, including land that overlapped with the park. Only one Yaku Igua community had formal land rights as of 2013; in 2001 it had acquired title to three hundred hectares, following violence among ranchers, migrant farmers, and Guaraní (D. H. Bebbington 2010, 180–81; 2013, 443).

Yaku Igua already had experienced the impacts of extraction in Aguaragüe when the Timboy X-2 conflict commenced. Hydrocarbon development in the park began with exploration by Standard Oil during 1926–36 and continued. In 1996, before the area was granted park status, the state declared the park region a traditional hydrocarbon area (Bebbington 2013, 443). Abandoned oil wells that were not sealed properly posed the most serious environmental problem in Aguaragüe. In many cases, the wells continued releasing hydrocarbons, with adverse impacts on the environment, including water. An estimated sixty-six abandoned wells were scattered throughout the park at the time of the Timboy X-2 conflict, with most contamination generated in areas that had been in operation until the 1990s (Seas Yelma 1/23/2013; Campanini et al. 2014, 89, 94).

The Guaraní fought for mitigation measures on an ongoing basis (Campanini et al. 2014, 94). They also endeavored to protect Aguaragüe by working through the national parks structure, though unsuccessfully. In December 2008, after learning about a planned exploration project of Eastern Petrogas in Aguaragüe's buffer zone, the APG Yaku Igua and leaders of the Council of Guaraní Captains of Tarija (Consejo de Capitanes Guaraníes de Tarija, CCGT) signed an agreement with SERNAP to manage jointly Aguaragüe. Neither YPFB nor the hydrocarbon ministry was aware of the Guaraní-SERNAP arrangement (Bebbington 2013, 443–44).

It was within this context that YPFB Petroandina S.A.M., a joint venture between YPFB and the Venezuelan state oil company Petróleos de Venezuela, S.A., proposed Timboy X-2, to identify new gas and oil reserves. The project consisted of the drilling of and seismic testing from Timboy X-2, in the Aguaragüe Sur "A" field (Luksic 8/30/2010; SENA 5/21/2010). The Guaraní worried about the well's potential impacts on community water sources and on agriculture (Luksic 8/30/2010).

Emergence of Conflict

Yaku Igua organized to demand prior consultation for Timboy X-2 starting in 2010 (Cox A. et al. 2013, 71–72). The conflict was part of a wave of Guaraní mobilizing over Aguaragüe that began when communities learned of twenty-three oil contracts for exploration and extraction in the park. In April 2010, three hundred people from seventeen capitanías marched one hundred kilometers to protest nonconsulted projects in the park and the government's disregard for the protection of park resources, including water (Luksic 8/30/2010; Seas Yelma 1/23/2013).

Immediately after the march, on April 14 and 15, Guaraní leaders in Tarija (with APG support) held the "Great Assembly" (Gran Asamblea), a meeting in the community of San Antonio, in the Villa Montes municipality. Assembly participants told the hydrocarbon minister, who was in attendance, that they disapproved of any exploration or extraction in Aguaragüe. They also wanted mitigation of the damages from previous hydrocarbon development. An APG leader highlighted the Guaraní's experience with seismic studies that had reduced water flows and his concern that the Timboy X-2 seismic work would bring more of the same (SENA 5/21/2010).

Leverage: The Juana Azurduy Consultation

As a strategy to push for a prior consultation on Timboy X-2, the APG Yaku Igua asked for a new consultation process for a separate project. The government had consulted Yaku Igua about the Bolivia-Argentina Juana Azurduy pipeline, which ran through Yaku Igua territory (and not through Aguaragüe). The pipeline was to transport up to 27.7 million cubic meters of gas daily until the year 2026. It had a planned start date of May 2011 (Luksic 8/30/2010; *Eju!* 11/12/2010).

The APG Yaku Igua accepted Juana Azurduy (SENA 5/21/2010; *Eju!* 11/12/2010) but argued that the pipeline consultation had been faulty. In the April 2010 Gran Asamblea, Yaku Igua leadership said the state had consulted community members agreeable to the project and not the actual community leaders. The capitanía made the Timboy X-2 project conditional on a correct prior consultation process for the pipeline. The hydrocarbon minister promised the new consultation but insisted that it be efficient (SENA 5/21/2010).

Leading up to the new Juana Azurduy consultation, Yaku Igua continued using the pipeline in their effort to be consulted about Timboy X-2. In July 2010—after the Gran Asamblea and before the second pipeline consultation—the APG Yaku Igua learned that the environment ministry had issued the Timboy X-2 environmental license. The organization responded by threatening to block the Juana Azurduy project (Luksic 8/30/2010).

After the state had administered a second consultation on the pipeline, the APG Yaku Igua still wanted to be consulted about Timboy X-2. According to a newspaper report, Yaku Igua's capitán grande "assured that it had not yet been decided" whether YPFB Petroandina S.A.M. would be allowed to carry out its exploration plans in Aguaragüe (*Eju!* 11/12/2010).

Limited Mitigation of Environmental Harms and Continued Gas Development in the Park

Exploration work continued in Aguaragüe, backed by the October 2010 decree authorizing hydrocarbon exploration in protected areas (DS 0676), including, specifically, more than 75 percent of the park (Campanini et al. 2014, 79).[39] Confronting pressure from the APG Yaku Igua—especially its role in several marches and strikes against new gas projects—YPFB began remediation activities in Aguaragüe in 2011; work to close three wells began that year (Bebbington 2013, 444; Campanini et al. 2014, 95).

Despite the capitanía's persistent organizing against extraction in Aguaragüe (e.g., see Luksic 7/3/2012), hydrocarbon development in the park progressed. Drilling for Timboy X-2 began in September 2013. The well was declared dry in 2015 (*Los Tiempos* 3/23/2016). Exploration in the Caigua field, which also was in the park and which had the potential to produce thirty-five million cubic feet of gas per day for fifteen years, proved successful. Production in Caigua began in 2016 (YPFB 1/19/2016).

Gran Chaco Plant

As in the Timboy X-2 case, Yaku Igua did not hold title to land impacted by the Gran Chaco gas plant, which was close to Aguaragüe (Campanini et al. 2014, 108). Yaku Igua blocked access to the Gran Chaco project to compel a prior consultation process. The capitanía failed in that effort, and the conflict was resolved through negotiations about compensation and land titling.

State Denial of the Right to Prior Consultation

The Gran Chaco Liquid Separation Plant (Planta Separadora de Líquidos Gran Chaco) would separate liquefied natural gas for export. With construction estimated at $500 million, the plant was projected to be the third largest of its kind in Latin America, based on its size and operations (*El País* 5/16/2013; Campanini et al. 2014, 80, 110). The state awarded the plant construction to

39. On DS 0676, see also Chapter 2.

the Spanish firm Técnicas Reunidas (Campanini et al. 2014, 109), although YPFB was the face of the project in discussions with Yaku Igua.[40]

The Bolivian state and Yaku Igua disagreed about whether Gran Chaco warranted prior consultation. Affected communities, dependent on agriculture and livestock and disturbed by the project's potential environmental harms, viewed lands impacted by the project as theirs and wanted to be consulted. However, the state ruled out prior consultation, on two grounds. First, the environment ministry had classified the project as Category 2, whereas only Category 1 projects could require prior consultation (see Chapter 3). Second, there was the question of land rights. YPFB reported that the plant was on titled, private land, and the city of Yacuiba deemed the land within its "urban radius" and not in TCO Yaku Igua (Luksic 6/28/2012, 7/3/2012).

Yaku Igua first protested for a consultation on Gran Chaco in 2010, with a blockade. Leading up to that action, the capitanía had expected to be consulted about the plant, for several reasons: INRA had made an early assessment that the project was on Yaku Igua lands (conflicting with YPFB's later determination), the state had consulted the Guaraní about other hydrocarbon projects in the area, and Yaku Igua previously had received documentation that the Gran Chaco plant was a Category 1 project (Cox A. et al. 2013, 84).

The environment ministry issued a license for Gran Chaco in April 2012 without prior consultation, causing renewed organizing (Luksic 7/3/2012). The APG Yaku Igua asked to meet with the state. In April–June 2012 discussions, officials of INRA, YPFB, and the environment and hydrocarbon ministries explained the process of licensing and Gran Chaco's Category 2 status. On June 25, 2012, a government commission traveled to the Yaku Igua community of Yerobiarenda, which neighbored the plant site. The team aimed to negotiate social investment plans with the APG Yaku Igua, to compensate the capitanía for project impacts. The APG Yaku Igua was determined to be consulted and refused to discuss compensation (Luksic 6/28/2012, 7/3/2012; Cox A. et al. 2013, 82).

The same day of the government's failed Yerobiarenda visit, Yaku Igua blocked the Gran Chaco project; and the CCGT, the APG, and the leaders of Yaku Igua's eighteen communities, held an "emergency meeting." Meeting participants agreed to continue the blockade and to threaten to close the valves of the Juana Azurduy pipeline, to ensure a prior consultation on Gran Chaco (Luksic 6/28/2012, 7/3/2012).

The conflict abated days later, at the end of June, with a signed agreement between the APG Yaku Igua and the hydrocarbon minister, who had traveled to the region. The document obliged the minister to address the APG Yaku

40. Técnicas Reunidas' contract stipulated that YPFB would manage community relations (Campanini et al. 2014, 112).

Igua's demands for (1) social investment programs for the Guaraní and (2) a review of the Gran Chaco environmental license and of ten properties that neighbored the plant, to determine Indigenous land allocations (Luksic 9/30/2012; Cox A. et al. 2013, 84). In the negotiations, the APG Yaku Igua representatives clarified that they did not oppose the Gran Chaco project but demanded respect for Yaku Igua's rights (Cox A. et al. 2013, 84). Conflict over prior consultation was now resolved, without an actual consultation process.

At the end of 2012, YPFB, the hydrocarbon ministry, and the APG Yaku Igua signed an agreement ("Acta de Conclusión del Proceso de Socialización del Estudio de Evaluación de Impacto Ambiental—Analítico Específico") concluding the socialization of the Gran Chaco EEIA (Cox A. et al. 2013, 84–85).

The Compensation Agreement

The last cycle of the Gran Chaco conflict centered on compensation. In 2012, the APG Yaku Igua proposed that YPFB pay the capitanía five million bolivianos annually in compensation for the plant. YPFB responded by requesting from Yaku Igua plans for social investments and socioenvironmental monitoring, as a condition for the transfer of any funds. In early 2013, the head of Yaku Igua insisted on five million bolivianos in compensation to the capitanía for Gran Chaco's construction, and negotiations to determine compensation for the remaining phases of the project. YPFB's offer at the time was five million bolivianos in social programs, as compensation for the entire project. The company had not paid the capitanía any compensation. Yaku Igua's capitán grande claimed that the APG Yaku Igua had produced the plans previously requested by YPFB (Paredes 4/4/2013; *El País* 5/16/2013).

On April 2, 2013, once again Yaku Igua community members cut off access to Gran Chaco. The state's response was immediate: still on April 2, the national government inaugurated a roundtable to resolve the matter. When on April 5 the government announced that roundtable discussions would begin the next day, Yaku Igua lifted the blockade. At the April 6 meeting, YPFB increased its compensation offer to six million bolivianos. Yaku Igua rejected it (*El País* 5/16/2013).

The situation remained tense during the roundtable. When for a period the dialogue was suspended, the capitanía threatened to block Gran Chaco again, and police were deployed to guard the plant. YPFB's offer of a one-time payment of fourteen million bolivianos resolved the conflict—unofficially in late April, and formally in May, with a signed agreement. The compensation structure assigned state agencies to design and pay for social and economic development projects that Yaku Igua would propose (*El País* 5/16/2013).

Gran Chaco began its test operations in October 2014 (*El Día* 10/16/2014). As of early 2020, the plant was producing liquefied natural gas for export, mainly to Paraguay and Peru. The value of the gas exported in 2019 surpassed $44 million (*Eju!* 2/3/2020).

Magallanes

Organizing to block the Colombian Magallanes gas exploration project is a final case in which outsider Indigenous communities used direct action as their main tactic.

Despite the nonrigid nature of Indigenous boundaries in Colombian prior consultation, communities of the U'wa nation could not claim rights to the Magallanes project area using legal-administrative justifications. The U'wa already had gauged the geographic reach of their authority in a legal dispute over prior consultation, for a different hydrocarbon project. Communities thus resorted to a blockade and, later, a plant occupation, to hold up Magallanes. Through that direct action, the U'wa did not achieve a prior consultation process for the project. However, they did stall the project indefinitely, and negotiate the rerouting of part of an oil pipeline and a path toward recognized rights to more land.

The Rigidity of U'wa Boundaries

The U'wa resided in Colombia's Arauca, Boyacá, Santander, and Norte de Santander departments (Rodríguez et al. 2010, 184). They rejected any oil development on their lands. This position was consistent with their cultural view that oil and other natural resources in U'wa territory needed to remain undisturbed; and with the value they placed on maintaining their traditional practices of agriculture complemented by hunting and fishing (Ávila 2002, 84; Arenas 2007, 125–26). The Magallanes project was near the U'wa resguardo. One of the two main U'wa organizations, the Association of U'wa Traditional Authorities and Councils (Asociación de Autoridades Tradicionales y Cabildos U'wa, ASOU'WA, representing the U'wa communities in Boyacá and Norte de Santander), led the organizing against Magallanes (Rodríguez et al. 2010, 188; *The Guardian* 3/26/2015).

The U'wa already had lost, in 2000, a legal effort to be consulted about the Gibraltar 1 gas exploration project, which was just outside of their resguardo. That struggle had occurred shortly after the resguardo's expansion.[41] As of the 2010s, the state had continued issuing licenses for exploration in areas that

41. The Samoré case study in Chapter 6 discusses Gibraltar 1.

the U'wa viewed as sacred but that were beyond the resguardo boundaries (Orduz Salinas 2014, 33–34). In that context, the U'wa fell back on direct action to obstruct Magallanes.

Direct Action

The Magallanes conflict was brought on when ANLA issued an environmental license to Ecopetrol for three new exploratory gas wells. The project, which abutted U'wa lands, was in the Troya vereda, in the municipality of Toledo, in Norte de Santander (Gómez Nadal 4/18/2014; Hill 6/17/2014). The U'wa learned about the license in 2013, at which point they began devising a response, working through the U'wa authority structure. They settled on direct action as the means to protest Magallanes, a decision that was "socialized" in late 2013, at the nation's Eighth Congress.[42]

The U'wa ultimately took action when the FARC attacked a critical pipeline. Ecopetrol transported heavy equipment to the Magallanes project site in February 2014 (*The Guardian* 3/26/2015). The following month, the FARC sabotaged the major Caño Limón pipeline. The resulting oil spill was a mere one hundred meters from an U'wa community and caused serious environmental damage (Gómez Nadal 4/18/2014). The U'wa responded by closing off access to both the Magallanes project and the pipeline. The loss in crude production due to the pipeline incident and the forty-day U'wa blockade amounted to approximately 2.4 million barrels (*Dinero* 8/21/2014).

The blockade succeeded in getting the state's attention. A team of high-level government officials negotiated a solution to the standoff. The talks produced, by May 2014, several obligations: the U'wa would allow Ecopetrol to access (and repair) the pipeline, the company would rebuild the section of damaged pipeline underground, and the government would suspend Magallanes for one month and pay for both a review of the Magallanes EIA and, within two years, the titling of all U'wa territory (*W Radio* 5/2/2014; Chato 7/21/2016). Ecopetrol removed its equipment from Magallanes in late 2014.[43] National and international Indigenous-rights groups touted the case as an U'wa victory (e.g., *The Guardian* 3/26/2015).

As of mid-2016, the state still had not fulfilled many of its 2014 promises. To force the government's hand, the U'wa occupied and shut down the

42. The U'wa began serious organizing in the Magallanes case in 2013, after learning of the license. However, previously they discussed the new gas development, based on Ecopetrol's preliminary visits and studies; that work alerted the nation of a new project. Interview with Aura Tegría, Legal Advisor of the U'wa nation; by phone from Bogotá, July 29, 2016 (Interview C16).

43. Interview C16.

important, producing Gibraltar gas plant. The May–July 2016 occupation ended only after a new understanding was reached. The state committed to clarifying the areas of the U'wa resguardo that overlapped with national parklands, agreed to U'wa participation in managing those same areas, and promised to complete the Caño Limón pipeline work (Chato 7/21/2016; *Portafolio* 7/28/2016).

At that time, Magallanes remained on hold. The U'wa had filed a complaint in February 2015 with the Consejo de Estado, asking the state to rescind the Magallanes environmental license. In July 2016, the case was pending, the environmental license was still in place, and the project location remained empty of equipment.[44]

OUTLIER: GASODUCTO DEL SUR

A final conflict involving outsider communities is an outlier. Like in other cases in this chapter, the state classified the communities that protested over the Gasoducto Sur Peruano pipeline ("Gasoducto del Sur") as residing outside the a project's area of influence. The state consequently did not include the communities in the EIA workshops, or in the public hearings held for the EIA and a MEIA, for the pipeline. However, in this case the communities were sufficiently far from the project's area of influence that their position as outsiders was not in question.[45] That is, the mobilized communities in the Gasoducto del Sur conflict did not contest the geographic boundaries that defined them as outsiders. Rather, EIA participation proved irrelevant in their organizing.

As discussed in this case study, the EIA participatory process was not conflictual. Whereas outsider communities staged the explosive protests that characterized the Gasoducto del Sur conflict, insider community organizing was minimal, and the EIA participatory process took place with few incidents. Some insider communities delayed an EIA hearing through protest, in following with the pattern by which insiders have blocked or otherwise interfered with participatory events (see Chapter 6).

When research for this study was concluding, the state had canceled Gasoducto del Sur, and efforts to design a replacement project were not progressing.

44. Interview C16.

45. Interview with José Victor Salcedo Ccama, journalist for *La República*; by phone from Lima, August 1, 2018 (Interview P10); and Interview with Valerio Paucarmayta, Director, Centro Bartolomé de las Casas del Cusco; by phone from Lima, August 2, 2018 (Interview P11).

Overview

Gasoducto Sur Peruano—originally, Gasoducto Sur Andino—began as a project of the national Private Investment Promotion Agency (Agencia de Promoción de la Inversión Privada, Proinversión). The state transferred the project to Kuntur Transportadora de Gas S.A.C. in 2010. When negotiations between Kuntur and the state over contract changes broke down, Proinversión developed a replacement project, which it licensed to Gasoducto Sur Peruano S.A. in 2014. The Brazilian conglomerate Odebrecht was the main shareholder in both Kuntur and Gasoducto Sur Peruano (Gamboa Balbín 2017, 13, 15–16).

Gasoducto del Sur was to transport gas from the Camisea reserves in the southern highland region of Cusco for distribution throughout Peru's south (Gamboa Balbín 2017, 15–17).[46] The government wavered in its commitment to this plan during the conflict, amid doubts about whether Camisea produced sufficient gas for both export and domestic use, and whether demand in the south justified the cost of the distribution. Communities in Cusco wanted the project to advance. The epicenter of the conflict was Cusco's La Convención province.[47]

The 2010 and 2014 Protests

The first large mobilization over Gasoducto del Sur occurred in September 2010. People protested in La Convención for more than two weeks that month, for a project design that included a local fractionation plant for gas distribution. Two protesters were killed in the events. In response to the violence, the García government began discussions with Camisea about domestic gas provision (Salcedo 7/31/2013). The executive also promised La Convención a fractionation plant, in the town of Kepashiato (Salcedo 9/7/2014).

Like García before him, President Humala conveyed dedication to a pipeline with fractionation plants (Salcedo 7/31/2013). To celebrate the beginning of project construction, he oversaw the symbolic placement of a portion of pipeline in a March 2012 ceremony in Quillabamba, La Convención's capital. Kuntur's preliminary work was scheduled to begin the following month (Salcedo 9/26/2013).

As of September 2013, the pipeline project, now awaiting a February 2014 transfer to its new owner, was delayed, and people in La Convención had grown impatient. Led by the La Convención Central Committee

46. On the development of the Camisea gas fields, see the analysis of the Camisea Block 56 conflict in Chapter 6.

47. Ordóñez 9/14/2009; Álvarez 11/26/2017; and Interview P11.

(Comité Central de Lucha de La Convención), residents launched a forty-eight-hour strike to compel an expedited ownership transfer and the construction of the pipeline and the Kepashiato fractionation plant (Salcedo 9/26/2013).

More protests began when the state signed the July 2014 contract with Gasoducto Sur Peruano for a project that did not include the plant. Mobilizing, which was strongest in Quillabamba, reached its zenith during two weeks in August–September 2014. An indefinite strike began on August 27, with the Comité Central again playing a leading role. Protests blocked main access roads and closed schools. Four people died and several went missing. In one confusing incident, a car occupied by the Kepashiato mayor fell or, according to strikers, was pushed, into a river. The mayor's death caused more people to join the protests (Salcedo 9/7/2014; *La República* 9/9/2014; Defensoría del Pueblo 2015, 108–10).

Added to dissatisfaction with the project's pace and design, other factors contributed to the 2014 mobilization: allegations of corruption in La Convención (Defensoría del Pueblo 2015, 109), anticipated changes to the gas canon that would mean cuts to the province's share,[48] and unease about the project's impacts on the environment, which, without the fractionation plant, would not be counterbalanced by gas provision. Simultaneous environmental activism in Cusco against the immense Central Hidroeléctrica hydroelectric project further energized organizing over the pipeline (Defensoría del Pueblo 2015, 108–9).

The Comité Central suspended the protests on September 9, 2014, to allow for negotiations. The government created several national working groups (*mesas de trabajo*) to address energy, mining, environmental, and social concerns. In early 2015 the Comité Central, MINEM, and Cusco's regional president discussed the construction of a fractionation plant (*La República* 9/9/2014; Tecsi 1/27/2015).

Post-2014 Project Delays

After the 2014 events, the pipeline project faced further delays. The state finally canceled it in 2017, during the "Lava Jato" international corruption scandal, in which Odebrecht was embroiled (Gamboa Balbín 2017, 31).[49]

48. Salcedo 9/7/2014; and Interview P11.

49. Lava Jato implicated high-level officials across Latin America and the Caribbean, including multiple Peruvian presidents. Pedro Pablo Kuczynski (2016–18), Peru's president during the cancellation of Gasoducto del Sur, faced accusations about his relationship with Odebrecht, before he resigned over a vote-buying scandal (Rochabrún and Casey 3/21/2018).

The state attempted yet another version of the pipeline, and there was renewed mobilizing in the south for domestic gas provision. For instance, in June 2019 people took to the streets in a twenty-four-hour strike that affected Cusco most severely. The strike caused a halt to all public transportation in the region and blocked interregional highways (Motta 5/25/2019; *La República* 6/6/2019). As of March 2020, pipeline planning was stalled (*La República* 3/12/2020).

The Area of Influence: EIA and MEIA Participation

Protesters in the Gasoducto del Sur conflict resided outside of the project's area of influence and did not question that geographic relationship; nor did they use the EIA participatory process in their organizing.[50] In the actual project area, mobilizing was limited and localized, and it focused on impacts and compensation rather than on gas for the southern regions. The EIA participatory stage was relatively smooth, as discussed here.

The state led fifteen EIA hearings for Gasoducto del Sur, in December 2010, following 246 EIA workshops. Twenty-five thousand people from communities within the project's area of influence attended those participatory events, held in the Arequipa, Cusco, Moquegua, and Puno regions (Chief Resolution [Resolución Directoral, RD] 173-2011-MEM/AAE, 13–14; *Mining.com* 6/8/2011). After MINEM approved the EIA in June 2011 (with RD 173-2011-MEM/AAE), a MEIA and several ITSs modified the project.[51] The January–July 2015 MEIA review and approval process included workshops and public hearings (Gamboa Balbín 2017, 15–16, 39, 48–51).

EIA and MEIA participation was orderly, especially in impacted Indigenous communities, which mainly desired compensation for the project.[52] During the development and review of the EIA, Kuntur successfully won over Indigenous communities with gifts that included community-wide parties.[53] The Machiguenga Council of the Urubamba River (Consejo Machiguenga del Río Urubamba, COMARU), an Indigenous organization, in collaboration with the NGO Law, Environment, and Natural Resources (Derecho, Ambiente y

50. The two La Convención public hearings were held in the Native communities of Monte Carmelo and Ticumpinia, both in the Echarate district, some distance from Quillabamba. RD 173–2011-MEM/AAE, 13–14; and Interview P11.

51. Sixteen ITSs had been submitted for the project as of August 2015, and twenty-two as of 2017 (Gamboa Balbín 2017, 38, 46).

52. Indigenous residents of affected areas also wanted access to gas but did not participate in the main Gasoducto del Sur conflict that serves as the focus of this case study. Interview P11.

53. Interview with a Specialist of the Rights and Amazon Program, Derecho, Ambiente y Recursos Naturales; via Skype, Lima, April 10, 2018 (Interview P12).

Recursos Naturales), advised communities in the MEIA process to help them obtain more compensation.[54]

The most noteworthy organizing in the pipeline's area of influence came from non-Indigenous communities in Cusco's Calca province, through which the pipeline was to pass and where two EIA hearings were held (RD 173-2011-MEM/AAE). Calca residents wanted a gas distribution point for the province. Community mobilizing led to multiple postponements of one EIA hearing. When the MEIA was under review, Calca continued clamoring for the distribution plant and for investments in development to compensate the province for the pipeline's impacts.[55]

SUMMARY

With the exception of the Gasoducto del Sur case, mobilized outsider communities in this chapter responded to the inclusion challenge—that is, the hurdle of accessing participatory processes. This challenge was produced by disagreement between communities and the state about the geographic boundaries that defined which communities were impacted by extraction. Communities that had been "drawn outside of" impacted areas insisted that they were affected by planned development and for that reason needed to be included in state review processes, through either prior consultation or the EIA hearing.

The first part of the chapter examined conflicts in which outsiders objected to state-recognized boundaries after the EIA process (Conga, Santa Ana), or after the state had bypassed prior consultation (Afrodita, Block 116, Putumayo). In these Colombian and Peruvian cases, formal institutions allowed for debate about the correct placement of the lines defining areas impacted by extraction and the territory to which Indigenous communities had rights. Communities contested the geographic boundaries after the fact, relying on legal-administrative processes and arguments.

By contrast, borders that marked Indigenous lands in Bolivian prior consultation were rigid, because the boundaries were based on formal title. Therefore, Guaraní outsiders who wished to be consulted had the sole recourse of physically holding up hydrocarbon activities to try to secure prior consultation processes. In the Colombian Magallanes conflict, the U'wa similarly used direct action to achieve negotiations with the state about gas exploration outside of their recently extended resguardo.

54. Interview P12.
55. Tecsi 3/25/2015; and Interview P11.

Having analyzed how outsider communities used participatory institutions in extractive conflict, the book turns, in Chapter 6, to conflicts involving members of insider communities, which, from the start, had access to participatory institutions. As that chapter will show, insiders grappled with the challenge of voicing their position on extraction. While some communities did so within the formally provided participatory spaces, others organized around them.

CHAPTER 6

The Articulation Challenge and Contested Community Representatives

In the final set of conflicts in this book, the communities that mobilized were classified by the state as impacted by hydrocarbon or mining plans. Therefore, they were eligible to participate in approval processes for the extractive activities. Insider communities had to decide how they would express their stance on the new projects. That is, they confronted the *articulation challenge*.

In some cases, the articulation challenge was exacerbated by debate over who spoke on behalf of a community, or disagreement over the boundary that delineated insider community representatives. As this chapter will demonstrate, and as illustrated in Figure 6.1, that boundary contestation had implications for how activists used participatory institutions.

Where there was no salient debate over insider representation, cohesive communities held up the participatory stage either by interrupting participatory events or by blocking them entirely. Strife within communities ruled out such unified action. In divided contexts, community uses of a participatory institution depended on its definition of participation. Participation within the EIA hearing meant convening a meeting for residents. This institutional design feature encouraged activist insiders to participate vocally in the hearings, in competition with project supporters. Different from EIA hearing procedures, participation in prior consultation consisted of Indigenous leaders signing agreements. Discord over Indigenous community representation allowed the state to pursue a fraudulent consultation by gathering signatures from people who posed as community representatives. Community members averse to

The Politics of Extraction. Maiah Jaskoski, Oxford University Press. © Oxford University Press 2022.
DOI: 10.1093/oso/9780197568927.003.0006

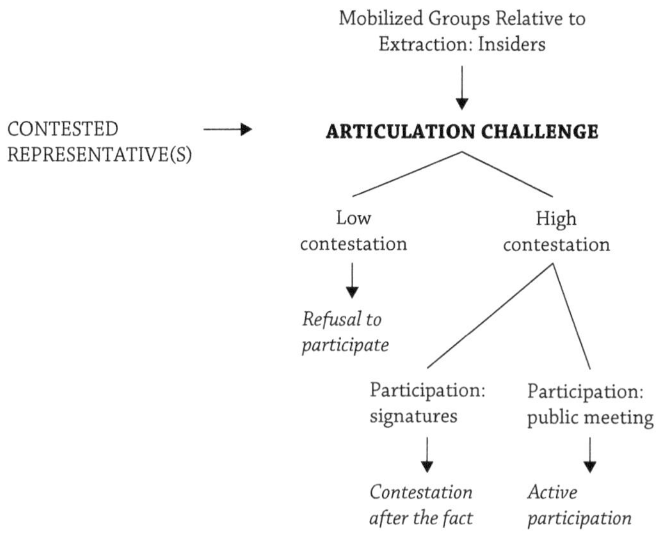

Figure 6.1 Articulation Challenge Intensified by Contested Community Representation

extraction, whom the state did not consult, later disputed the consultation's legitimacy.

To complement these prevailing patterns in the employment of prior consultation and EIA hearings, the conflicts in this chapter offer examples of additional applications of these and other participatory institutions, as summarized in Table 6.1 and discussed in the case studies.

This chapter begins by examining how unified communities interrupted or prevented participatory events. It then takes up the strategies of activists residing in fragmented communities. The analysis concludes with three outlier cases in which conflict transpired before the state would have scheduled either prior consultation or EIA hearings for the planned development. Nevertheless, and as shown in Table 6.1 and the analysis to come, insider communities in those cases did make use of available participatory institutions to prevent extraction.

BLOCKING PARTICIPATORY PROCESSES

Cohesive insider communities interfered with extractive plans by preventing or interrupting mandatory participatory processes. In the Ranchería, Samoré, and San Antonio conflicts, communities refused to be consulted; and communities boycotted EIA hearings for the development of Camisea Block 56 and the Tambo Grande mine, and interrupted a hearing with violent protest, in the Tía María case.

Table 6.1 THE ARTICULATION CHALLENGE: CASES

Conflict	Goal of mobilizing	Dominant participatory institution			Other uses of participatory institutions
		Institution	Contested representation	Use of institution	
Samoré (Colombia; hydrocarbons; 1995–2006)	Block oil exploration	Prior consultation	n/a	Refusal to participate	Contestation of lack of prior consultation; participation in prior consultation
Diversion of Ranchería (Colombia; mining; 2011–12)	Block mine expansion	Prior consultation	n/a	Refusal to participate	n/a
San Antonio (Bolivia; hydrocarbons; 2010–14)	Compensation	Prior consultation	n/a	Refusal to participate	n/a
Camisea Block 56 (Peru; hydrocarbons; 2004–5)	Compensation; mitigation	EIA hearing	n/a	Refusal to participate	Postponement of EIA hearing
Tambo Grande (Peru; mining; 1999–2003)	Block mine	EIA hearing	n/a	Refusal to participate	Informal popular consultation; refusal to participate in EIA workshops
Tía María (Peru; mining; 2009–11; 2013–	Block mine	EIA hearing	n/a	Interruption of hearing	Informal popular consultations; attempt to interrupt EIA workshop and second EIA hearing; attempt to prevent EIA workshop
Quellaveco (Peru; mining; 2008–12)	Block mine	MEIA hearing	Intra-communal disagreement about costs and benefits of mine	Active engagement in hearing	Active engagement in MEIA workshops; attempts to postpone MEIA hearings

Las Bambas (Peru; mining; 2003–13; 2015–)	Compensation	EIA hearing	Community competition based on proximity to mine and associated compensation and social investments	Active engagement in hearing	Active engagement in EIA workshops; contestation of exclusion from project revision process
Mandé Norte (Colombia; mining; 2009)	Block mine	Prior consultation	Staged community representatives	Contestation of legitimacy of sham consultation	Informal popular consultation
Cosigo (Colombia; mining; 2007–14; *outlier*)	Block mine	n/a	n/a	n/a	Prior consultation to create park
Río Blanco (Peru; mining; 2003–; *outlier*)	Block mine	n/a	n/a	n/a	Active engagement in EIA workshops; informal popular consultation; submission of written critiques of draft EIA
Quilish (Peru; mining; 1999–2004; *outlier*)	Block mine expansion	n/a	n/a	n/a	Submission of written critiques of exploration plans

In three of the Indigenous conflicts in this section, any valid participatory event for project approval needed to include multiple, individually cohesive communities or organizations. Therefore, one such community or organization on its own could stall the participatory stage. Concretely, the Machiguenga communities impacted by the development of Peru's Camisea Block 56 were represented by two organizations, both of which had to agree to the project's EIA hearing in order for it to take place. All of the actors in the Colombian Samoré oil conflict recognized that the state had to consult the U'wa's two main organizations in any consultation process for the proposed oil exploration. In a mining case involving the diversion of the Ranchería River in northern Colombia, each individual impacted Wayúu community required its own prior consultation, due to the dispersed nature of the Wayúu governance structure.

In addition to illustrating how communities prevented prior consultations and EIA hearings, this analysis will show other types of insider organizing around—and also through—participatory institutions. In the Samoré conflict, the U'wa contested the legitimacy of a consultation process that took place before prior consultation was regulated. Later, while one of the U'wa organizations refused to be consulted, the other vehemently opposed oil exploration within a consultation process. The Machiguenga postponed, by request, the Camisea Block 56 EIA hearing before boycotting it. Multiple districts held informal popular consultations on the Peruvian Tía María mine. Also in the Tía María conflict, groups attempted to prevent one EIA workshop and interrupt another; and to interfere in the project's second EIA hearing. In the Tambo Grande case in Peru, activists refused to participate in the EIA workshops. They also voted down the Tambo Grande mine in an informal popular consultation.

Samoré

The Colombian U'wa famously held up oil development in the Samoré block by refusing to be consulted in the 2000s. The U'wa's rejection of prior consultation delayed but did not prevent oil development; the state permitted exploration just outside of the U'wa resguardo, and also exploration within the resguardo's boundaries—after the interior ministry had gone to great lengths to consult the nation about the work.

The Fight for Prior Consultation

The conflict began in the mid-1990s when the Colombian state issued an environmental license to Occidental Petroleum for exploration in Samoré, which straddled Arauca, Boyacá, and Norte de Santander, and overlapped with U'wa lands. Occidental won over some members of the U'wa through early public relations programs (Arenas 2007, 126), and the U'wa participated in January 1995 discussions with representatives of Occidental, Ecopetrol, and the environment, government, and mining and energy ministries. At a time when prior consultation was mandated by the national environmental law but still unregulated (see Chapter 3), state and company officials regarded the two-day meeting as a prior consultation. The state granted an environmental license for the project in February 1995 (Arenas 2007, 126–27; Rodríguez et al. 2010, 177–78).

The U'wa thought the January 1995 meeting had not fulfilled the prior consultation requirement and threatened collective suicide should oil exploration occur in their territory. Two legal struggles proceeded that resulted in conflicting rulings. The Defensoría del Pueblo filed a tutela against Occidental and the environment ministry in 1995 on behalf of nineteen U'wa individuals, to object to the issuance of the environmental license without prior consultation. Also in 1995, the Defensoría pursued an action through the Consejo de Estado to suspend Occidental's environmental license. The tutela reached the Constitutional Court, which ruled for the U'wa (with Constitutional Court Sentence SU-039) in February 1997. In contrast, in its decision the next month, the Consejo de Estado found that the state had satisfied its requirement to inform the U'wa about extraction and that the environmental license was legal (Rodríguez-Garavito and Arenas 2005, 251–52; Rodríguez et al. 2010, 177–79).

While the domestic legal battles were underway, a global coalition of actors ranging from international NGOs to European political parties formed out of concern for the U'wa. Transnational advocacy gained impressive momentum after a May 1997 visit to the United States by leaders of the U'wa and of the National Indigenous Organization of Colombia (Organización Nacional Indígena de Colombia, ONIC), invited by the US-based Amazon Coalition. During that trip, NGO allies of the U'wa drafted a complaint against the Colombian state. An U'wa representative and the head of ONIC filed it with the IACHR (Rodríguez-Garavito and Arenas 2005, 253–55; Rodríguez et al. 2010, 179–80).

The Colombian government, which faced the IACHR filing, a national and international movement in support of the U'wa, and the conflicting rulings of the Constitutional Court and Consejo de Estado, asked the OAS to review the U'wa case, in May 1997 (Rodríguez-Garavito and Arenas 2005, 255). An OAS–Harvard University investigation produced several recommendations, including that the state consult the U'wa and expand their resguardo. The government issued the 1998 Decree 1320 to regulate prior consultation, hoping to expedite development.[1] In August 1999, the U'wa resguardo boundaries were redrawn, making the territory 3.6 times its previous size (Rodríguez et al. 2010, 180–81, 183–84).

Occidental attempted to advance in its work during the uncertainty surrounding prior consultation. The company modified its Gibraltar Well 1 oil

1. On Decree 1320, see also Chapter 3.

exploration project so as to situate it outside of the U'wa resguardo. The project was located just beyond the boundary of the recently expanded resguardo but in ancestral lands of the U'wa. At the environmental licensing stage for the Gibraltar exploration, the interior ministry determined that the U'wa did not have "regular permanent" presence in the project area. The state issued the license in 1999, without consulting the nation. The license held up. In March 2000, the U'wa filed a tutela. A court decided in their favor, but, still in 2000, Cundinamarca's departmental tribunal overturned that ruling (*El Tiempo* 5/23/2000; Rodríguez et al. 2010, 184–87; Orduz Salinas 2014, 33).

Standoffs

When it came to development *within* their resguardo, the U'wa refused the very participation for which they had fought. After the 1997 Constitutional Court decision,

> The U'wa surprised their allies who were celebrating this "legal victory" by issuing a communiqué expressing their rejection of the Court's ruling and reiterating that their goal was not that the oil project be consulted or negotiated, but rather that it simply be cancelled for attacking their most profound cultural convictions. (Rodríguez-Garavito 2011, 296)

The U'wa continued delaying hydrocarbon development in the 2000s by refusing to be consulted. Occidental, which had not found oil, departed, and in May 2002, the 1995 environmental license and the 1999 license for Gibraltar Well 1 were transferred to Ecopetrol. The state company discovered natural gas reserves. In 2003 Ecopetrol asked the interior ministry to hold a prior consultation for exploration in areas that overlapped with the U'wa resguardo (Rodríguez et al. 2010, 187–88; Orduz Salinas 2014, 33). The interior ministry initiated the consultation process, with mixed results. One of the U'wa's two representative bodies, the Association of Traditional Indigenous Councils and Authorities of the Arauca Department (Asociación de Cabildos y Autoridades Tradicionales Indígenas del Departamento de Arauca, ASCATIDAR), participated in a 2004–5 consultation in which the organization firmly objected to exploration. However, ASOU'WA (introduced in Chapter 5) refused the consultation process (Rodríguez et al. 2010, 188). According to the interior ministry, in striving to consult ASOU'WA, the state sent more than one hundred communications to the organization across two years, and for six months the ministry operated a local informational office (in Boyacá) that residents did not visit (Meléndez P. 12/16/2006).

Encountering ASOU'WA's continued refusal to be consulted, the interior and justice ministries asked the Consejo de Estado for guidance on how to develop the project, given the U'wa's intransigence. The Consejo de Estado ruled in 2006 that the state's earnest, multiyear endeavor to consult the U'wa had satisfied the prior consultation requirement, and that the exploration could take place without an agreement between the government and impacted communities (Rodríguez et al. 2010, 189–90; Orduz Salinas 2014, 34).

Diversion of the Ranchería River

Like the U'wa, Colombian Wayúu communities of the dry, northern department of La Guajira declined prior consultation in order to thwart extractive development—specifically, a coal-mine expansion project that required diverting the major Ranchería River. When the Wayúu succeeded in preventing the project, the mining company moved forward with an alternative expansion plan that caused further conflict.

The Expansion Project

Carbones del Cerrejón Limited proposed diverting the Ranchería in order to expand its immense open-pit coal mine, Cerrejón, which had operated in La Guajira since the 1980s. By 2011, when Cerrejón was pursuing the expansion, the mine had produced five hundred million tons of coal for export (Coronado Delgado et al. 2014, 33). The $4.5 million expansion project aimed to extract from two new sites and increase production by an estimated five hundred million tons of coal, across approximately twenty years (Herrera 6/10/2012). To access the new sites, Cerrejón proposed diverting twenty-six kilometers of the Ranchería River, a crucial water source for the region (Orduz 8/20/2012).

The diversion troubled local Wayúu communities that relied on agriculture and, consequently, the river. Communities were familiar with Cerrejón's environmental impacts. The mine generated noise pollution and, through the release of carbon particles, polluted the air and the river. Contamination from the mine harmed wildlife, crops, and natural plant species (Orduz 8/20/2012; Coronado Delgado et al. 2014, 41–43). Local communities also worried about a possible relocation, given their proximity to the project (Orduz 8/20/2012).

Opposition from Cohesive, Separate Communities

The Wayúu authority structure was based on matrilineal extended families (Premauer and Berkes 2012, 57). This configuration meant that the mine expansion required a prior consultation with each Wayúu community. At the time of the conflict, prior consultation was progressing without incident in most cases. Cerrejón had won over many communities by promising material benefits—for example, boats, fishing equipment, and the installation of community soccer fields (Herrera 6/10/2012). Of the 115 affected Wayúu communities, 103 participated in prior consultations during 2011 and 2012 that consisted of approximately six hundred meetings in total. The state reached the penultimate agreement (preacuerdo) with each of the 103 communities.[2]

The other communities would not participate. In a context in which Cerrejón's social investment pledges had caused splits among communities, some communities objected to the Ranchería diversion (Arboleda Mutis 2015, 184) and refused to be consulted. One explanation they gave for impeding the consultation process was that they needed first to carry out the Wayúu cultural practice of internal reflection (Orduz 8/20/2012).

With the consultation stalled and after a 35 percent drop in global coal prices, Cerrejón suspended its expansion project in 2012 (*El Tiempo* 11/9/2012; Arboleda Mutis 2015, 187). A Cerrejón community relations official framed the decision as follows:

> There were six hundred meetings—we have recordings of all of them. At each meeting, the preacuerdo memorandum [*acta*] was signed. Twelve communities refused to participate in the consultation—those united with NGOs, supported by international NGOs. It was a scandal, because 103 communities were angry about [the position of those few communities]. In this context, the price of coal dropped. We can't risk spending all that money on the project in this context. First, we have uncertainty with the communities. Second, we don't know if we'll make money off the project.[3]

The Bruno Alternative

After shelving the Ranchería project, Cerrejón occupied itself with a different plan to expand production: the diversion of the Bruno tributary, which fed into the Ranchería (Betancur Alarcón 5/24/2016).[4] According to the Cerrejón community relations official interviewed in 2016, at that time the Bruno project was proving difficult for Cerrejón, because the company encountered

2. Interview with a high-level community relations employee, Carbones del Cerrejón; Bogotá, July 21, 2016 (Interview C17). During the interview, the employee produced photographs and signed documents from meetings held with several of the communities as part of the prior consultations.

3. Interview C17.

4. This study's bundling of the Ranchería and Bruno conflicts, with the latter an offshoot of the former, is consistent with the treatment of the two conflicts by experts interviewed in Colombia for this book in 2016 and by analyses of the Ranchería case (e.g., Arboleda Mutis 2015).

civil-society groups that already were organized, due to their activism around the Ranchería diversion.[5]

Local community members who were disturbed by the Bruno proposal's impacts on health, water, and food sources, filed tutelas to block the project. The Consejo de Estado decided on one tutela at the end of 2016, in the communities' favor. The Consejo ordered the government to (1) create a roundtable to facilitate dialogue among Cerrejón, the government, and communities; and (2) consult the impacted Indigenous communities that had not been consulted about the project. One year later, the Constitutional Court also ruled for the communities, on a second tutela. By that time, the diversion work was nearly complete. The court ordered that the project be halted based on several technical uncertainties, and that the roundtable address whether Bruno should be returned to its natural course (*Semana sostenible* 12/21/2016; *UN periódico digital* 7/29/2019; *Radio France internationale* 7/18/2020).

No project reversal was on the horizon as of mid-2020. The environment ministry, ANLA, the La Guajira CAR (CORPOGUAJIRA), and Cerrejón opted not to undo the Bruno diversion, a choice they justified in a report. According to the Contraloría in its review of the report, the document was based on deficient information and did not consider the irreversible damage of the Bruno diversion for local populations (Rojas Hernández 7/15/2020).

San Antonio

As in the Samoré and Ranchería cases, cohesive Indigenous communities refused to be consulted in a standoff between the APG Itika Guasu and the Bolivian state over gas exploration in the San Antonio megacampo, in northern Tarija. Aspiring to secure compensation and other investments from Petrobras—the San Antonio operator—Itika Guasu spurned the state's prior consultation initiative, wanting only to negotiate with the Brazilian firm. After four years, the capitanía agreed to participate in a state-led prior consultation and, afterward, compensation discussions with Petrobras.

At the time of the San Antonio conflict, Itika Guasu comprised thirty-eight communities—two of which were new—in the provinces of O'Connor and Gran Chaco in Tarija (Bebbington 2013, 441–42; Ministerio de Hidrocarburos 11/14/2014). The state recognized Itika Guasu's rights to land impacted by the San Antonio project and hence acknowledged the need for prior consultation.

More generally, Itika Guasu had difficulty acquiring land. The capitanía had sought title to more than 290,000 hectares (Bebbington 2013, 442) but had formal rights to only 90,540 hectares as of 2012. Those titled lands were

5. Interview C18.

exceptionally noncontiguous: counting pending claims, third-party claims—of cattle ranchers and peasants—made up 42 percent of the total area on which titled TCO lands were located (Anthias 2018, 83–86).

Itika Guasu's Perspectives on Prior Consultation and Compensation Agreements

The basis of the San Antonio conflict was that the APG Itika Guasu wanted to work directly with Petrobras to fulfill the prior consultation requirement, when in fact regulations required that the hydrocarbon ministry lead consultations (in coordination with Indigenous communities; see Chapter 3). Itika Guasu's approach to prior consultation in this case can be explained by the following factors, on which this discussion will elaborate: (1) the community's extensive experience with contamination from gas extraction and previous success negotiating a sizable compensation package with a hydrocarbon firm; and (2) the connection Itika Guasu drew between those negotiations, and the concept of prior consultation.

The capitanía's experience with gas development dated to the late 1990s, when the Margarita megacampo was discovered in TCO Itika Guasu (Perreault 2008, 9–10). Maxus Energy Corporation of Repsol YPF began exploration work in Margarita in 1997. Itika Guasu initially rejected exploration and extraction in their territory, but in 2001 they abandoned that position, as they "came to view that complete resistance to the presence of hydrocarbon companies that had discovered sizeable gas reserves was not a politically viable option" (Bebbington 2013, 442).

Itika Guasu shifted their focus to obtaining compensation for damages from gas development, successfully. Lengthy talks between Itika Guasu and Repsol YPF produced in 2010 a $14.8 million compensation agreement.[6] The amount far surpassed what hydrocarbon companies previously had invested in Bolivian Indigenous communities (Bebbington 2013, 442–43; Schilling-Vacaflor 2017b, 1067). Indeed, industry actors worried that the Repsol YPF investment could set a precedent for other hydrocarbon firms that operated in Bolivia.[7]

After finalizing the accord with Repsol YPF, Itika Guasu leaders articulated a connection between the private deal and prior consultation, in their reaction to a recent watershed decision issued by Bolivia's Constitutional Tribunal. In its ruling on a (different) case involving Itika Guasu, the tribunal

6. The agreement was finalized at the end of December 2010 and announced in 2011 (*Observatorio petrolero sur* 5/19/2011; Bebbington 2013, 443).

7. Interview with an environmental engineer who had fourteen years of experience working for private companies in Bolivia's gas sector (and not for Repsol YPF); Santa Cruz, June 15, 2017 (Interview B15).

defended the right to prior consultation and considered scenarios that would demand community consent. The decision drew on ILO 169, UNDRIP, and the IACHR's 2007 decision on *Saramaka People v. Surinam*—which identified conditions under which prior consultation on its own was insufficient, and FPIC was warranted.[8] The APG Itika Guasu touted the agreement with YPF as having respected Itika Guasu's rights as articulated by the tribunal, including their rights to possess, use, and control their traditional lands and territories (*Observatorio petrolero sur* 5/19/2011).[9]

Refusal to Be Consulted

Having made an association between, on one hand, prior consultation, and on the other, compensation arrangements, Itika Guasu refused to be consulted by the state about Petrobras's $50 million San Antonio exploration project ("Exploración Sísmica 3D, en el Bloque San Antonio"; Barriga 8/19/2014).

San Antonio entailed laying four thousand kilometers of seismic lines, creating new exploratory wells and more than two hundred seismic trenches, and building base camps, helicopter pads, and other infrastructure. Twenty percent of the project was located within TCO Itika Guasu (D. H. Bebbington 2010, 184; Barriga 8/19/2014).

The project required prior consultation with Itika Guasu and with two impacted campesino communities. The consultations with the campesino communities concluded in December 2010 (*La Andalucía boliviana* 12/7/2012; Ministerio de Hidrocarburos 11/14/2014). For its part, the APG Itika Guasu refused to be consulted, throughout the 2010–14 term of Capitán Grande Never Barrientos, who insisted on direct negotiations with Petrobras. May 2011 proved to be a critical moment in the conflict. In a communication that month to the APG Itika Guasu, Petrobras explained that, as per instructions from the Bolivian state, the hydrocarbon ministry would head the prior consultation process. Itika Guasu leaders balked at Petrobras's refusal to consult the community and blamed the hydrocarbon ministry for interrupting what they viewed as prior consultation (Equipo Nizkor and Derechos Human Rights 1/21/2013; *Eju!* 3/11/2013; Barriga 8/19/2014).

In mid-2014, Hugo Arebayo was elected to replace Barrientos, bringing an end to the impasse. Arebayo agreed to a prior consultation for San Antonio,

8. The tribunal mandated consent if a development project required the relocation of Indigenous communities or the storage or disposal of dangerous materials on Indigenous territories or lands; or if the project had an especially large impact on Indigenous territory (*Servindi* 9/6/2011, referencing the Constitutional Tribunal's Constitutional Sentence 2003/2010-R).

9. On the 2010 Repsol YPF-Itika Guasu agreement and its importance to Itika Guasu as a demonstration of the capitanía's autonomy, see also Anthias 2018, 202–11.

to advance to compensation discussions about investment in basic education, health, and other services for the community (Barriga 8/19/2014; *Eju!* 9/6/2014). The San Antonio consultation concluded in November 2014 (Ministry of Hydrocarbons and Energy 11/14/2014).[10]

Camisea Block 56

The Peruvian Camisea Block 56 natural gas conflict moves this discussion of unified insider strategies from the refusal of prior consultation, to interference in the EIA hearing process. Communities of the Machiguenga nation delayed the Block 56 hearing through one postponement and two boycotts. Eager to receive compensation payments, the communities eventually permitted the hearing, and the project proceeded.

Camisea and the Machiguenga

The Shell Corporation discovered the Camisea gas reserves in Cusco in the 1980s. Camisea multiplied Peru's total natural gas reserves by eleven times (Bruijn and Whiteman 2010, 482). Public officials referred to the 1996 contract between Shell and the Peruvian government as "the contract of the century" (Ross 2008, 202–3). That contract fell through in 1998, and in 2000 a consortium headed by the Argentine Pluspetrol took over Camisea production. A second consortium—led by Techint (also Argentine)—acquired the downstream operations (i.e., transportation and distribution; Ross 2008, 208).

The Camisea fields were located in a part of Cusco classified as rainforest and valued by conservationists for its biodiversity. The area encompassed the Lower Urubamba River Basin (Bajo Urubamba), which was populated by Indigenous communities, mainly of the Machiguenga (Ross 2008, 203–5). By the time the Block 56 project was under review, the development of Camisea Block 88—which had begun producing in August 2004—had transformed the Machiguenga's social and economic realities; communities previously had relied on traditional hunting, gathering, farming, and fishing, but now they depended significantly on the gas industry (Earle and Pratt 2009, 18, 57; Bruijn and Whiteman 2010).

Three Indigenous organizations participated in the Block 56 conflict. COMARU, of AIDESEP, represented thirty communities. Speaking for eight other communities was COMARU's competing organization, the Council

10. On the leadership struggle within the APG Itika Guasu, including divergent views on prior consultation and concerns about the use and transparency of the Repsol YPF funds, see Anthias 2018, 227–41.

of Native Machiguenga Communities (Central de Comunidades Nativas Machiguengas, CECONAMA), a CONAP affiliate. The Yine Yane Indigenous Communities Federation (Federación de Comunidades Nativas Yine Yane, FECONAYY) represented twenty communities, most of which resided outside of the Urubamba sector. In their organizing over Block 56, the Machiguenga received support from the Catholic Church, NGOs, and the local government (Ross 2008, 216–17; Earle and Pratt 2009, 17–18).

Independent of those allies, the Machiguenga chose to hold up the Block 56 EIA hearing, to delay gas development (Ross 2008, 261). They entered the Block 56 conflict with experience postponing EIA participation, for Block 88. By request, the state had rescheduled the first EIA hearing for the Block 88 pipeline so that the meeting would not coincide with an annual meeting of Machiguenga communities (Johnson 2005, 76, 105–6; Bruijn and Whiteman 2010, 482).

The EIA Hearing: Postponement and Boycotts

The development of the Block 56 EIA was contentious, due to contamination from the Block 88 operations.[11] A December 2004 pipeline break and resulting spill led COMARU and CECONAMA to unite for the first time in Camisea-related advocacy (Ross 2008, 249).

MINEM planned to hold the Block 56 EIA hearing in the community of Shivankoreni. The ministry initially scheduled the meeting for December 2004. Machiguenga communities called for the event's deferment on the grounds that the state had denied residents the minimum required period of ninety days to review the EIA. They succeeded: the state postponed the hearing to January 2005.

In January 2005 and still before the meeting date, communities were dismayed by the December pipeline break and the state's handling of it. Discussions among COMARU, CECONAMA, and their member communities produced a plan to boycott the hearing. COMARU and CECONAMA also submitted a joint letter to MINEM in which they demanded more information about the cause of the pipeline break and about its continuing environmental impacts. In the letter, the organizations also warned that until their concerns about the break were addressed, they would reject any development in Block 56, including by obstructing the EIA hearing. The Machiguenga boycotted the January hearing and protested loudly outside the meeting location. MINEM rescheduled the hearing again, for May 2005.

11. This section is based on Earle and Pratt 2009, 57–58, and the other referenced sources.

When in May 2005 MINEM had not fulfilled the demands in the January COMARU-CECONAMA letter (Griffiths 2007, 13), Shivankoreni's leadership informed the companies and MINEM in writing that the timing of the hearing was not appropriate (Ross 2008, 251). MINEM and company officials nonetheless traveled to Shivankoreni, on May 8. They found no community members; the day had been allocated for work at the Shivankoreni communal plot (*chacra*), some distance away.

Conflict Resolution and Community Divisions

Directly after finding Shivankoreni deserted, Camisea officials invited the leaders of COMARU and CECONAMA to their local headquarters and persuaded them to allow the EIA hearing. The head of COMARU then returned to Shivankoreni, where he convinced community leaders to participate in the hearing by suggesting that compensation for the Block 56 development would depend on their cooperation. The EIA hearing was held on May 9, 2005, though without representation from some communities. Now distrustful of COMARU due to its reversal, member communities made individual compensation deals with the companies. MINEM approved the EIA that July (Griffiths 2007, 13–14; Ross 2008, 250–51; Earle and Pratt 2009, 58–60).

The Machiguenga were disgruntled with the COMARU and CECONAMA leadership for folding at the EIA stage. Approximately one month after the public hearing, COMARU held a special meeting at which the head of the organization was replaced. Soon after, CECONAMA did the same (Ross 2008, 251).

In spite of the serious fissures caused by the Block 56 EIA hearing process, the Machiguenga organized in response to three Block 88 gas spills that occurred between August and November 2005. COMARU, CECONAMA, and FECONAYY requested an environmental audit, a halt to gas transport, and the implementation of environmental protections; and twenty-five hundred Machiguenga participated in a five-day strike (Ross 2008, 251–52).

Production in Block 56 began in 2008 (Suárez 10/13/2008).

Tambo Grande

Organizing against the proposed Tambo Grande mine in northern Peru was like the Camisea Block 56 case, in that unified communities planned to boycott the scheduled EIA public hearings for Tambo Grande. The broader dynamic of the mine conflict consisted of violent protests and an informal popular consultation that was pivotal in bringing about Tambo Grande's cancellation.

Emergence of Conflict and Violent Protest

Manhattan Minerals Corporation's Tambo Grande project—acquired from the Peruvian state in 1996—was to produce ten thousand tons of minerals per day and generate $100 million in revenue (De Echave et al. 2009, 27, 29). Residents of the Tambogrande district in Piura opposed the planned open-pit mine mainly due to its threat to the vibrant agricultural sector and the possible displacement of eight thousand people—one-half the population of the town of Tambogrande—for the project. In the conflict, the antimine San Lorenzo and Tambogrande Valley Defense Front (Frente de Defensa del Valle de San Lorenzo y Tambogrande, FDVSLT) had the backing of national and international NGOs (De Echave et al. 2009, 31–33; Arce 2014, 71, 75–77).

Serious organizing against Manhattan Minerals began in May 1999, when MINEM granted the company permission to carry out a feasibility study and develop a financing plan for the development and construction of a mining complex. Manhattan Minerals subsequently began exploration (De Echave et al. 2009, 29). Having progressed in that work, the company submitted its baseline study for the project in July 2000. The FDVSLT was troubled by what it viewed as progress toward the authorization of extraction. In August 2000, the organization led the first district strike against Tambo Grande (De Echave et al. 2009, 33–34).

Conflict broke out again when Manhattan Minerals began an information campaign about new model homes for the resettlement scheme. The campaign incited protest during two days in February 2001. Mobilizing in urban areas of the district led to clashes between residents and the three hundred police personnel who were guarding Manhattan Minerals' facilities. Fifteen demonstrators and twenty-five policemen were wounded. Shortly afterward, the Manhattan Minerals encampment was ransacked, and the houses that the company had constructed to serve as examples for the relocation were burned. Damages totaled approximately $600,000 (De Echave et al. 2009, 34–35). After the February 2001 uprising, violence spiraled, with a key event being the assassination of a prominent activist and local agricultural association leader, Godofredo García Baca (Arce 2014, 73).

The Popular Consultation

García Baca's death caused the FDVSLT to prioritize peaceful organizing (Arce 2014, 73). The major component of this shift was an informal popular consultation that the organization held, working with the Tambogrande municipal mayor's office. A municipal ordinance (Ordenanza Municipal 012-2001-MDT-C) provided for the "neighbors' consultation" (*consulta vecinal*), a mechanism for district-level participation. The ordinance was based in national and municipal laws, the environment code, and constitutional articles pertaining to citizen participation. The National Office of Electoral Processes (Oficina Nacional de Procesos Electorales, ONPE) initially recognized the consultation but then reversed its position one month before the vote, in response to a formal challenge by MINEM (Paredes 2008, 293–95; Walter and Urkidi 2017, 269).

The consultation moved forward in June 2002, with participation by 73 percent of the thirty-six thousand eligible voters. Ninety-eight percent of participants voted against the mine. When MINEM declared the referendum results nonbinding and reaffirmed Manhattan Minerals' extraction rights, protest intensified. In one march, more than seven thousand Tambogrande residents took to the streets (De Echave et al. 2009, 37–41, 41; Arce 2014, 73). Although the vote was not legally enforceable, it evinced local antipathy toward the mine and spawned greater national and international support for the Tambogrande district's plight (Paredes 2008, 296–98).

The Suspension of EIA Hearings, and Project Cancellation

Tambo Grande was canceled while the EIA was under review. During a series of FDVSLT mobilizations in 2003, MINEM and INRENA raised technical questions about the project. The FDVSLT scheduled protests that overlapped with the three EIA public hearings planned for November 2003 (to be held in Piura, Tambogrande, and Lima); the organization intended for the protests to dissuade people from attending and thereby validating the meetings and the mine project (De Echave et al. 2009, 40–42; Arce 2014, 74). As described by De Echave et al., the FDVSLT rejected the EIA participatory process, because the organization believed that "the culmination of the EIA review process inevitably would lead to the approval of the mining project" (2009, 42). Before the scheduled dates of the hearings, they were postponed, due to protests (De Echave et al. 2009, 43; Arce 2014, 74).

In December 2003, the state mining company Centromín—Manhattan Minerals' partner—issued a surprising press release stating that Manhattan Minerals had not fulfilled its contract obligations. Manhattan Minerals closed its Piura offices in July 2004 and left Peru in February 2005. In June 2005, MINEM archived permanently the Tambo Grande EIA (De Echave et al. 2009, 43; Arce 2014, 74).

Tía María

Tía María is a final case in which unified insiders interfered with participatory processes. Specifically, residents violently interrupted the EIA hearing held for a first version of the Tía María mine, causing the hearing's suspension. The mine conflict made the convening of a new hearing, and the project itself, politically impracticable.

After the initial mine project was canceled, Tía María's owner, Southern Copper Corporation, prepared another EIA, for a new project design. In that process, residents tried to interfere with the EIA participatory process, but their efforts were foiled by the national police. Although MINEM approved the new EIA, community organizing continued holding up the mine project when research for this study was concluding.

The First EIA

The $950 million open-pit Tía María mine project near the coast of Peru's southern region of Arequipa had the promise of producing approximately 120,000 tons of copper per year. In late 2009, several months into the conflict, Southern planned to begin construction in 2010 and production in 2012 (Kozak 9/28/2009; Chauca 12/19/2013).

Although some local groups endorsed Tía María (Bárcena Carpio 12/15/2014), antimine sentiment overwhelmingly dominated local and regional politics surrounding the project. The mine site was in the province of Islay and near the agricultural Tambo Valley. The central issue for activists was that the project could harm agriculture, principally through its use of large volumes of water.[12] Communities already had grievances about contamination from Southern's activities: air pollution from the company's smelter, which was located in the coastal city of Ilo, in the Moquegua region.[13] Serious contamination from the smelter had impacted crops in the Tambo Valley for decades (Perla 2012, 164–67). The Tambo Valley Defense Front (Frente de Defensa del Valle de Tambo) and the Tambo Valley Water Use Board (Junta de Usuarios del Valle de Tambo) were civil-society groups active in the Tía María conflict (Pinto Herrera 2016).

Following a limited community relations campaign,[14] Southern held three EIA workshops for Tía María, between November 2007 and July 2009 (*Enlace*

12. Pinto Herrera 2016; and Interview with a mining company official close to the Tía María case; Lima, March 30, 2012 (Interview P13).
13. Interview with a mining company official who had close knowledge of the Quellaveco and Tía María mine conflicts; Lima, March 27, 2012 (Interview P14).
14. Interview P14.

nacional 11/16/2007; *Revista la punta* 7/31/2009). At each of the meetings, the company discussed two possible water sources for the mine: river and underground water. At the last workshop, Southern introduced the concept of constructing a desalination plant and using seawater, a project design that would have left community freshwater sources untouched.[15]

Conflict over Tía María emerged at the public hearing, in August 2009. The presentation of the EIA covered all three water options for the mine but favored the use of river water. That emphasis surprised and frustrated community members in attendance, because they had come to expect desalination.[16] Residents at the meeting threw chairs and other furniture. They also attempted to stone mining company officials and, upon their arrival, national police personnel. The hearing was adjourned prematurely due to the violence, in which fifteen individuals were wounded. The public hearing stage for Tía María remained incomplete (*Perú 21* 8/28/2009).

Disagreement about desalination led to Tía María's suspension. After the interrupted public hearing, Arequipa's regional president, Juan Manuel Guillén Benavides, asked Southern to adopt the desalination plan, hoping the project could advance (*Dow Jones* 9/15/2009). When in September 2009 the company still would not commit to that option, citing its cost, the rural district of Cocachacra held a (nonbinding) popular consultation on the project. More than 90 percent of the 3,131 participants voted against the mine, which also was voted down in four other districts (Kozak 9/28/2009).

After several postponements of the hearing and in response to an indefinite strike in Islay over Tía María, Southern asked that MINEM call off the EIA hearing. The ministry did so in April 2010 (*El Comercio* 4/17/2010). The same month, the government suspended the project for ninety days and formed a roundtable to review the EIA (*El Comercio* 5/2/2010; *Reuters* 5/24/2010).

In November 2010, six months into the government-led roundtable, Southern announced it would invest $50 million to construct a desalination plant (*Minería y progreso* 11/12/2010; *El Comercio* 11/20/2010). However, opposition to the mine had consolidated. Frente de Defensa leaders announced later that same month that they would resume protests against Tía María. The Frente's president said, "We don't want them to explain where they will get the water from, or the technology that they will use to avoid pollution. We only want them to leave the valley and let us live in peace" (*El Comercio* 11/20/2010).

15. Interview P13.

16. Interview P13. A mining conflict consultant and mediator said Southern had "lied" to the population by promising the desalination plant (interview, Lima, March 28, 2012; Interview P15).

The state canceled the mine project following an independent review of the EIA. During heightened protest in late 2010, MINEM contracted a team from the UN Office for Project Services (UNOPS) to review the document. The external review process temporarily appeased activists, but when the UNOPS study was leaked to the Frente de Defensa in March 2011, protests resumed. The UNOPS report identified 138 problems with the EIA, including the absence of a hydrogeological study and of details on the desalination option. MINEM paused its review of the EIA for 180 days in response to the protests (Pinto Herrera 2016, 202).

Hostility toward the mine only grew. By early April 2011, three people had been killed in encounters with the police, and several others were in critical condition. Arequipa president Guillén asked, for the first time, that Tía María be canceled (*El Comercio* 4/7/2011). MINEM canceled Tía María, stating that the EIA contained "unsalvageable elements" (Prado 4/9/2011).[17]

The Second EIA

Southern announced in 2012 that it was working on a revised EIA (*La República* 2/9/2012). The new version of Tía María relied on seawater and included a desalination plant. Yet the project remained controversial, due to anticipated contamination and impacts on agriculture. Furthermore, pollution from the Ilo smelter was still a reference point for the local population (Pinto Herrera 2016, 206–8).

The first incident registered by the Defensoría del Pueblo in this second chapter of the Tía María conflict was violence at an EIA workshop in late October 2013, in the district of Deán Valdivia, in Islay. Residents complained that many workshop attendees were not from the area and had been paid 150 *soles* each to attend, to legitimize the event. Furious protesters from Deán Valdivia—supported by the Frente de Defensa—were met by national police personnel outside the meeting. Nine officers were wounded.[18]

Communities then tried to prevent the second workshop, also in Deán Valdivia, in October 2013. Before that meeting, Tambo Valley residents cut off a connector route to the Pan-American Highway in a twenty-four-hour strike. The police opened the highway, but then the Deán Valdivia municipal government warned that it would cancel the workshop if Southern did not submit missing required paperwork, within hours. Simultaneously, approximately one hundred farmers assembled outside the workshop site to demand that

17. On the project cancellation, see also Pinto Herrera 2016, 202; and Defensoría del Pueblo, Adjuntía para la Prevención de Conflictos Sociales y la Gobernabilidad 2017d, 1.

18. Pinto Herrera 2016, 202–3; and Defensoría del Pueblo, Adjuntía para la Prevención de Conflictos Sociales y la Gobernabilidad 2017d, 2.

the event be canceled. Due to the protest and the earlier roadblock, four hundred national police agents guarded the meeting location and other "strategic points" in the Tambo Valley, to prevent more blockades (*Perú 21* 10/30/2013). The workshop was convened on schedule (Pinto Herrera 2016, 203).

The December 2013 EIA hearing, in Cocachacra, also was conflict-ridden. Two thousand police personnel were deployed to prevent interference with the hearing (Chauca 12/19/2013; Pinto Herrera 2016, 203). While the meeting of twelve hundred to sixteen hundred people was in progress, the police barred a group of residents—among them the Frente de Defensa's leader—from entering. Confrontations followed, between four hundred community members and the police. Three protesters were wounded and another ten detained. Hearing attendees who rejected the project reported that Southern had transported people from outside of the area in taxis and buses to the meeting, to fill the venue. Noting the large number of hearing attendees, the energy and mining minister declared that the Arequipa population accepted the project (Chauca 12/19/2013; Pinto Herrera 2016, 203, 209). On August 1, 2014, MINEM granted the Tía María environmental license (Pinto Herrera 2016, 203).

Post-EIA Conflict

Tensions increased over the mine in late 2014, after the EIA approval and with construction for the mine projected to start before the end of the year (CooperAcción 2014, 19; Bárcena Carpio 12/15/2014). That phase of conflict culminated in March–May 2015 protests, the longest and most violent interval of organizing against Tía María; across the two months, there were clashes between police and activists almost daily (Malpartida Tabuchi 3/3/2018).

During a strike in April 2015, the government made several attempts to de-escalate the conflict through talks. The agriculture, environment, interior, and energy and mining ministers traveled to the city of Arequipa to speak with subnational political authorities, and a MINEM team led a meeting with Arequipa residents to discuss the EIA. The PCM instated two working groups in Islay that included local authorities and representatives of MINAM, MINEM, and the agriculture and interior ministries. Another meeting brought together the agriculture minister, Arequipa's regional governor, the Islay provincial mayor, the leaders of the Frente de Defensa and the Junta de Usuarios del Valle de Tambo, and the mayors of the Cocachacra, Deán Valdivia, and Punto de Bombón districts (Defensoría del Pueblo, Adjuntía para la Prevención de Conflictos Sociales y la Gobernabilidad 2017d, 6).

Resistance to Tía María mounted, now with participation by labor unions. Protests and the coercive police response resulted in four deaths and more than one hundred injuries by late May 2015.[19] To calm protest and facilitate dialogue, Southern announced it would stop work on the project for sixty days, but to no avail (*SPDA actualidad ambiental* 5/15/2015). The government ended the violence by placing Islay under a sixty-day state of emergency (Defensoría del Pueblo, Adjuntía para la Prevención de Conflictos Sociales y la Gobernabilidad 2017d, 9). After the crackdown, Southern embarked on social relations campaigns in Islay that reduced antagonism toward the mine,[20] though communities continued to stage intermittent mobilizations.[21]

As of this writing, Tía María was on hold, due to an incendiary licensing process for the mine's construction. Protest exploded in mid-2019 when the state authorized the license. The mobilizing led to the project's suspension, in August 2019 (*Bloomberg* 7/24/2019; Cervantes 10/30/2019). In late October 2019, the state mining council (Consejo de Minería, independent of the executive) affirmed that the construction plan was sound, but President Martín Vizcarra's (2018–20) prime minister announced that the government would not press forward with Tía María without the necessary environmental and social conditions. Southern Copper issued a communication that the company planned to develop the project when there was a "more favorable social climate" (Cervantes 10/30/2019). In January 2020, Vizcarra announced that, due to local opposition, the project was not viable at the time (*RPP noticias* 1/29/2020). The prime minister reiterated that message several months later, in July (*La Mula* 7/5/2020).

COMPETITION AMONG INSIDER GROUPS

In the conflicts analyzed thus far in this chapter, unified insider communities prevented or interfered with participatory procedures that were integral to project approvals. This section analyzes the strategies of activists in fractured insider communities—specifically, where there was contestation over who spoke for communities when it came to planned extraction. These divisions foreclosed the possibility for mobilized groups to hold up participatory events, because people agreeable to development willingly participated in them.

Where community representation was debated, organized insiders either participated in the formal participatory process, or were excluded from it and later claimed it to have been illegitimate. Their choice depended on the

19. Defensoría del Pueblo, Adjuntía para la Prevención de Conflictos Sociales y la Gobernabilidad 2017d, 7–9; and Malpartida Tabuchi 3/3/2018.

20. *El Comercio* 9/1/2015; CooperAcción 2018a, 10; and Malpartida Tabuchi 3/3/2018.

21. See, for example, *La República* 4/27/2016; *SPDA actualidad ambiental* 5/11/2016; and *El Comercio* 7/29/2016.

design of the participatory institution, and especially how the institution defined participation. Participation in an EIA hearing meant the convening of a meeting for local residents. This design feature encouraged activists to attend and communicate their positions at the meeting, to compete with participants that held other positions on extraction, in the Peruvian Las Bambas and Quellaveco mining cases. In contrast to EIA hearing rules, participation in prior consultation meant the attendance and certification of meetings by community leaders. The state therefore was able to consult residents who were open to extraction and who claimed to represent their communities, in the Colombian conflict over the Mandé Norte mine project. Later, impacted communities argued that the consultation process had been a sham, because their true representatives had not been included.

Communities supplemented their participation in and organizing around the EIA hearing and prior consultation, respectively, with additional uses of participatory institutions. Activists participated in MEIA workshops and tried (unsuccessfully) to compel the state to postpone MEIA hearings, for the Quellaveco mine. In the Las Bambas case, communities participated in EIA workshops but also disputed their exclusion from a project revision. Finally, communities held an informal popular consultation about Mandé Norte.

Quellaveco

Residents impacted by Anglo American's proposed Quellaveco copper mine in southern Peru protested the project in part by participating in public hearings for modifications to it. Groups that wanted the mine also participated. The project modifications were approved.

After analyzing citizen participation in and approvals of the MEIAs, this case study examines how residents who were uneasy about Quellaveco's environmental and social impacts held up the mine during water licensing. A drawn-out roundtable led to changes to the project, which moved forward.

Organizing against Quellaveco took place in both the Moquegua region—where the project was located—and neighboring Arequipa, and it overlapped temporally with the conflict in that region over Tía María, analyzed in the first part of this chapter. Communities affected by Quellaveco primarily worried that the mine would cause water depletion and thereby harm agriculture. They entered the Quellaveco conflict well aware of the impacts of mining: Moquegua was a traditional mining region, and Southern Copper's large, producing Cuajone mine was a mere fifteen kilometers from the Quellaveco site (Arellano Yanguas 2011, 152).

In 1992, Anglo American acquired the Quellaveco concession, which had the potential to produce 225,000 tons of copper annually for twenty-eight years (Inoue 2/17/2012). The state approved the Quellaveco EIA in 2000, but communities considered the water plan inadequate. In response, the government instructed Anglo American to revise the document.[22] A rise in copper prices motivated the company to present a new project design in the late 2000s.[23] The conflict analyzed here was about that design.

Conflict over the MEIAs, Expressed in Public Hearings

Many local communities were hopeful that Quellaveco would bring investment to the region, and/or already had benefited from Anglo American's social programs (Arellano Yanguas 2011, 152–53). Yet agricultural groups with misgivings about contamination and water diminution from the mine rejected the project, which made the review of the two MEIAs conflictual.

There was noteworthy participation by communities in the workshops and public hearing for the first MEIA, which dealt with water-related aspects of the project. Mine supporters and opponents attended the series of workshops led by Anglo American in May–September 2008.[24] Among other items, farmers questioned Anglo American's proposal to divert the local Asana River and the possibility of water contamination from the mine's waste dump, which was to be situated at the end of the Asana riverbed. Quellaveco advocates directed their attention toward the jobs that the mine might generate. Animated debate between the two sides in an August 2008 workshop reached a level of intensity that prompted the director of energy and mines to intervene to calm participants.[25]

The Cocachacra district government and civil-society organizations asked that the MEIA hearing be postponed, but DGAAM denied their request. The hearing was held in December 2008 in San Cristóbal-Calacoa, a district in the Mariscal Nieto province, in Moquegua (Report 389-2010/MEM-AAM/CAG/WAL/CMC, 4). More than three hundred people attended from Deán Valdivia and several other districts. Participants posed fifty-three questions—twenty-six in writing and twenty-seven orally. Of the topics raised in the oral interjections, most pertained to the mine's environmental impacts—above all, on water.[26]

22. Vega Nieto 8/22/2008; and Interview P14.
23. Arellano Yanguas 2011, 152; and Interview P14.
24. Report 531-2009/MEM-AAM/PRN/WAL/EA/WBF/PRR/RC, Section II; and Report 389-2010/MEM-AAM/CAG/WAL/CMC, 2.
25. Vega Nieto 8/22/2008; and *Coordinadora nacional de radio* 4/14/2010.
26. Report 531-2009/MEM-AAM/PRN/WAL/EA/WBF/PRR/RC, Appendix I.

Besides participating in the workshops and the hearing, antimine residents protested. Approximately two hundred people, including representatives of several civil-society groups, attended a March 2008 mobilization spearheaded by the Moquegua Water and Environment Defense Front (Frente de Defensa del Agua y del Medioambiente de Moquegua), a prominent organization in the Quellaveco conflict. The protest was motivated primarily by disquiet over contamination from Quellaveco and over the mine's water use. In early December 2008, farmers held another protest (Defensoría del Pueblo, Adjuntía para la Prevención de Conflictos Sociales y la Gobernabilidad 2015, 3–4).

After the public hearing for the first MEIA, reservations about that modification merged with apprehension about a second one, which altered copper transport routes (*Coordinadora nacional de radio* 4/9/2010). The Frente de Defensa marched through the streets of the city of Moquegua in late January 2009 to protest both MEIAs. Days after that mobilization, the regional council (Consejo Regional de Moquegua) ratified an ordinance declaring the Quellaveco project a public necessity and in the region's interest (Defensoría del Pueblo, Adjuntía para la Prevención de Conflictos Sociales y la Gobernabilidad 2015, 4, 5).

Groups approached the second MEIA public hearing the same way they had the first: they tried to delay the hearing and then participated in it. The hearing was scheduled for April 9, 2010, in Ilo (Defensoría del Pueblo, Adjuntía para la Prevención de Conflictos Sociales y la Gobernabilidad 2015, 6). The state declined civil-society groups' request for a thirty-day postponement of the meeting. The night before the event, municipal authorities and civil-society leaders insisted that the hearing be pushed back and threatened to cut off access to it (*Coordinadora nacional de radio* 4/9/2010). The hearing was held on schedule. It was attended by 432 individuals, including representatives of MEM, DREM Moquegua, the Defensoría del Pueblo, the Ilo provincial government, the government of the Torata district (in Mariscal Nieto), Anglo American, and civil-society organizations, and members of the general public. Participants delivered twenty-six oral interventions and submitted forty-nine questions in writing (*Andina* 4/16/2010).

Days after the hearing, on April 14, 2010, farmers mobilized in the city of Moquegua. The protest, which paralyzed interprovincial bus routes, focused on the mine's impacts on water and agriculture. In addition, protest leaders expressed solidarity with residents of the Cocachacra district, who at the time were organizing against Tía María; the Moquegua protesters underscored their own grievances with Southern, blaming the firm for Cuajone's damage to the environment, including water contamination (*Coordinadora nacional de radio* 4/14/2010; Arellano Yanguas 2011, 152).

MINEM approved both MEIAs in 2010—the first in late April, and the second in October (*La Mula* 5/2/2012).

The Moquegua Working Group

After the MEIA process concluded, agricultural groups used a roundtable in conjunction with protest to alter Quellaveco, to make it palatable.

Civil-society groups pressed for a roundtable to discuss Quellaveco with Anglo American during a window of opportunity in the water-licensing process: the National Water Authority (Autoridad Nacional del Agua, ANA) had disallowed an agreement between Anglo American and Moquegua's agricultural water authority (Proyecto Especial Regional Pasto Grande) about the firm's water plan (Motta 7/4/2010).

In March 2011, Moquegua's new regional president (and a future president of Peru) Martín Vizcarra Cornejo assembled a working group of government, company, and civil-society actors to resolve the water problem.[27] Their work was underway when, in June 2011, ANA deemed technically viable and approved the Quellaveco water plan. Mobilizing, primarily by farmers, forced ANA to reverse the authorization two months later (Motta 1/10/2012). Anglo American adjusted its project substantially based on the working group's discussions, for instance proposing a dam that would provide more than twice the amount of water to Moquegua communities than expected from the previous version of the project.[28]

The regional working group met twelve times by January 2012 (Gobierno Regional Moquegua n.d., 7–20) and proved so successful in promoting dialogue that a March 2012 MINEM resolution transformed it into a national roundtable that included representatives of ANA, MINAM, MINEM, OEFA, and the PCM (*Los Andes* 3/13/2012). That same month, the body decided to hire, with MINEM funding, UNOPS—which had reviewed the Tía María EIA—to study the hydrogeological portion of the Quellaveco EIA (*Tiempominero.com* 4/2/2012). The roundtable produced agreements about water, the environment, and corporate social responsibility. In July 2012 the Defensoría del Pueblo proclaimed the Quellaveco conflict "resolved" (Defensoría del Pueblo, Adjuntía para la Prevención de Conflictos Sociales y la Gobernabilidad 2015, 10).

As of April 2020, production from Quellaveco was expected to begin in 2022 (*Reuters* 4/23/2020).

27. Interview P14; see also Dirección Regional, Energía y Minas–Moquegua n.d., especially 17.

28. Interview P14; see also Dirección Regional, Energía y Minas–Moquegua n.d., especially 17.

Las Bambas

Alongside the Quellaveco case, the other instance of participation in environmental licensing by competing insider communities in this study occurred during the first of two main periods of conflict over the Las Bambas mine, located in Peru's southern highland region of Apurímac. Representatives of all communities impacted by Las Bambas participated in the EIA public hearing for the mine.

In the second cycle of conflict over Las Bambas, which was unresolved when this research was concluding, communities protested a new project design and their exclusion from the project modifications. That is, the conflict dynamic mirrored that of outsider conflicts analyzed in Chapter 5.

Throughout both conflict periods, communities held major demonstrations in their desire for compensation and company investments in local development.

The Fideicomiso and Participation in the EIA Hearing

Communities responded to the initial version of Las Bambas by seeking greater benefits from a large social investment fund associated with the mine, the *fideicomiso* (Gustafsson 2018, 149). The communities most active in the conflict resided in the project's area of influence but not at the planned mine site.

Las Bambas was part of a mining boom in Apurímac. The project was in Challhuahuacho, a district in the Cotabambas province that bordered the Grau province (Gustafsson 2018, 136, 141). Conceived of by the state, Las Bambas was to produce 324,000 tons of copper per year for eighteen years, which would make it one of the world's biggest copper mines (*Andina* 3/7/2011; Damonte 2013, 80). In August 2004, the state transferred the project to Xstrata AG Suiza (CooperAcción 2015, 5).

Prior to the Las Bambas conflict, civil society in Apurímac generally had been weak, due to 1980s civil-war violence. Certain local groups became stronger through, and proved consequential in, organizing over the mine. Especially salient during the first conflict period were the Provincial Federation of Cotabambas Campesinos (Federación Provincial de Campesinos de Cotabambas), established in 1999; and the District Federation of Challhuahuacho Campesinos (Federación Distrital de Campesinos de Challhuahuacho), formed in 2003 to increase peasant solidarity in response to Las Bambas. The two organizations overlapped in their structures and purposes and have been treated as a single federation (Gustafsson 2018, 139–40, 143).

Ruptures among communities in the Las Bambas area of influence stemmed importantly from the resources offered to the community of Fuerabamba. As the only community to be resettled for the mine, Fuerabamba received more social investments than the other impacted communities. That favoritism was evident in the social programs that Proinversión coordinated with other public institutions (Gustafsson 2018, 141, 145–46). The community also received attention from Xstrata, which negotiated the community's relocation. After years of negotiations, a 2010 agreement between Fuerabamba and the company guaranteed the community generous monetary compensation and other benefits that included land, jobs, pensions, education facilities, and new houses. Residents moved to Nueva Fuerabamba during 2014–15 (CooperAcción 2015, 16; Gustafsson 2018, 142, 167–68).

Initial organizing over Las Bambas emerged during 2003–4, when communities were looking ahead to the project's transfer to Xstrata. Impacted communities wanted the handover to be postponed, to give them time to gather information and form opinions about the mine. They did not achieve the delay, but they did alter the contract terms. A new appendix, "Anexo K," outlined seventeen points that covered the company's obligations to tackle cultural, economic, environmental, and social issues (CooperAcción 2015, 14).

The first substantive protests over Las Bambas were about the $64 million fideicomiso, which the government created when it transferred the mine to Xstrata (Gustafsson 2018, 146, 149). Organizers believed Proinversión managed the fund poorly; they wanted more investment in agriculture, increased efficiency in the implementation of projects, and greater investment in Cotabambas at large. A forty-eight-hour strike in Apurímac in March 2005 was followed by strikes in February 2006 and July 2007 (CooperAcción 2015, 14–15; Gustafsson 2018, 147–51).

After the 2007 mobilization, talks between activists and a government commission led the government to commit to transferring fideicomiso oversight to the Cotabambas provincial mayor (Gustafsson 2018, 151). In 2009, the fideicomiso became the Las Bambas Social Fund (Fondo Social Las Bambas, FOSBAM), as part of a national move—formalized through the 2008 Legislative Decree 996—to end the central government's control over private extractive firms' social investments. The fund's board consisted of six mayors and two Xstrata employees. FOSBAM still did not orient assistance toward the province as a whole; according to Decree 996, 85 percent of investment from the fund was to benefit areas directly influenced by the mine (CooperAcción 2015, 15; Gustafsson 2018, 151–53).

In this context, the EIA participatory process took place, with citizen engagement. The Apurímac and Cusco DREMs led EIA workshops in 2009 and 2010 in the vicinity of the mine and also on the route of a planned pipeline for transporting minerals from Las Bambas to Xstrata's Tintaya mine site in Cusco, for processing. At the workshops, local political authorities, civil-society groups, and members of the public articulated reservations about environmental and socioeconomic matters (Moreno Hermoza 2014, 138–40; CooperAcción 2015, 3).

Approximately forty-five hundred people attended the July 2010 EIA hearing, in Challhuahaucho. Every community in the project's area of influence was represented at the event, where participants openly exchanged ideas. MINEM approved the EIA in March 2011 (with RD 073-2011-MEM/AAM).[29]

In May 2011, communities struck over the initial Las Bambas project again, this time demanding jobs and the implementation of Anexo K (CooperAcción 2015, 16). The strike illuminated residents' focus on compensation and material benefits, and the mine's divisiveness. Communities in the mine's area of direct influence had participated in the 2005–7 protests. Those communities were to receive more resources from Las Bambas than the fourteen highland communities that planned the 2011 strike; the latter resided in an area demarcated as only minimally impacted. These more remote communities lacked the support of the directly impacted communities and of the federation (which had been central in the previous strikes) but made a temporary alliance with urban groups for the mobilization (Gustafsson 2018, 177–82). In the two-day strike in May 2011, activists kidnapped a company engineer, and the national police repressed protesters violently (CooperAcción 2015, 16). Xstrata resolved the conflict by agreeing to invest in social development and provide jobs (Defensoría del Pueblo, Adjuntía para la Prevención de Conflictos Sociales y la Gobernabilidad 2017b, 3–4; Gustafsson 2018, 182).

The next year, after coordinating with local authorities in Cotabambas, MINEM created the Working Group for the Development of Cotabambas (Mesa de Trabajo para el Desarrollo de Cotabambas) as a longer-term measure to address grievances in the province. Central government officials and Cotabambas mayors negotiated state investment plans in the twelve-session working group, which operated until December 2013 (CooperAcción 2015, 16).

Project Changes, Community Exclusion, and More Conflict

The first period of conflict over Las Bambas, then, was characterized by the actions of competing insiders. By contrast, the second period fits the outsider pattern in this study: communities protested because they were infuriated by their exclusion from a project revision process that eliminated compensation opportunities while introducing new environmental impacts.

As mentioned, according to the original project, Xstrata would transport via a pipeline Las Bambas minerals, to the location of Tintaya in Cusco. The

29. Moreno Hermoza 2014, 139; and CooperAcción 2015, 6.

pipeline was no longer logical when in 2014 the MMG Limited consortium, led by China Minmetals, acquired Las Bambas (Gustafsson 2018, 143), because the project transfer split the two mines between different owners. The revised Las Bambas design situated molybdenum and filtration plants and other infrastructure at the mine site and provided for the transport of Las Bambas minerals via trucks on public roads, in place of the pipeline plan (CooperAcción 2015, 3–5, 13).

The project changes upset communities that lost anticipated compensation for the pipeline's impacts and brought new impacts, from the planned infrastructure in the area of Las Bambas, and from overwhelming amounts of dust along the transport route, due to truck traffic (CooperAcción 2015, 2, 13; del Río 11/15/2015).

Poor transparency surrounding the revisions was as perturbing to communities as the project changes themselves. Two modifications to the 2011 EIA, and three ITSs, altered Las Bambas, between mid-April 2013 and late February 2015. Neither workshops nor public hearings were held for the changes. The revision process overlapped with the MMG transfer (CooperAcción n.d.; 2015, 3–5, 13; del Río 11/15/2015).

Frustrated by the opaque modification process, increased environmental impacts, and reduced compensation, communities set off new conflict cycles. Protest was met by state repression and negotiations with the government about investment in development. Conflict first soared in late September 2015, when the recently formed Central Committee of the Grau and Cotabambas Provinces (Comité Central de Lucha de las Provincias de Grau y Cotabambas) led an indefinite strike (CooperAcción 2015, 17). Several days into the strike, on September 28, actions by approximately ten thousand protesters and two thousand national police personnel left three people dead and fifteen others with bullet wounds. The government declared a state of emergency the next day in the provinces of Andahuaylas, Chincheros, Cotabambas, and Grau in Apurímac; and in the provinces of Chumbivilcas and Espinar in Cusco (CooperAcción 2015, 17).

The strike was paused on September 30 to allow for dialogue (CooperAcción 2015, 17). During the first week of October, several ministers met in Cotabambas with residents and the district and provincial mayors. The ministers agreed to (1) lift the state of emergency pending the strike's conclusion; (2) attend to the families of the people who had died in the September 28 violence; and (3) hold workshops in every Cotabambas district on the ITSs that had modified Las Bambas. Later that month, a gathering in Lima of central government officials and the provincial and district mayors of Grau produced a commitment to local development planning and to a roundtable. The participants also planned for an informational meeting about the Las Bambas modifications and a meeting between MMG and local authorities in Grau.

On October 28, civil-society groups in Cotabambas and Grau agreed to lift the strike (Defensoría del Pueblo, Adjuntía para la Prevención de Conflictos Sociales y la Gobernabilidad 2017b, 13–14).

By December 1, 2015, roundtables had been installed for Cotabambas and Grau. Dialogue was ongoing in August 2016, when commercial production from Las Bambas began (Defensoría del Pueblo, Adjuntía para la Prevención de Conflictos Sociales y la Gobernabilidad 2017b, 14–23; De Echave C. 1/23/2018).

Another mobilization commenced in 2018.[30] At issue was a stretch of road used by the company to reach its encampment in Nueva Fuerabamba. The transportation and communication ministry declared the road public in May 2018. In response, Nueva Fuerabamba claimed ownership of the road, denounced contamination from passing company vehicles, and insisted on company payments for road access. A series of roadblocks, states of emergency, and negotiation efforts followed. In one particularly visible case, Fuerabamba residents set up a blockade in February 2019, which they sustained for sixty-eight days. They withdrew in April, after the government lifted the state of emergency that had been in place and inaugurated a roundtable. The dialogue was tense. Las Bambas, which was now a global leader in copper production, lost more than $300 million due to the February–April standoff.

During the extended conflict over the altered Las Bambas design, communities in Apurímac and Cusco went to the courts to contest the government's use of states of emergency to prevent organizing. In October 2017, three Apurímac organizations represented by the Legal Defense Institute (Instituto de Defensa Legal) and the Apurímac branch of the Pro-Human Rights Association (Asociación Pro Derechos Humanos) submitted a habeas corpus demand against the PCM for continuous states of emergency in Cotabambas. The organizations, which resided in the Las Bambas area of influence, claimed that the states of emergency unjustly criminalized social protest. Three years later, the Constitutional Tribunal, which confirmed that the state of exception in the zone had been extended fifteen times with only slight geographic changes, ruled for the Apurímac groups (*Servindi* 1/6/2021).

When this research was being completed, the most recent cycle of mobilizing over Las Bambas had begun in February 2020, with protests in Cusco. In response, the government instituted a state of emergency, which it later extended through successive decrees. The United Defense Front of the Chumbivilcas Province (Frente Único de Defensa de los Intereses de la Provincia de Chumbivilcas) filed an amparo against the PCM and the interior

30. This paragraph is based on Machacuay 3/27/2019; Ortiz 3/27/2019; Fowks 4/11/2019; and *El Comercio* 5/21/2019, 2/10/2020.

and justice ministries regarding the suspension of the rights to protest and associate (*La República* 5/14/2020; *Servindi* 5/15/2020).

Mandé Norte

The Colombian Mandé Norte mine conflict is another case of insider mobilizing within non-cohesive communities. Whereas in the Quellaveco and Las Bambas conflicts the relevant participatory institution was the EIA (or MEIA) hearing, the Embera Indigenous communities that opposed the open-pit Mandé Norte copper and gold mine project had at their disposal prior consultation. Because participation in prior consultation consisted of community leaders ratifying consultations—and not a public assembly, as with EIA hearings—community behavior at the participatory stage for Mandé Norte differed relative to that in the Las Bambas and Quellaveco cases. The Colombian state held a consultation on Mandé Norte that left out the true leaders of impacted communities. Embera communities later condemned the deficient consultation, through the courts. With that tutela filing, they brought the project to an indefinite halt.

A Sham Consultation and Indignant Excluded Communities

In 2005, the Colombian state granted the Mandé Norte concession—located in the municipalities of Murindó in the Antioquia department, and Carmen del Darién in Chocó—to the Denver-based Muriel Mining Company (Comisión Intereclesial de Justicia y Paz 12/23/2008; Congote Gutiérrez 11/29/2012). The mine would have affected Afro-Colombian, Embera, and peasant communities (Sentence T-769-09, Section I.A). Prior to Muriel Mining's arrival, ethnic communities in the region had been fractured by the intersection of political decentralization, the strengthening of Indigenous authority structures, and violence associated with Colombia's civil war (Velasco Jaramillo 2014).

That weak community cohesion facilitated a faulty prior consultation for Mandé Norte. Officials from Ingeominas and the interior and energy and mining ministries met with members of some impacted communities about Mandé Norte on multiple occasions, in 2006 and 2007, a process that participants treated as a prior consultation (Sentence T-769-09, Section I.A; Velasco Jaramillo 2014, 143).

Conflict over the mine began in January 2009, when a team of Muriel Mining geologists came to Carmen del Darién to conduct exploratory drilling. Upon arriving by helicopter, the geologists presented community members a written description of the exploration. The document had been signed by Embera individuals who had participated in the 2006–7 process and whom the community did not recognize as its representatives. Days later, company employees set up camp on Careperro Mountain, the exploration site. For the Embera, the mountain was sacred and a vital water source for crops that were part of the traditional local economy.[31]

The company's arrival prompted twelve hundred people from multiple Embera communities to congregate in the hamlet of Coredocito, accompanied by representatives of Chilean and Guatemalan Indigenous groups and German, Honduran, and Spanish NGOs. One month of daily planning sessions ensued (Congote Gutiérrez 11/29/2012).

Conflict and Project Suspension

The Coredocito meetings gave rise to a two-pronged course of action to prevent the development of Mandé Norte: a popular vote and a tutela filing. In February 2009, the Embera held the informal referendum, which was framed as an exercise of their right to consultation. Individuals ages ten and older participated. There were 798 votes against mining and zero in favor. The consultation motivated direct action. Community members ascended Careperro and camped outside the mining installation for one month, holding demonstrations that included dances and prayers. The activists told Muriel Mining—via a message to the local military battalion—that the company had two days to leave, or else they would seize its equipment to prevent further exploration. At that point, the company suspended its helicopter flights (Comisión Intereclesial de Justicia y Paz 12/23/2008; Congote Gutiérrez 11/29/2012).

The Embera also turned to the judicial system, a course that successfully stopped the project. In April 2009, members of the Bachidubi Embera community filed a tutela that detailed how they had not been consulted about Mandé Norte. Later that year, the Constitutional Court ruled in a landmark decision that the state had not consulted affected communities and that, due to the gravity of the mine's expected harm to the communities, the case demanded FPIC.[32] Specifically, the court found the impacts of Mandé Norte on Colombian communities to be as significant as those that the IACHR had ruled warranted FPIC in its *Saramaka People v. Surinam* decision. Taking into account this resemblance, the Constitutional Court found that the Mandé Norte case required that principles of good faith and free and informed consent govern the prior consultation process.[33]

31. Sentence T-769-09, Section I; Congote Gutiérrez 11/29/2012; and Velasco Jaramillo 2014, 143.

32. Sentence T-769-09, especially Section II.6.3; Rodríguez 2014, 189; and Interview with Gloria Amparo Rodríguez; Bogotá, July 6, 2016 (Interview C18).

33. Sentence T-769-09, Section II.6.3.

OUTLIERS

Three mining conflicts that involved mobilizing by insider communities serve as outliers in this study: the successful struggles to prevent the Quilish expansion project in Peru and the development of the Colombian Cosigo and Peruvian Río Blanco mines. Activist groups in these conflicts did not use the EIA hearing or prior consultation. In each of the cases, the state suspended the project before planning either participatory process; insiders therefore could not organize through or around the institutions.

Communities did, however, take advantage of available participatory institutions. Indigenous communities participated in a prior consultation to establish a protected national park that made Cosigo infeasible. Organizers submitted to the state written comments on the Quilish and Río Blanco projects, and, in the Río Blanco conflict, residents participated in EIA workshops and coordinated an informal popular consultation.

Cosigo

The Canadian Cosigo Frontier Mining Corporation's open-pit gold mine project was shelved long before Colombia's interior ministry would have consulted the impacted Indigenous communities about the mine. However, local communities still employed prior consultation, to create a national park so as to preempt large-scale mining in the region. Consistent with this study's findings about how activist insiders in divided communities organize around prior consultation, a member of a local community that did not want the park claimed the consultation had been carried out incorrectly and thereby tried (unsuccessfully) to revert the parkland to its former status.

The Protected Park Debate and Cosigo's Arrival

Cosigo planned to construct its gold mine in a remote area in southeastern Colombia, near Brazil. The mine promised to produce two million ounces of high-quality gold. The Cosigo site was in the municipality of Taraira in the Vaupés department and neighbored two towns in the department of Amazonas (*El Tiempo* 4/30/2014, 9/24/2014).

The possibility of the mine prompted local Indigenous communities to launch a park project, to prevent the Cosigo development through environmental protections. Notably, the idea of instituting a park had existed for decades (*Semana* 5/21/2011). Before Cosigo's arrival, communities ruled out that avenue, viewing it as a threat to their autonomy, in two ways. First, the central state, and not local communities, oversaw SPNN (Rodríguez-Franco

2017, 150–53). Second, because "conservation"—a main objective of national parks—was associated with the preservation of spaces as pristine,[34] communities thought that a park could interfere with their traditional economy, which included hunting and fishing.[35] In important ways to protect those traditional practices from the impacts of informal mining, instead of pursuing a park, local communities expanded their resguardo. The local Association of Yaigojé Apaporis Indigenous Leaders (Asociación de Capitanes Indígenas de Yaigojé Apaporis, ACIYA), and Fundación Gaia Amazonas, an NGO that had long-standing presence in the area, achieved the resguardo expansion in 1998.[36]

Communities finally embraced the park concept once Cosigo arrived and, in 2007, began offering community leaders gifts in return for their support for the mine, which was to be constructed at the site of a sacred waterfall.[37] By that time, the communities found the park route less worrisome due to changes in the meaning of conservation; the concept had come to encompass communities living in and from parks and participating in park management.[38]

Conflict over the Park

ACIYA and Gaia Amazonas successfully led the park initiative, using prior consultation. From mid-2007 to mid-2009, local communities discussed and settled on the park plan, requested a prior consultation, and participated in socialization, internal deliberations, and the actual consultation. In October 2009, MAVDT established Yaigojé Apaporis National Park (Parque Nacional Natural Yaigojé Apaporis, PNNYA), Colombia's third largest national park (*El Tiempo* 7/13/2011, 4/30/2014; Rodríguez-Franco 2017, 162–66).

Conflict arose when, two days after MAVDT's decision, Cosigo obtained a mining title for exploration in the park. Communities represented by ACIYA challenged the title transfer. However, that five Apaporis communities had not wanted PNNYA provided Cosigo a proxy—a local community leader—for a tutela process. That individual claimed in the tutela filing that the park consultation had been unrepresentative, to try

34. "It was a 'conservation' without people [*sin gente*]." Interview with a former Fundación Gaia Amazonas lawyer; by phone from Bogotá, August 5, 2016 (Interview C19).

35. *Semana* 5/21/2011; and Interview C19.

36. Rodríguez-Franco 2017, 150–53; and Interview C19.

37. Rodríguez-Franco 2017, 153–56; and Interview with a lawyer at Fundación Gaia Amazonas who had worked for the organization during the Cosigo conflict; by phone from Bogotá, August 5, 2016 (Interview C20).

38. Interview C19.

to nullify the park status and facilitate the Cosigo mine (Rodríguez-Franco 2017, 166–68).

The tutela was denied at all three levels of the judicial process. When the case reached the Constitutional Court, three court magistrates traveled to PNNYA to speak with community members and assess the quality of the prior consultation process. In 2014, the court upheld the PNNYA consultation and ordered the immediate suspension of all mining activities in the park (*El Tiempo* 9/24/2014; Rodríguez-Franco 2017, 168).

Río Blanco

The main period of organizing against the Peruvian Río Blanco mine project occurred during the development of the EIA, though still before the state would have programmed an EIA hearing.

Environmental licensing shaped the Río Blanco conflict substantially. The mining company and the state were looking ahead to the EIA when they pursued dialogue with communities, which began organizing only after the company had submitted the EA for exploration privileges. In addition, communities and their allies criticized the project at EIA workshops and in written comments on a draft of the EIA.

Most prominently, communities used protest and an informal popular consultation to prevent the development of Río Blanco. Local opposition continued to hold up the mine project when research for this study was concluding.

Communities Primed for Conflict

Minera Coripacha S.A. discovered the Río Blanco copper-molybdenum deposit in Piura in 1994. Minera Majaz S.A.—a subsidiary of the British company Monterrico Metals—bought the project in 2002 and then, in June 2003, transferred it to the newly formed Río Blanco Copper Limited. The foreign-owned mine project was in international borderlands, near Ecuador; the project was allowed by a government decree that declared it of national interest. Total investment for the open-pit Río Blanco mine was estimated at $1.5 billion. Project development was expected to begin in 2008 and extraction in 2010 (De Echave et al. 2009, 49–50; Gustafsson 2018, 78).

The Río Blanco project area was conducive to mining conflict. The mine threatened the important agricultural economies of Piura and of the mine site, which spanned the communities of Yanta in the Ayabaca province and Segunda y Cajas in Huancabamba (Bebbington et al. 2007, 13–14; A. Bebbington 2012, 72–73; Gustafsson 2018, 74). Communities also worried that the mine could be a first step in Piura's transformation into a mining region by bringing more mining investment, in following with development goals of the national and regional governments (Bebbington et al. 2007, 15; Gustafsson 2018, 78–79).

Added to Río Blanco's serious consequences for agriculture, another factor that contributed to mobilizing against the mine was a strong civil society. The Tambo Grande conflict, also in Piura, had produced activists and groups that participated in the struggle against Río Blanco, including Red Muqui, a national network of NGOs that helped communities affected by mining (Bebbington et al. 2007, 17; Gustafsson 2018, 80). In addition, Piura's rondas campesinas had ties to the powerful rondas of neighboring Cajamarca (Gustafsson 2018, 76–77)—a relationship worth noting in part because Cajamarca communities, which had experience with large-scale mining, believed that Río Blanco could contaminate water flowing into their region (Bebbington et al. 2007, 22).

The Land-Use Permissions Debate

Yanta and Segunda y Cajas argued throughout the Río Blanco conflict that Majaz had not followed proper procedures to obtain land permissions for exploration, and hence that any work on the project was illegal. The company lacked the required approval from each community's general assembly (*asamblea general*) and an affirmative vote by at least two-thirds of each community (Defensoría del Pueblo 2006, 4–5, 7– 9; see also Bebbington et al. 2007, 21–23).

In January 2003, Majaz submitted the project EA, for exploration privileges. After reviewed the submission, DGAA requested more information from the company, including evidence that the firm had negotiated surface rights with local communities. In response, Majaz presented agreements it had made in 2002 with community leaders in Yanta and Segunda y Cajas (leaving out the general assemblies; Defensoría del Pueblo 2006, 7–9; Bebbington et al. 2007, 23); and referred to a 1997 agreement between Segunda y Cajas and Minera Coripacha S.A. that had given the firm exploration, construction, and extractive rights (Defensoría del Pueblo 2006, 6–7, 9; see also Bebbington et al. 2007, 40–41). MINEM approved the EA in late November 2003 (De Echave et al. 2009, 51).

Distressed by Majaz's exploration plans, Segunda y Cajas and Yanta held assemblies in May 2003 and January 2004, respectively. At the meetings, the communities rescinded any permissions their leaders had conferred to the company in 2002 and called for its departure. The communities followed up by filing complaints with MINEM (Bebbington et al. 2007, 23, 39). Yanta and Segunda y Cajas also communicated their stance against the project during EIA workshops held in Segunda y Cajas, in August 2003; and in Yanta, in January 2004 (De Echave et al. 2009, 51; Gustafsson 2018, 86–87).

Protests and Collapsed Dialogues

The two main waves of mobilizing against Río Blanco took place in 2004 and 2005. In April 2004, community members held a three-day march to the company encampment, where police officers killed an activist with a tear-gas grenade. In the coming months, organizing continued, one visible event being the kidnapping of company employees by ronderos (De Echave et al. 2009, 54–55; Gustafsson 2018, 91–92).

Piura's regional president, César Trelles Lara, responded to the April 2004 march by creating the Río Blanco Negotiation Table (Mesa de Concertación Río Blanco) to help facilitate the project and incorporate more participation into the development of the EIA. The roundtable, formed in July 2004, was short-lived; community representatives withdrew, resentful that the body included few community representatives, left out the rondas campesinas, and neglected the themes of environmental impacts and the (il)legality of the company's exploration privileges (A. Bebbington 2012, 75; Gustafsson 2018, 92–93).

The second noteworthy mobilization against Río Blanco erupted in July 2005. Three thousand people marched to the mining camp. They were met by national police and private security forces. Two protesters were killed in the consequent violence, and thirty-two people were detained in the next two days. The physical and psychological harm to detainees attracted international attention, including from European NGOs that would help bring a human rights case against Monterrico Metals before the High Court in London (A. Bebbington 2012, 75–76; Gustafsson 2018, 94).

After the 2005 events, the company and the central government—through its regional representatives—tried to manipulate the local political environment to facilitate Río Blanco's development. They supported the formation of local groups that rivaled existing civil-society organizations. This strategy contributed to community divisions while also hardening the antimine position and militancy of certain groups, most notably ronderos. A regional coalition against mining formed of Yanta and Segunda y Cajas, campesino groups, and subnational governments. The Front for the Sustainable Development of the Northern Border of Peru (Frente por el Desarrollo Sostenible de la Frontera Norte del Perú, FDSFNP) led the movement (Gustafsson 2018, 104–7).

The central government initiated a dialogue on Río Blanco in 2006. The inclusion of the FDSFNP—formed the same year—made the endeavor more representative relative to the 2004 roundtable. However, as in those previous negotiations, the 2006 agenda omitted the theme of land permissions and communities' associated insistence that the company leave. Deadlock caused MINEM to give up on the dialogue after three meetings (De Echave et al. 2009, 62–63; Gustafsson 2018, 82, 114–15).

When the 2006 talks collapsed, the FDSFNP, aided by the Defensoría del Pueblo, concentrated on the company's unsanctioned presence in Yanta and Segunda y Cajas. In two reports, the Defensoría maintained that the 2002 agreements had not followed correct procedure and argued that Segunda y Cajas's 1997 agreement with Coripacha was irrelevant, as Coripacha no longer owned the project. In the end MINEM responded to the matter by denying, in 2006, that community permission was needed for the company to carry out exploration.[39]

The Informal Popular Consultation and Project Suspension

A 2007 informal popular consultation stalled Río Blanco. The FDSFNP initiative utilized the consulta vecinal, as activists had done in the Tambo Grande case.

The FDSFNP knew that the vote outcome could not be enforced. Indeed, days before the consultation, the national elections agency (the Jurada Nacional de Elecciones) deemed it nonbinding (De Echave et al. 2009, 68–69; Gustafsson 2018, 116). Nevertheless, the state and company tried to block the vote. Monterrico Metals offered to establish an $80 million development fund. The Piura government tried to make the local consultation regional. In the central government, the vice minister of mines spoke out against the consultation, and the education ministry prohibited voting at schools. The consultation went forward on September 16, 2007, in three districts. Ninety-eight percent of participants voted against Río Blanco (De Echave et al. 2009, 69–71).

After the consulta vecinal, the prime minister initiated yet another dialogue process, which failed due to participants' conflicting goals: the FDSFNP remained adamant that the company did not hold land-use rights, whereas MINEM focused on details about Río Blanco's development (Gustafsson 2018, 120–21).

In 2007, a Chinese consortium led by Zijin Mining acquired Monterrico Metals and, with it, Río Blanco (A. Bebbington 2012, 77). The new owners persevered in the effort to acquire an environmental license for the mine (García 12/30/2013). Groups associated with Red Muqui took advantage of participatory channels by submitting comments on a draft EIA (A. Bebbington 2012, 78). Río Blanco Copper continued infiltrating and weakening civil society—for instance by investing in local social programs. As in previous years, that maneuver deepened ronderos' animosity toward the mine. People who rejected the mine, including subnational political officials, had as an important reference the 2007 popular consultation, on the basis of which they

39. Defensoría del Pueblo 2006; Bebbington et al. 2007, 32, 40; De Echave et al. 2009, 63–64; and A. Bebbington 2012, 77.

thought Río Blanco should be canceled (*Servindi* 7/12/2018, 6/8/2020; *El Comercio* 4/24/2019). In late 2020, the project remained at a standstill due to community resistance, and the company had yet to submit the EIA for review (Observatorio de Conflictos Mineros en el Perú 2020, 13–14; *Business News Americas* 11/26/2020).

Quilish

Whereas the Cosigo and Río Blanco conflicts were over new mines, in a final outlier case, activists stopped a mine expansion: the Quilish project, to expand the Peruvian Yanacocha mine. Communities blocked the project at the exploration stage through protest.

Project Opposition

Minera Yanacocha's plan to extract from Mount Quilish (Cerro Quilish) prompted widespread outrage, despite the company's history of successfully co-opting local communities; in general, community organizing over Yanacocha's operations had been disjointed (De Echave et al. 2009, 78–81).

Opposition to the Quilish project emerged in 1999, taking the form of intermittent mobilizations. It would then consolidate, amassing farmers, rondas campesinas, university students, unions, and different urban sectors in the city of Cajamarca. The regional movement was encouraged by the framing of Quilish as an intangible aquifer and sacred mountain, and of mining and gold as inherently incompatible with the protection of water. Also contributing to the broad, intense reaction to the Quilish project were two events that alarmed communities about Yanacocha's environmental and social practices: a mercury spill in June 2000 and the company's poor handling of it; and the sudden death of large populations of trout, in January 2001 (Lingán 2008, 44–46; De Echave et al. 2009, 81–84; Arce 2014, 88–91; Li 2015, chs. 2, 3).

There were several attempts at dialogue over the course of the Quilish conflict, including three roundtables that together engaged Yanacocha, civil society, subnational political authorities, and ministerial representatives (Lingán 2008, 47–51, 54–56; De Echave et al. 2009, 85–87, 92–93).

The Issuance and Withdrawal of Exploration Privileges

The two major periods of protest against the Quilish development occurred in 2001 and 2004 (Lingán 2008, 33). The 2001 trout incident in the district of Bambamarca, in the Hualgayoc province, ignited a March 2001 mobilization, led by the Hualgayoc rondas campesinas. Months later, in September, activists set fire to Yanacocha's offices in the city of Cajamarca (GRUFIDES 8/21/2004; Lingán 2008, 45–46).

The 2004 protests were tied to a multiyear struggle over Yanacocha's exploration privileges. MINEM authorized the Quilish exploration EA in May 2000 (Lingán 2008, 45). In the wake of the EA approval and the mercury spill, the Cajamarca provincial government declared Quilish a protected reserve in October 2000 to prevent the mine expansion (with Municipal Ordinance 012-2000-CMPC). Yanacocha challenged the ordinance, claiming that municipalities did not have the authority to institute protected areas. Two courts ruled against the firm, but in 2003 the Constitutional Tribunal upheld Yanacocha's rights to the concession and to exploration, on the grounds that new protected areas could not have retroactive effects (Lingán 2008, 45–46; Arce 2014, 92–93).

After the tribunal issued its decision, Yanacocha needed permission from MINEM to resume exploration. Civil-society actors used the available participatory mechanism: in January 2004, groups that included the Peruvian NGOs Ecovida, GRUFIDES, and the Ecumenical Foundation for Development and Peace (Fundación Ecuménica para el Desarrollo y la Paz) submitted comments on a MINEM document describing the exploration. The organizations found MINEM's product incomplete and not credible (GRUFIDES 8/21/2004; Lingán 2008, 45; De Echave et al. 2009, 87).

In July 2004, MINEM gave Yanacocha permission to recommence exploration (Arce 2014, 93; GRUFIDES 9/4/2016), and shortly thereafter Yanacocha brought exploration equipment to Quilish. Amid mobilizing within the local population, an August 2004 dialogue between movement leaders and MINEM representatives failed (Arce 2014, 93–94).

The Quilish conflict reached its height during two weeks of protest in September 2004. Activism scaled up from a roadblock, to the cutting off of the water supply to the city of Cajamarca, to a region-wide strike that caused Yanacocha to suspend its operations. Tens of thousands of people participated in the protests. On September 16, MINEM reversed its approval of the Quilish exploration, directly after which organizers lifted the strike (De Echave et al. 2009, 87, 92; Arce 2014, 93–98).

SUMMARY

This chapter has analyzed activism within insider communities—that is, communities eligible to participate in formal participatory spaces for new extraction. With the exception of communities in the three outlier cases, insiders confronted the challenge of articulating their positions on planned development, at the prior consultation or EIA hearing stage. In response to this articulation challenge, they varied in how they drew on the participatory institutions. Some communities prevented participatory events, others participated in them, and still others cast doubt on the legitimacy of a completed participatory process.

The chapter explained this variation in community strategies by focusing importantly on whether the lines defining community representatives in relation to the larger community were debated. Where representation was not contested, cohesive insider communities interrupted, postponed, or boycotted participatory processes. By contrast, local activists who competed with pro-development insiders could not interfere with participatory events. Instead, they either participated in the EIA public hearing, to be heard over project advocates, or, in the Mandé Norte conflict, decried a faulty prior consultation that had included only pro-development community members.

This treatment of insider conflicts completes the book's analysis of the thirty cases under study for purposes of explaining community strategies. Chapter 7 will review the three challenges that communities in extractive zones encountered, and how those challenges were caused or exacerbated by boundary struggles. It also will explore potential intersections among different community characteristics, goals, and strategies, based on an examination of the full conflict sample.

PART IV

Conclusions

CHAPTER 7

Boundary Struggles in Latin America's Extractive Zones

This book has shown how participatory institutions shape social conflict over new hydrocarbon and mining development in Latin America. It centers on the ways local communities in extractive zones use participatory institutions: they voice complaints within formally provided spaces of participation, and mobilize around them. Following a summary of the book's findings, this chapter extends the analysis in two ways. First, using the sample of thirty conflicts, it explores relationships among several factors that have received attention in the literature on conflict in mining and hydrocarbons—community cohesion, goals, experience with extraction, and strategies with regard to participatory institutions.

Second, the chapter examines insights from the study about the power of institutional procedures, including those that appear empty of substance. The discussion highlights the potential for tight, ongoing linkages between, on one hand, formal institutional procedures, and on the other, multiple behaviors by societal actors that those procedures may effect. It also elaborates on how strictly procedural participation can be grounded in lines and categories that trigger and exacerbate societal conflict, with ramifications for state building: ultimately, the procedures that states have implemented to organize and manage society in extractive regions to further hydrocarbon and mining development, might make such control elusive, due to boundary contestation.

The Politics of Extraction. Maiah Jaskoski, Oxford University Press. © Oxford University Press 2022.
DOI: 10.1093/oso/9780197568927.003.0007

SUMMARY OF THE ARGUMENT: CONTESTED BOUNDARIES AND COMMUNITY CHALLENGES

This research identified three challenges to participation with which communities in extractive areas grapple. In the study's sample of thirty hydrocarbon and mining conflicts in Bolivia, Colombia, and Peru, the particular challenge a community confronted helped explain how the community used a participatory institution in its mobilizing. Each challenge was either intensified or caused by disagreement over a boundary that determined institutional access.

The book first analyzed conflicts in which communities encountered the *event initiation challenge*, or the challenge of prompting a participatory process. That challenge was present in Colombian cases in which the pertinent participatory institution was the popular consultation or the EIA hearing, because regulations required the submission of requests to activate either process. Faced with the event initiation challenge, mobilized communities had the single option of organizing through the participatory institutions by asking for a participatory process and then taking part in it. That sequence of events played out in six Colombian extractive conflicts—those surrounding the Lorito 1 oil well, the Angostura and La Colosa mines, the Nogal and Odisea 3D oil exploration projects, and fracking in San Martín.

The event initiation challenge was more severe where actors disputed the boundary that separated subnational from central state jurisdictions. Colombian municipalities claimed the authority to hold popular consultations about mining and hydrocarbon development, whereas extractive firms and the national government maintained that only the central state had a say over subsoil resources. Given this boundary contestation, communities rallied energetically to hold popular consultations on extraction, most notably in the La Colosa and Odisea 3D cases. In addition, communities achieved public hearings in their home municipalities for Angostura and for Lorito 1 only through considerable mobilizing.

The book also analyzed the *inclusion challenge*, experienced by communities left out of the participatory stage of project approvals. This challenge arose from disagreement over boundaries that demarcated Indigenous communities and the areas of influence and direct influence of projects. Communities claimed that the state (1) inaccurately had defined them as residing outside of areas impacted by development, and (2) in that way unjustly had denied them participatory opportunities.

Confronted with the inclusion challenge, outsider communities demanded the right to participate. Their timing and tactics depended on the rigidity of the geographic boundaries in question. If the lines were non-rigid—that is, if there was legal or regulatory latitude to debate a boundary's placement—then communities fought for inclusion after the fact, using legal-administrative arguments and processes. Peruvian communities situated outside of EIA-defined areas of influence or direct influence (in the Conga and Santa Ana conflicts, respectively), contended that they would experience significant project impacts. Based on various connections to lands, Indigenous communities claimed rights to impacted areas in the Peruvian cases of Afrodita and Block 116, and in the conflict over expanded production in Colombia's Putumayo oil fields.

Bolivia differed from its counterparts. Indigenous territorial boundaries in that country were rigid, because only communities with legal title to impacted land could participate in prior consultations. Similarly, in the Magallanes gas conflict, it was impracticable for the Colombian U'wa to claim rights to lands beyond their resguardo, which the state had expanded. In these cases of rigid boundaries, Indigenous communities could not contest effectively their outsider status after the state had finished reviewing a project. Instead, they physically obstructed development to demand inclusion, at or just after the participatory moment. Communities took this approach in the Magallanes conflict and in the Bolivian cases of the Percheles and El Dorado fields, the El Dorado and Timboy X-2 wells, and the Río Grande and Gran Chaco plants.

A third and final challenge, which was encountered by insider communities, was the *articulation challenge*, or the undertaking of expressing a position on new extraction. This challenge was made greater by disagreement over the boundary that defined an impacted community's representative(s) relative to the overall community—that is, the line that determined who legitimately could speak on behalf of a community. This boundary contestation was tied directly to community divisions over extraction.

Where community representation was uncontested, communities held up extraction by interfering with or refusing to take part in participatory events, a strategy pursued in the Ranchería and Samoré cases in Colombia; the Bolivian San Antonio conflict; and the Camisea, Tambo Grande, and Tía María conflicts in Peru.

In contrast to situations of community cohesion, discord within an insider community over its representative(s) meant that actors amenable to the planned extractive development showed up to participatory events, which consequently proceeded. The strategy of activist insiders in divided settings depended on the formal rules of the applicable institution and, specifically, the definition of participation. Participation within the EIA hearing structure was the holding of a public meeting. That institutional design feature limited groups in fractured communities to a single option: participating actively in the meeting, to be heard over residents that held other positions on extraction, as observed in the Las Bambas and Quellaveco conflicts in Peru. Unlike EIA hearings, prior consultations consisted of community leaders attending meetings and signing agreements. The state exploited community divisions by consulting community members who accepted a mine project, leaving other residents to condemn, afterward, that exclusionary process, in the Colombian Mandé Norte case.

COHESION, GOALS, STRATEGY, AND EXTRACTIVE EXPERIENCE

Chapter 1 situated this research within the literature on extractive conflict. It devoted special attention to studies about how participatory institutions may streamline the approval of new mining and hydrocarbon development, by dividing communities and deterring them from trying to prevent extraction. This section revisits these dynamics. It first reviews potential causal relationships among community cohesion, goals, and uses of participatory institutions, while considering a fourth variable: extractive experience. It then explores empirical relationships, using the thirty cases in the book.

Causal Connections in the Literature

As introduced in Chapter 1, the literature on participation and conflict in mining and hydrocarbons has evolved mainly as in-depth case studies and small-*n* comparisons. We can pull from that body of work possible causal relationships among community cohesion, goals, and mobilizing in and around formal participatory institutions.

Studies suggest that cohesion and participation strategies may interact. Engagement in formally provided participatory events might encourage cohesion because, as examined by McAdam et al. (2010), communities come to know and take a position on extraction through participation. Yet scholars also have observed the opposite: states cleaving communities within participatory settings (e.g., Pellegrini and Ribera Arismendi 2012). Communities that choose to organize around rather than through formal participatory processes therefore might retain more cohesion than those that suffer divisions caused by participating. If we follow the logic of this more pessimistic view about participation and cohesion, the causal arrow might also point in the other direction, from cohesion to strategy: more cohesive communities might have enough strength to refuse to participate in established participatory events. For instance, Chapter 6 observed this causal connection for insider conflicts.

In terms of the relationship between strategy and goals, in some cases, communities that oppose extraction have found prior consultation and EIA hearings inadequate for not formally ascribing them power to influence development outcomes. Therefore, communities trying to prevent extraction have chosen to act outside of the institutions, by protesting or refusing to participate (e.g., Walter and Martinez-Alier 2010; Rodríguez-Garavito 2011; Li 2015). We can construct the reverse causal story, as well: over the course of the participatory process, companies and the state may co-opt participating communities and, in turn, change the latter's goal from thwarting extraction, to receiving compensation for the new hydrocarbon or mining development.

Work that is skeptical about the possibility of community empowerment within formal participatory frameworks also seems to suggest interactions between cohesion and goals: perhaps more unified communities have greater capacity to sustain an antiextractivist position in their interactions with companies and state agencies. Conversely, communities motivated to impede development could be more likely to retain their cohesion than communities focused on compensation or project adjustments.

A final possible correlation worth contemplating, though not addressed in Chapter 1, is that between goals and prior experience with extraction. Impacted communities in a region with an established mining or hydrocarbon industry might be accustomed to its impacts and thus not oppose new development (McAdam and Boudet 2012, 51, 182–83; Eisenstadt and West, especially 62 and ch. 4). If experience with hydrocarbon and mining development has complicated organizing against extraction, at the same time, impacted communities still could have unusually strong motivations to rein in future development. This was apparent in the case of Quilish, in which residents of Cajamarca who resented Yanacocha's poor environmental record caused the cancellation of a mine expansion.

Empirical Relationships

The book's conflict sample provides the opportunity to explore possible relationships among cohesion, goals, extractive experience, and participation, through medium-*n* analysis. This discussion uses the scoring presented in Table 7.1 of the thirty conflicts, along the four dimensions.

Cohesion and Goals

Data on the full sample do not align with the expectation that greater community cohesion and the goal of impeding extraction will go together. Community divisions caused by extraction were central in twelve (57 percent) of the twenty-one cases of community opposition to planned development and in five of the nine (56 percent) conflicts in which activists worked toward different aims.

Table 7.1 COHESION, GOALS, STRATEGY, AND EXTRACTIVE EXPERIENCE IN THE THIRTY CONFLICTS

Use of participatory institution	**Goal of mobilizing**		
	Impede extraction	Compensation	Mitigation and either project design change or compensation
Organizing through	*Fracking in San Martín* *Quellaveco* Odisea 3D *Nogal* *Angostura* La Colosa Lorito 1	*Las Bambas*	
Refusal to participate/ interference	Diversion of Ranchería *Tía María* Samoré Tambo Grande	San Antonio	*Camisea Block 56*
Contestation of process after the fact	*Conga* *Afrodita* *Lote 116* *Santa Ana* *Mandé Norte*		Putumayo fields
Direct action to demand participation	Magallanes Timboy X-2	*Percheles and El Dorado fields* *El Dorado exploratory wells* *Río Grande plant* Gran Chaco plant	
N/A (outliers)	Quilish *Cosigo* *Río Blanco*		Gasoducto del Sur†

Note: Conflicts above the diagonal line in each cell involved mobilized communities that had previous, direct experience with large-scale extraction. Italics indicate that community divisions were central to the extractive conflict.

†In the Gasoducto del Sur case, activists focused on project design changes and not also on mitigation.

Extractive Experience and Goals

The data do, however, support the idea that experience with extraction makes a community less likely to try to impede future mining and hydrocarbon development. In six of the sixteen conflicts (38 percent) in which communities had experience with large-scale extraction, they pursued goals other than the prevention of development, as compared to only two of the fourteen communities (14 percent) without such experience.

Interestingly, in several cases, communities that had been exposed to impacts from mining or hydrocarbon development organized against projects at least partly *because of* those experiences and concerns about future contamination—for example, in the Magallanes, Odisea 3D, Quilish, Ranchería, and Timboy X-2 conflicts.

Cohesion, Goals, and Strategic Use of Participatory Institutions

Finally, in the conflict sample, community strategy with regard to participatory institutions is correlated with goals, but not with cohesion. Communities opposed extraction in seven of the eight cases (88 percent) in which they mobilized through the relevant participatory institution, and in eleven of the eighteen cases (61 percent) in which they organized around it; that is, communities that participated in formal structures were somewhat more likely to reject the new extractive plans. Although this study's paradigm incorporates community cohesion to explain community uses of participatory institutions—specifically, splits between insiders and outsiders and among insiders—cohesion on its own did not predict strategy within the full sample. Community divisions caused by extraction were paramount in five of the eight (62 percent) conflicts in which communities participated in formally provided channels and in ten of the eighteen (56 percent) cases of communities acting around participatory institutions.

Summary

This examination of community cohesion, goals, extractive experience, and uses of participatory institutions reveals an expected finding: communities that had previous experience with extraction and its impacts were less likely to try to hinder new development. The absence of certain other relationships is noteworthy. At odds with the literature, extraction seemed equally divisive when comparing communities that tried to stave off extraction to those that worked toward other ends. Particularly relevant to this research are observations about cohesion, goals, and uses of participatory institutions. Communities that took part in formal participatory processes were not more likely to be organizationally weaker, or to be convinced or coerced into accepting extraction, relative to communities that organized around participatory institutions.

Above all, the analysis here and throughout the book demonstrates how communities have utilized formal participatory institutions powerfully, in creative ways. In cohesive and divided contexts alike, communities strategically employed the EIA hearing, prior consultation, and popular consultation to help achieve their objectives, which ranged from hindering extraction to changing the design of extractive projects to reaping material benefits from hydrocarbon and mining development. In the thirty conflicts, formal participatory institutions that in "normal times" might serve as tools of the state and of extractive firms to co-opt, weaken, and control communities were assets for mobilized communities.

Measurement Choices

A brief discussion about measurement choices concludes this empirical analysis of the sample. Because the book already has examined in detail communities' varying strategies, the comments address the other three dimensions.

Experience with Large-Scale Extraction

Table 7.1 captures whether communities were accustomed to impacts from large-scale mining or hydrocarbon development. Experience is measured as the nearby presence of an extractive operation or project. Several conflicts are classified as involving communities that had no direct experience with extraction, even though the communities had substantial knowledge about its impacts through their ties to communities in nearby areas impacted by hydrocarbon or mining development (e.g., in the Lorito 1, Nogal, and Río Blanco cases).

Goals

When it comes to measuring goals, one distinction in the literature, made by Moisés Arce, is between the aims of impeding extraction, "demands for rights"; and obtaining services or compensation payments, "demands for services" (2014, 50–54). Pellegrini and Arsel differentiate between the "green objectives" of reducing environmental harms—for instance through mitigation, limits to extraction in certain areas, or blocking extraction entirely; "brown motives," to include investments in the region; and a combination of the two (2018, 213–14). Javier Arellano Yanguas identifies four possible community goals: (1) the prevention of extraction, (2) the implementation of environmental safeguards, (3) compensation, and (4) changes to the formula for allocating state revenue from extraction (2014, 64–65).

Drawing on previous typologies, Table 7.1 denotes whether communities strived to avert the proposed extraction (twenty-one cases), sought compensation (six cases), or fought for some other outcome—project revisions (Gasoducto del Sur), revisions with environmental mitigation (Putumayo), or compensation and mitigation (Camisea Block 56).

The sorting of cases according to goals in Table 7.1 is necessarily crude, given empirical complexities. For example, sometimes communities adjusted their focus over time. Communities impacted by Tía María first complained about the project's water plan, insisting on the construction of a desalination plant. Similarly, early in the Conga conflict, the state and company had a window of opportunity to negotiate project elements with activists, including the project's use of certain mountain lakes. Communities in each of the two conflicts eventually opposed the project entirely. In Moquegua, communities that rejected the Quellaveco mine later participated in a regional roundtable and agreed to a new project design.[1]

As a final note about the characterization of goals, Table 7.1 emphasizes community objectives with regard to planned extraction and its impacts, and not another prominent aspiration in many of the cases: to secure the right to participate. This measurement choice does not intend to downplay the importance to many communities of gaining access to formal participatory processes, a theme incorporated explicitly into the book's causal framework. Specifically, outsider communities confronting the inclusion challenge struggled for the right to participate; Colombian residents mobilized to initiate EIA hearings and popular consultations; and Embera communities challenged the legitimacy of an unrepresentative consultation process in the Mandé Norte case.

Cohesion

The measure for cohesion employed in Table 7.1 is whether community divisions brought on by extraction were key in the unfolding of a conflict.

Level of cohesion mattered a great deal in this study, with fissures between insiders and outsiders and within insider communities proving decisive. Beyond the communal fragmentation that is built into the book's paradigm, other divisions came through in the analysis that are captured in Table 7.1. Extraction threatened cohesion in mining and hydrocarbon areas by straining relations within some outsider communities. That logic was evident in the

1. Arellano Yanguas (2014, 65) and Gustafsson (2018, 9) also discuss challenges to classifying activist goals in extractive conflict.

Bolivian Takovo Mora conflicts: the APG broke with Takovo Mora and aligned with the Morales government in the cases of the Río Grande plant and the Percheles and El Dorado gas fields. The Río Grande conflict also created serious internal division within Takovo Mora over whether to accept as legitimate a prior consultation process that concluded after the issuance of an environmental license. Takovo Mora fractured again in the El Dorado wells case, resulting in the temporary appointment of a MAS supporter to lead the capitanía.

Even some insider communities that were sufficiently cohesive to take a unified stance against extraction underwent splits over the course of conflicts. The Peruvian Machiguenga acted with cohesion during the Camisea Block 56 conflict, including through coordinated efforts by their two main, competing representative bodies. However, community leaders grew distrustful of the organizations and negotiated compensation directly with consortium members. Likewise, while opposition to Tía María dominated local and regional politics surrounding the mine, Southern Copper drew enough citizens to the second EIA hearing to give the event the appearance of legitimacy, for EIA approval.

Table 7.1 omits declining community cohesion that was not pivotal in the conflicts but that nonetheless evinces the divisive nature of hydrocarbons and mining. For example, the table scores the Colombian Samoré and Ranchería conflicts as cases of community cohesion, though extraction called attention to, and contributed to, intracommunity differences within both the U'wa and the Wayúu. In the Samoré case, Occidental's early conversations with the U'wa weakened their unity. Subsequently, the U'wa's two main, cohesive organizations diverged in how they employed prior consultation to oppose oil development: one agreed to being consulted, whereas the other did not. Impacted Wayúu communities retained internal unity throughout the Ranchería conflict. However, the Cerrejón expansion separated the few communities that opposed the project from the majority, which had accepted company gifts.

Significantly, in these cases of conflict over hydrocarbons and mining, divisions among and within communities did not necessarily reduce the influence of activists. In fact, groups in fragmented communities sometimes held up extraction in part *because* divisions fueled mobilizing (e.g., in the Peruvian mining cases of Las Bambas, Río Blanco, and Santa Ana).

THE POWER OF PROCEDURE: EXTENSIONS

Neither EIA hearings nor prior consultation formally offered communities the possibility of vetoing or even altering extractive plans; and the norms underpinning Colombia's local popular consultation did not outline how municipalities might use the referendum to vote down large-scale hydrocarbon and mining development. Nonetheless, communities have utilized these participatory institutions to affect extraction. Communities that from the start pursued compensation and/or social investments obtained such commitments in the conflicts over Las Bambas, San Antonio, the Percheles and El Dorado fields, and the Gran Chaco and Río Grande plants. (In general, communities sought more compensation and other investments than they received.) Communities that fought extraction achieved the complete withdrawal of the project owner, and/or the cancellation or indefinite suspension of the project, in thirteen cases: Afrodita, Angostura, Block 116, Conga, Cosigo, the diversion of the Ranchería, La Colosa, Mandé Norte, Quilish, San Martín, Santa Ana, Tambo Grande, and Tía María. Antiproject communities delayed projects that later moved forward or that appeared positioned to do so in the future, in the cases of Lorito 1, Magallanes, Odisea 3D, Quellaveco, Río Blanco, and Samoré.

It is striking that "mere" participatory procedures mattered in the high-stakes realm of hydrocarbons and mining; one might expect wealthy companies and extractivist states to bypass or ignore inconvenient participatory procedures in their efforts to advance development. Yet even when trying to sidestep participation, state actors and companies justified doing so while respecting the procedural scaffolding of the institutions, especially the basic entitlement of impacted communities to participate. State agencies claimed that no Indigenous communities were present in project areas, and companies narrowly defined areas of influence. Occidental altered the Colombian Gibraltar 1 project to locate it outside of U'wa lands. Also in Colombia, companies and the central government went to great lengths to argue that applicable legal and regulatory structures ruled out municipal popular consultations in extractives, and to obstruct scheduled consultations.

The presence of participatory procedures also generated for states a new, arduous task: balancing the right of impacted communities to participate in hydrocarbons and mining, against national development interests. Colombia's Constitutional Court tackled tensions between Indigenous rights and development when it required prior consultation with the Nasa and Awá but did not, in the meantime, halt oil expansion in Puerto Asís, Putumayo. Similarly, the Colombian Consejo de Estado ruled that, after several years of trying to consult the U'wa about exploration in the Samoré oil block, the interior ministry had fulfilled the prior consultation requirement, and therefore Ecopetrol could move forward with the project. Courts in all three countries painstakingly defined levels and types of impacts that would justify allowing Indigenous communities to veto development.

In addition to demonstrating the power of participatory procedures to shape extractive conflict, this study also illuminates two facets of that power: (1) the linkage between the formal procedures, and the actual, varying community behavior that they support; and (2) the contentious lines and boundaries that form the basis of the procedures.

Stable Institutions with Multiple Uses

In this book, participatory institutions caused different community behaviors that were tightly bound to—though often not written into—the institutions' formal rules.

The connection between formal institutions and the ways communities use them demands that we move beyond scholarship on institutional change. While offering invaluable insights into how an institution might serve multiple purposes, that literature does not account for the trajectories of the extractive conflicts analyzed here. Studies of institutional change theorize how an institution that exhibits greater ambiguity in its formal rules should be more likely to serve more than one purpose, during the institutional change process (see Chapter 1). Yet the degree of precision in rules and categories did not predict the extent to which communities deviated from formal participatory procedures in this study's conflict sample. For instance, outsider Indigenous communities in Bolivia, Colombia, and Peru mobilized around prior consultation by challenging their outsider status, although inclusion in Bolivia depended on the unambiguous holding of title to land, whereas Indigenous land rights were debatable in the Colombian and Peruvian cases. In fact, where there was consensus on procedures—specifically, where all actors concerned agreed upon which participatory events were required, which communities were impacted, and who represented insider communities—insiders refused to participate in prior consultation and the EIA hearing, a use of the institutions not envisioned by their creators.

More fundamentally, rather than investigating institutional change, this research explores the connection between formal institutions that generally function as designed, and the ways communities organize through or around those institutions amid major conflict. Indeed, choices of communities in this book frequently related to dissatisfaction with the recognized institutions. For instance, several communities acted around prior consultation and EIA hearings because those institutions did not give them veto power. In sum, the legitimate, known rules of EIA hearings, prior consultation, and in Colombia, popular consultation, patterned community behavior.

Due to the identified relationship between formal rules and community strategies, the research does not treat community uses of participatory institutions as separate, informal institutions themselves. This analytical choice is consistent with research on informal institutions; communities' creative treatment of participatory institutions did not meet Helmke and Levitsky's threshold for informal institutions, "the violation of which generates some kind of external sanction" (2006, 7).

To theorize satisfactorily the multiple purposes that participatory institutions can serve, we might turn to work from literary theory, and specifically Caroline Levine's concept of "affordances." In *Forms: Whole, Rhythm, Hierarchy, Network*, Levine vividly introduces how a political institution can have different affordances, through her discussion of everyday objects:

> A doorknob affords . . . turning, pushing, and pulling. Designed things may also have unexpected affordances generated by imaginative users: we may hang signs or clothes on a doorknob, for example, or use a fork to pry open a lid, and so expand the intended affordances of an object. (Levine 2015, 6)

In Levine's terms, then, this book identifies and explains patterns in how communities activated different affordances of participatory institutions, in extractive conflict.

Boundary Struggles and State Building in Latin America's Extractive Zones

The power of participatory procedures in this book rested importantly on their underlying boundaries, and especially conflict around the drawing of those lines and the prioritization of some of the resulting categories over others. That conflict helped explain how communities appropriated participatory institutions in their resistance to state-sanctioned development in hydrocarbons and mining, often resulting in delayed or canceled development plans. That is, the participatory institutions that extractivist states have adopted to streamline hydrocarbon and mining development, have helped to hinder extraction.

The EIA hearing and prior consultation emphasize impacted territory and communities, bringing to the fore questions about what constitutes an impact, where to draw borders around projects and communities, and how to define Indigeneity. The two institutions also contain definitions of participation that generate disagreements about, in the case of EIA hearings, the minimum number of local residents that must attend a hearing; and, in prior consultation, which individuals speak on behalf of Indigenous communities. Colombian decentralization gave municipalities a say in their development trajectories, provoking debates about just how much authority municipalities have and, in particular, whether their power extends to the subsoil. Only after we resolve such issues pertaining to boundaries and associated categories can we answer questions of procedure: Was a participatory event appropriate? For participation that moved forward, were the actual representatives of a community, or enough community members, included, and therefore did the participatory process in fact take place? In short, state-drawn lines for purposes of participation in new extraction have been consequential in mining and hydrocarbon conflicts.

The dynamics of boundary conflict in extraction illustrate a broader phenomenon: the unanticipated outcomes of state initiatives to manage people and resources, as part of state building. In James C. Scott's *Seeing Like a State: How Certain Schemes to Improve the Human Condition Have Failed*, state building entails the creation of categories to make society and its resources "legible," for purposes of documenting, monitoring, and taxing the population (1998, 183). Scott's research brings to light how those top-down state ventures may cause surprising reactions in society that derail the original project. An aggressive Ethiopian resettlement project led to inefficient agriculture, because relocated populations lacked knowledge of their new surroundings that would have increased their effectiveness in farming (1998, 251). That mixed-use spaces were absent from Brazil's planned capital, Brasilia, caused people to live in the periphery of the sterile city, which they left underpopulated (1998, 129–30, 136–37).

In line with Scott, the introduction of participatory procedures—with accompanying lines and categories—has affected the politics of extraction in ways neither intended nor desired by state actors. The boundaries that underlie participatory procedures have produced, structured, and aggravated conflict. The very placement of the lines can cause strife over who represents communities, the policy jurisdiction of the municipality vis-à-vis the central state, and the reach of project impacts and communal territorial rights.

Added to the struggles that stand at the core of this study's analytical framework, conflicts in this book showed how extractivism incited other boundary tensions, which forced the state to choose between extraction and its contributions to national and subnational economies, and other ends. One such boundary defined international borderlands. In the Afrodita, Río Blanco, and Santa Ana mining conflicts, the Peruvian state weighed government interests in extraction, against constitutionally based national security interests in barring foreign enterprises from operating too close to the border.

In several conflicts, actors debated whether proposed hydrocarbon or mining development was in environmentally sensitive areas, a status that could rule out the extractive activities. Communities defended the original border of a national park, in the Peruvian Afrodita case. The Angostura project owner abandoned its Colombian mine site in response to a new demarcation of a páramo, the protection of which was reinforced by a Constitutional Court decision. Civil-society groups argued that the Caquetá department qualified as part of Colombia's Amazon region, to try to preclude oil extraction in the Nogal block. Communities established a protected park in the area of the Colombian Cosigo project and in that way thwarted the open-pit mine. The Cajamarca province tried to create a local protected park to preempt the Quilish expansion of Peru's Yanacocha mine, though unsuccessfully. In the case of the Conga expansion of Yanacocha, the regional government of Cajamarca tried, also in vain, to protect all basin headwaters in that region. In another regional effort, the Bucaramanga CAR defined a portion of the Santurbán páramo as a natural park to preclude the development of Angostura. Defining areas as off limits to extraction not only involved the definition of park boundaries, but also decisions about how much or whether to protect parkland; in Bolivia, sequential regulations opened previously protected areas to extraction.

Overall, then, the current era of extractivism has brought new challenges for Latin American states and state building in resource-rich areas of the region, by creating new boundaries and increasing the salience of certain existing ones. Those borders and related categories generate conflict, as communities in extractive zones call into question lines that delineate subnational policy jurisdictions, project impacts, environmentally protected areas, communal lands, and local authority structures.

APPENDIX A

Omission of the Tintaya/Antapaccay Conflict

During the case-selection phase of this study, the author omitted one potential conflict only after carrying out considerable research on it: a 2011–13 conflict in the Espinar province, in Cusco, Peru, over the Tintaya mine and its Antapaccay expansion project. This appendix discusses the conflict to substantiate its exclusion.

The author ruled out the case due to the timing of the conflict relative to the EIA process. This book analyzes extractive conflicts that took place up through the approval stage for new development. Although Espinar communities were apprehensive about Tintaya's ongoing environmental impacts while Antapaccay was under review, noteworthy activism—focused on both Tintaya and Antapaccay—began in 2011, more than a full year after MINEM already had approved, in July 2010, the Antapaccay EIA (RD 225-2010-MEM/AAM).

The Tintaya/Antapaccay mobilizing focused on the management of a large social investment fund associated with Tintaya, as well as the environmental and health impacts of the mine and of Antapaccay. The conflict was part of longer-term tensions over the social fund and Tintaya's environmental harms. Antapaccay moved forward during a lengthy dialogue that settled the 2011–13 conflict episode.

EARLY GRIEVANCES ABOUT TINTAYA, RESOLVED BY THE CONVENIO MARCO

The Tintaya social investment fund was a product of early conflict over the mine, in the 2000s. By that time, communities resented the relocations and environmental impacts associated with Tintaya. In the 1980s–1990s, communities moved to make way for the new mine. Many families found themselves without land or work and also disgruntled, as the company had paid low prices for land and coerced communities during the resettlements (Sanborn and Dammert 2013, 56; Flores Unzaga 2016, 27–28). Communities also had experienced contamination from Tintaya, which had become the third largest copper producer in Peru (Flores Unzaga 2016, 27).

As of the 2000s, Espinar communities displayed organizational capacity. They were advised by the Peruvian NGO CooperAcción (by invitation of the Espinar mayor) and were part of the Regional Coordinating Committee of Communities Affected by Mining (Coordinadora Regional de Comunidades Afectadas por la Minería, CORECAMI) Cusco, a founding member of CONACAMI (Sanborn and Dammert 2013, 56).

CONACAMI filed a complaint in 2000 with Oxfam Australia's mining ombudsman, on behalf of communities impacted by Tintaya, which belonged to the Anglo-Australian firm BHP Billiton. The complaint focused on relocation issues and water and land contamination (Sanborn and Dammert 2013, 56). The ombudsman responded by convening a roundtable of subnational political officials, residents of five impacted communities near the town of Espinar (the mine site), and representatives of BHP, CONACAMI, CooperAcción, and Oxfam America (Anguelovski 2011, 389; Sanborn and Dammert 2013, 56–57).

The dialogue process resulted in the 2003 "Framework Agreement" (Convenio Marco), according to which BHP would contribute at least $1.5 million annually to development and environmental protections in Espinar. In December 2004, roundtable participants signed a second agreement that created a social fund for investment in local communities. The fund was to be managed by the new Tintaya Foundation (Fundación Tintaya; Anguelovski 2011, 389–90; Sanborn and Dammert 2013, 57). The dialogue table and the Convenio Marco were viewed internationally as an emblematic success story of corporate social responsibility, due to the high quality of participation and negotiation, and because the process had led to sizable company investments in communities (e.g., Sanborn and Dammert 2013, 55, 57).

THE 2005 CONFLICT

Complaints about the Tintaya Foundation and the mine's impacts soon emerged. Communities not in the mine's immediate vicinity resented the management of the social funds; they wanted more investment throughout the province, a company commitment to local contracts and purchases, and an independent study on the mine's environmental impacts (Anguelovski

2011, 390; Sanborn and Dammert 2013, 57). In May 2005, between twenty-five hundred and ten thousand protesters took over BHP facilities, halting production. Several activists were injured, and the police processed seventy-five protest leaders for theft, disturbances, and other crimes. New talks between BHP and community leaders began in early June 2005. After weeks of negotiations, BHP agreed to review the content of the Convenio Marco, which was the central concern of protesters (Anguelovski 2011, 390).

The 2006 transfer of Tintaya to Xstrata Copper only exacerbated local tensions. Xstrata confronted preexisting dissatisfaction over the Convenio Marco, and new complaints. Communities posited that any transfer in ownership of the mine warranted a replacement agreement, to ground community relations with the new firm. In addition, people resented that Xstrata favored some groups over others, through its clientelistic management of foundation resources (Sanborn and Dammert 2013, 58; Pinto Herrera 2015, 176).

THE 2011–13 CONFLICT

Conflict broke out again in 2011. It peaked as major protests during mid-2012, when negotiations to revise the Convenio Marco collapsed. The protests erupted when Antapaccay was on the horizon. The expansion was expected to operate for twenty-two years; it was to produce 160,000 tons of copper per year for the first five years and 143,000 tons per year for the remaining seventeen. Xstrata pursued Antapaccay while preparing for the 2012 closure of Tintaya, due to the exhaustion of the mine's reserves (Sanborn and Dammert 2013, 55, 58, 60; Zeisser Polatsik 2015, 15).

Political officials and local civil-society organizations worked to attain a revised Convenio Marco in 2011. An August 2011 gathering to alter the agreement (the Primer Congreso de Reformulación del Convenio Marco) was attended by the Espinar mayor, Óscar Mollohuanca; three national congresspeople; and representatives from nearly one hundred towns and communities, seventy-eight civil-society groups, and the neighboring Chumbivilcas province (Flores Unzaga 2016, 29). In November 2011, Mollohuanca's administration sent a letter to Xstrata representatives to propose that the Convenio Marco be revised (Sanborn and Dammert 2013, 58; Red Muqui 2016, 33).

Pressure built over the Convenio Marco during a time of local unease about the environmental and health impacts of Tintaya and of Antapaccay exploration work in Espinar. Beginning in 2009, there was a surge in complaints about air pollution and animal deaths. Research in 2010 that identified heavy metals in the blood of Espinar residents caused uncertainty and anger within the population. Well-publicized research by the Vicariate of Solidarity of the Sicuani District Prelature (Vicaría de Solidaridad de la Prelatura de Sicuani) found excessive levels of heavy metals in the water and soil in Tintaya's area of influence. In September 2011, the Vicaría presented its research, which it later published as a 2012 report. Also in 2012, the Espinar provincial government released its finding of heavy metals in the blood of livestock (Sanborn and Dammert 2013, 58; CooperAcción et al. 2016, 7, 11; Red Muqui 2016, 33).

In the lead-up to the 2012 protests, Espinar saw impressive civil-society organizing. Local environmental groups had mobilized during 2010–11 against the construction of the mammoth Angostura dam.[1] When in November 2011 a Constitutional Tribunal decision stalled the dam project, those organizations turned their attention to the Convenio Marco and environmental impacts from Tintaya (Zeisser Polatsik 2015, 16–17). Espinar's labor sector also was activated before the 2012 protests; demands for contracts from Xtrata contributed to an important January 2012 truck drivers' strike (Sanborn and Dammert 2013, 60).

Efforts to negotiate a revised Convenio Marco failed. In February 2012, Xstrata representatives met with Cusco's regional president and Mollohuanca and other Espinar provincial leaders to begin a dialogue process. The initiative was suspended amid disagreements. Espinar civil-society groups tried to restart talks but gave up in May 2012 (Zeisser Polatsik 2015, 20–21).

On May 21, 2012, the United Defense Front of the Interests of Espinar (Frente Unido de Defensa de los Intereses de Espinar, FUDIE) led a strike throughout Espinar, to advocate for an immediate solution to air, land, and water pollution; an international environmental audit of Tintaya; the mine's closure; Antapaccay's suspension; the guarantee of respect for the human rights of residents; and community participation in decisions surrounding the planned pipeline from the Las Bambas mine (Flores Unzaga 2016, 31).[2] The 2011–13 wave of organizing included participation by several communities directly impacted by mining, as well as more remote communities in the province.[3]

Between twelve hundred and fifteen hundred national police personnel were sent to Espinar to control the strike. On May 28, 2012, the prime minister declared a thirty-day state of emergency throughout the province. Tensions increased when the police arrested Mollohuanca, a key leader in the strike. The violence caused harm to public and private property, injuries, and deaths (Pinto Herrera 2015, 182; Flores Unzaga 2016, 31).

A June 2012–February 2013 roundtable resolved the conflict. The roundtable brought together Mollohuanca, Cusco's president, and other

1. The dam project in Arequipa was expected to reduce the volume of river water flowing to Espinar (Zeisser Polatsik 2015, 16–17; Red Muqui 2016, 33).

2. On the pipeline plan, see also the Las Bambas case study in Chapter 6.

3. Author communication with Maritza Paredes, April 12, 2021.

subnational government representatives, at the regional, provincial, and district levels; representatives from the PCM; several vice ministers; three congresspeople; the agriculture, environment, health, housing, interior, and energy and mining ministers; and civil-society organizations, including groups that had participated in the strike (Flores Unzaga 2016, 31–38).

Production from Antapaccay began in December 2012, while the roundtable was underway (Zeisser Polatsik 2015, 16).

APPENDIX B

Study Participants

Table B.1 STUDY PARTICIPANTS

Affiliation/profession	Bolivia	Colombia	Peru	Total
NGOs	13	8	14	35
Government				31
Office of the National Ombudsman	*2*	*1*	*6*	
Other	*13*	*4*	*5*	
Activist				27
Indigenous organization	*13*	*2*	*1*	
Other		*11*		
Research institution, including university	4	9	9	22
Consultant, lawyer, conflict mediator	3	3	5	11
Extractive firm	6	2	3	11
Journalist			4	4
Totals	54	40	47	141

Note: The author interviewed participants during 2012 and 2016–18.

REFERENCES

ARTICLES, BOOKS, AND OTHER PUBLISHED AND UNPUBLISHED DOCUMENTS

Abers, Rebecca Neaera. 2000. *Inventing Local Democracy: Grassroots Politics in Brazil.* Boulder, CO: Lynne Rienner.

Alberti, Carla. 2019. "Populist Multiculturalism in the Andes: Balancing Political Control and Societal Autonomy." *Comparative Politics* 52, no. 1 (October): 43–63.

Amengual, Matthew. 2018. "Buying Stability: The Distributive Outcomes of Private Politics in the Bolivian Mining Industry." *World Development* 104 (April): 31–45.

Andrade, Germán I. 2008. "Conducir el cambio: Hacia un modelo ecosistémico en la conservación del Sistema Nacional de Áreas Naturales Protegidas de Colombia." In Manuel Rodríguez Becerra, ed., *Gobernabilidad, instituciones y medio ambiente en Colombia*, 477–522. Bogotá: Foro Nacional Ambiental.

Anguelovski, Isabelle. 2011. "Understanding the Dynamics of Community Engagement of Corporations in Communities: The Iterative Relationship between Dialogue Processes and Local Protest at the Tintaya Copper Mine in Peru." *Society and Natural Resources* 24, no. 4: 384–99.

Anria, Santiago. 2016. "Delegative Democracy Revisited: More Inclusion, Less Liberalism in Bolivia." *Journal of Democracy* 27, no. 3 (July): 99–108.

Anria, Santiago. 2018. *When Movements Become Parties: The Bolivian MAS in Comparative Perspective.* Cambridge: Cambridge University Press.

Anthias, Penelope. 2012. "Territorializing Resource Conflicts in 'Post-neoliberal' Bolivia: Hydrocarbon Development and Indigenous Land Titling in TCO Itika Guasu." In Håvard Haarstad, ed., *New Political Spaces in Latin American Natural Resource Governance*, 129–53. New York: Palgrave Macmillan.

Anthias, Penelope. 2018. *Limits to Decolonization: Indigeneity, Territory, and Hydrocarbon Politics in the Bolivian Chaco.* Ithaca, NY: Cornell University Press.

Arboleda Mutis, Zohanny. 2015. "Territorio, consulta previa y autonomía." In Mauricio Archila, ed., *"Hasta cuando soñemos": Extractivismo e interculturalidad en el sur de La Guajira*, 159–203. Bogotá: Centro de Investigación y Educación Popular Programa por la Paz.

Arce, Moisés. 2014. *Resource Extraction and Protest in Peru.* Pittsburgh, PA: University of Pittsburgh Press.

Arellano Yanguas, Javier. 2011. *¿Minería sin fronteras? Conflicto y desarrollo en regiones mineras del Perú.* Lima: Instituto de Estudios Peruanos.

Arellano Yanguas, Javier. 2014. "Religion and Resistance to Extraction in Rural Peru: Is the Catholic Church Following the People?" *Latin American Research Review* 49: 61–80.

Arellano Yanguas, Javier, and Andrés Mejía Acosta. 2014. "Extractive Industries, Revenue Allocation and Local Politics." Working Paper 2014-4 (March). Geneva: United Nations Research Institute for Social Development.

Arenas, Luis Carlos. 2007. "The U'wa Community's Battle against the Oil Companies: A Local Struggle Turned Global." In Boaventura de Sousa Santos, ed., *Another Knowledge Is Possible: Beyond Northern Epistemologies*, 120–47. London: Verso.

Arribasplata, Juan. 2011. "Conga: Cronología de un conflicto." *Voces* 38 (December): 10–13.

Arsel, Murat, Carlos Mena, Lorenzo Pellegrini, and Isabella Radhuber. 2014. "Property Rights, Nationalisation and Extractive Industries in Bolivia and Ecuador." In Maarten Bavinck, Lorenzo Pellegrini, and Erik Mostert, eds., *Conflicts over Natural Resources in the Global South: Conceptual Approaches*, 109–28. London: CRC Press.

Assies, Willem. 2006. "Land Tenure Legislation in a Pluri-cultural and Multi-ethnic Society: The Case of Bolivia." *Journal of Peasant Studies* 33, no. 4: 569–611.

Asurza, Johana. 2015. "Informe sobre Máxima Acuña de Chaupe." In *Informe Anual 2014–2015*, 47–48. Lima: Coordinadora Nacional de Derechos Humanos.

Ávila, Ricardo. 2002. "El caso de la comunidad U'wa: Territorio y petróleo." In *Nuevos caminos para la resolución de conflictos: Experiencias latinoamericanas*, 77–100. Washington, DC: Organization of American States.

Avritzer, Leonardo. 2002. *Democracy and the Public Space in Latin America*. Princeton, NJ: Princeton University Press.

Baiocchi, Gianpaolo. 2005. *Militants and Citizens: The Politics of Participatory Democracy in Porto Alegre*. Stanford, CA: Stanford University Press.

Baiocchi, Gianpaolo, Patrick Heller, and Marcelo Silva. 2011. *Bootstrapping Democracy: Transforming Local Governance and Civil Society in Brazil*. Stanford, CA: Stanford University Press.

Banco Central de Reserva del Perú. 2012. *Memoria 2012*. Lima: Banco Central de Reserva del Perú.

Banco Central de Reserva del Perú. 2015. *Memoria 2015*. Lima: Banco Central de Reserva del Perú.

Banco Central de Reserva del Perú. 2017. *Memoria 2017*. Lima: Banco Central de Reserva del Perú.

Baquero Díaz, Carlos Andrés. 2014. "Contested Lands, Contested Laws." *Americas Quarterly* 8, no. 2 (Spring): 106–10.

Barandiarán, Javiera, and Sebastián Rubiano-Galvis. 2019. "An Empirical Study of EIA Litigation Involving Energy Facilities in Chile and Colombia." *Environmental Impact Assessment Review* 79 (November): https://doi.org/10.1016/j.eiar.2019.106311.

Barrera Ayala, José Antonio. 2008. "El reglamento de participación ciudadana para la realización de actividades de hidrocarburos." *Círculo de derecho administrativo* 6: 320–29.

Barrera-Hernández, Lila. 2009. "Recent Developments in Social Impact Management in Extractive Resource Development in Peru." *McGill International Journal of Sustainable Development Law and Policy* 5, no. 2: 155–69.

Bascopé Sanjinés, Iván. 2010. *Lecciones aprendidas sobre consulta previa*. La Paz: Centro de Estudios Jurídicos e Investigación Social.

Bebbington, Anthony. 2009. "The New Extraction: Rewriting the Political Ecology of the Andes?" *NACLA Report on the Americas* (September–October): 12–20.

Bebbington, Anthony. 2010. "Extractive Industries and Stunted States: Conflict, Responsibility and Institutional Change in the Andes." In K. Ravi Raman and Ronnie D. Lipschutz, eds., *Corporate Social Responsibility: Comparative Critiques*, 97–115. New York: Palgrave Macmillan.

Bebbington, Anthony. 2012. "Social Conflict and Emergent Institutions: Hypotheses from Piura, Peru." In Anthony Bebbington, ed., *Social Conflict, Economic Development and Extractive Industry: Evidence from South America*, 67–88. London: Routledge.

Bebbington, Anthony, Denise Humphreys Bebbington, and Jeffrey Bury. 2010. "Federating and Defending: Water, Territory and Extraction in the Andes." In Rutgerd Boelens, David Getches, and Armando Guevara-Gil, eds., *Out of the Mainstream: Water Rights, Politics and Identity*, 307–27. London: Earthscan.

Bebbington, Anthony, and Jeffrey Bury, eds. 2013. *Subterranean Struggles: New Dynamics of Mining, Oil, and Gas in Latin America*. Austin: University of Texas Press.

Bebbington, Anthony, Michael Connarty, Wendy Coxshall, Hugh O'Shaughnessy, and Mark Williams. 2007. *Minería y desarrollo en el Perú con especial referencia al Proyecto Río Blanco, Piura*. Lima: Oxfam Internacional, Instituto de Estudios Peruanos, Centro de Investigación y Promoción del Campesino, Peru Support Group.

Bebbington, Denise Humphreys. 2010. "The Political Ecology of Natural Gas Extraction in Southern Bolivia." PhD dissertation, University of Manchester.

Bebbington, Denise Humphreys. 2012a. "Consultation, Compensation and Conflict: Natural Gas Extraction in Weenhayek Territory, Bolivia." *Journal of Latin American Geography* 11, no. 2: 49–71.

Bebbington, Denise Humphreys. 2012b. "State-Indigenous Tensions over Hydrocarbon Expansion in the Bolivian Chaco." In Anthony Bebbington, ed., *Social Conflict, Economic Development and Extractive Industry: Evidence from South America*, 134–52. London: Routledge.

Bebbington, Denise Humphreys. 2013. "Extraction, Inequality and Indigenous Peoples: Insights from Bolivia." *Environmental Science and Policy* 33 (November): 438–46.

Bebbington, Denise Humphreys, and Anthony Bebbington. 2010. "Anatomy of a Regional Conflict: Tarija and Resource Grievances in Morales's Bolivia." *Latin American Perspectives* 37, no. 4 (July): 140–60.

Bejarano, Ana María, and Eduardo Pizarro. 2005. "From 'Restricted' to 'Besieged': The Changing Nature of the Limits to Democracy in Colombia." In Frances Hagopian and Scott P. Mainwaring, eds., *The Third Wave of Democratization in Latin America: Advances and Setbacks*, 235–60. Cambridge: Cambridge University Press.

Bruijn, Eveline, and Gail Whiteman. 2010. "That Which Doesn't Break Us: Identity Work by Local Indigenous 'Stakeholders'." *Journal of Business Ethics* 96, no. 3 (October): 479–95.

Buitrago, Emerson A. 2016. "Limitaciones y delimitaciones de los páramos en una Colombia posacuerdo." In Astrid Ulloa and Sergio Coronado, eds., *Extractivismos y posconflicto en Colombia: Retos para la paz territorial*, 137–66. Bogotá: Editorial Universidad Nacional de Colombia and Centro de Investigación y Educación Popular Programa por la Paz.

Bury, Jeffrey, and Timothy Norris. 2013. "Rocks, Rangers, and Resistance: Mining and Conservation Frontiers in the Cordillera Huayhuash, Peru." In Anthony

Bebbington and Jeffrey Bury, eds., *Subterranean Struggles: New Dynamics of Mining, Oil, and Gas in Latin America*, 91–118. Austin: University of Texas Press.

Caballero Argáez, Carlos, and Sebastián Bitar. 2016. "The Liberal Rarity of South America: Oil and Mining Policy Reform in Colombia in the 2000s." In Paul A. Haslam and Pablo Heidrich, eds., *The Political Economy of Natural Resources and Development: From Neoliberalism to Resource Nationalism*, 121–40. New York: Routledge.

Calle, Isabel, and Carol Mora. 2016. *Evaluación de impacto ambiental: Los ITS de proyectos de inversión en sectores estratégicos*. Cuaderno legal No. 2. Lima: Sociedad Peruana de Derecho Ambiental.

Campanini, Jorge, Pablo Villegas, Georgina Jiménez, Marco Gandarillas, and Silvia M. Pérez. 2014. *Los límites de las fronteras extractivas en Bolivia: El caso de la biodiversidad en el Aguaragüe*. Informe OMAL No. 12. Cochabamba: Centro de Documentación e Información Bolivia; Bilbao: Paz con Dignidad.

Canal Albán, Francisco, and Manuel Rodríguez Becerra. 2008. "Las corporaciones autónomas regionales, quince años después de la creación del SINA." In Manuel Rodríguez Becerra, ed., *Gobernabilidad, instituciones y medio ambiente en Colombia*, 303–89. Bogotá: Foro Nacional Ambiental.

Castillo Fernández, Marlene. 2016. *Disputa de representación de los pueblos Awajún y Wampis en la región Amazonas–Perú*. Lima: CooperAcción.

Cavero, Omar. 2014. *Hacia un entendimiento de la conflictividad social: Las protestas contra la minería en Puno–2011*. Cuaderno de trabajo No. 21 (December). Lima: Pontificia Universidad Católica del Perú, Departamento de Ciencias Sociales.

Centro Amazónico de Antropología y Aplicación Práctica (CAAAP). 2016. *¿Cómo va la aplicación de la consulta previa en el Perú? Avances y retos*. December. Lima: CAAAP.

Centro Amazónico de Antropología y Aplicación Práctica (CAAAP) and CooperAcción. 2015. *Estudio sobre la actuación de las empresas petroleras Perenco en el Lote 67 y Maurel Et Prom-Pacific Rubiales Energy en el Lote 116: Impactos socio-ambientales y afectación de derechos de los pueblos indígenas Awajun y Wampis en Amazonas y Kechwa y Arabela en Loreto*. Informe Final (April). Lima: CAAAP and CooperAcción.

Centro de Investigación y Educación Popular/Programa por la Paz (CINEP/PPP). 2012. *Minería, conflictos sociales y violación de derechos humanos en Colombia*. Informe Especial, October. Bogotá: CINEP/PPP.

Chernick, Marc W. 2003. "Colombia: Does Injustice Cause Violence?" In Susan Eva Eckstein and Timothy P. Wickham-Crowley, eds., *What Justice? Whose Justice? Fighting for Fairness in Latin America*, 185–214. Berkeley: University of California Press.

Ciro, Estefanía, Julián Barbosa, and Alejandra Ciro. 2016. "Mapa petrolero de la Amazonia y resistencia en el Caquetá: Retos de paz en el posconflicto." In Astrid Ulloa and Sergio Coronado, eds., *Extractivismos y posconflicto en Colombia: Retos para la paz territorial*, 413–40. Bogotá: Editorial Universidad Nacional de Colombia and Centro de Investigación y Educación Popular Programa por la Paz.

Collier, Ruth Berins. 1999. *Paths Toward Democracy: The Working Class and Elites in Western Europe and South America*. Cambridge: Cambridge University Press.

Contraloría General de la República. 2017. *El proceso administrativo de licenciamiento ambiental en Colombia*. Bogotá: Contraloría General de la República.

CooperAcción. n.d. "Las Bambas: Un proyecto que no para de cambiar; Cinco modificaciones en 20 meses." Pamphlet. Lima: CooperAcción.

CooperAcción. 2014. "Resumen de noticias." *Actualidad minera del Perú*. No. 185 (October): 18–23.

CooperAcción. 2015. *Caso "Las Bambas"*. Informe Especial. Lima: CooperAcción.

CooperAcción. 2018a. "Otra vez Tía María." *Actualidad minera del Perú*. No. 224 (February): 10–11.

CooperAcción. 2018b. "Editorial: ¿Qué nos dice el último reporte de conflictos de la Defensoría?" *Actualidad minera del Perú* 228 (June): 2–3.

CooperAcción. 2018c. "Sección económica." *Actualidad minera del Perú* 228 (June): 4–7.

CooperAcción, Derechos Humanos sin Fronteras, Instituto de Defensa Legal, and Broederlijk Delen. 2016. *Metales pesados tóxicos y salud pública: El caso Espinar*. Lima: CooperAcción.

Coronado Delgado, Sergio, Zohanny Catrileo-Arboleda Mutis, Martha Cecilia García Velandia, Ana María Restrepo, Álvaro Delgado, and Jerry de Jesús Garavito. 2014. *Minería y conflictos en el Caribe colombiano: Hacia una ecología política de la minería de carbón*. Documentos ocasionales No. 78. Bogotá: Centro de Investigación y Educación Popular Programa por la Paz.

Costanza, Jennifer N. 2015. "Indigenous Peoples' Right to Prior Consultation: Transforming Human Rights from the Grassroots in Guatemala." *Journal of Human Rights* 14, no. 2: 260–85.

Cox A., Ricardo, Jannette Giné L., Diego Andreucci, and Adriana Soto S. 2013. *Estado de la gestión socio-ambiental del sector hidrocarburos en pueblos indígenas del Chaco y Norte de La Paz*. Cochabamba: Centro de Estudios Aplicados a los Derechos Económicos, Sociales y Culturales.

Damonte, Gerardo. 2013. "Transformación de la representatividad política local en contextos extractivos a gran escala en los Andes peruanos." *Revista Iberoamericana* 24, no. 1: 65–104.

Dargent, Eduardo, José Carlos Orihuela, Maritza Paredes, and María Eugenia Ulfe. 2017. "Cycle of Abundance and Institutional Pathways." In Eduardo Dargent, José Carlos Orihuela, Maritza Paredes, and María Eugenia Ulfe, eds., *Resource Booms and Institutional Pathways: The Case of the Extractive Industry in Peru*, 1–40. Cham: Palgrave Macmillan.

De Echave C., José. 2018. *Diez años de minería en el Perú: 2008–2017*. Lima: CooperAcción.

De Echave, José, and Alejandro Diez. 2013. *Más allá de Conga*. Lima: CooperAcción.

De Echave, José, Alejandro Diez, Ludwig Huber, Bruno Revesz, Xavier Ricard Lanata, and Martín Tanaka. 2009. *Minería y conflicto social*. Lima: Instituto de Estudios Peruanos, Centro de Investigación y Promoción del Campesinado, Centro de Estudios Regionales Andinos Bartolomé de Las Casas, and Consorcio de Investigación Económica y Social.

Defensoría del Pueblo. 2006. *Informe No. 001-2006/ASPMA-MA*. November 14. Lima: Defensoría del Pueblo.

Defensoría del Pueblo. 2015. *Décimoctavo informe anual de la Defensoría del Pueblo: Enero–diciembre 2014*. May. Lima: Defensoría del Pueblo.

Defensoría del Pueblo. 2017. *Buenas prácticas de las defensorías del pueblo de Bolivia, Colombia, Ecuador y Perú en procesos de consulta previa*. Lima: Defensoría del Pueblo.

Defensoría del Pueblo, Adjuntía del Medio Ambiente, Servicios Públicos y Pueblos Indígenas. 2016. *El camino hacia proyectos de inversión sostenibles: Balance de la evaluación de impacto ambiental en el Perú*. Serie Informes de Adjuntía. Informe No. 006-2016-DP/AMASPPI.MA. December. Lima: Defensoría del Pueblo.

Defensoría del Pueblo, Adjuntía para la Prevención de Conflictos Sociales y la Gobernabilidad. 2012. *Violencia en los conflictos sociales*. Informe Defensorial No. 156. March. Lima: Defensoría del Peru.

Defensoría del Pueblo, Adjuntía para la Prevención de Conflictos Sociales y la Gobernabilidad. 2015. "Caso: Quellaveco." Ayuda memoria. Opened May 2007. Updated to RCS No. 132–February 2015. Lima: Defensoría del Pueblo.

Defensoría del Pueblo, Adjuntía para la Prevención de Conflictos Sociales y la Gobernabilidad. 2016. "Caso: Santa Ana—Huacullani." Ayuda memoria. RCS No. 57–November 2008. Updated to RCS No. 143–January 2016. Lima: Defensoría del Pueblo.

Defensoría del Pueblo, Adjuntía para la Prevención de Conflictos Sociales y la Gobernabilidad. 2017a. "Caso: Conga—Yanacocha." Ayuda memoria. RCS No. 74–April 2010. Updated to RCS No. 143–January 2016. Update through March 2017 obtained May 2017. Lima: Defensoría del Pueblo.

Defensoría del Pueblo, Adjuntía para la Prevención de Conflictos Sociales y la Gobernabilidad. 2017b. "Caso: Cotabambas—MMG proyecto minero Las Bambas." Ayuda memoria. RCS No. 87–May 2011, updated to RCS No. 157–March 2017. Lima: Defensoría del Pueblo.

Defensoría del Pueblo, Adjuntía para la Prevención de Conflictos Sociales y la Gobernabilidad. 2017c. "Caso: El Cenepa—Afrodita." Ayuda memoria. RCS No. 58–December 2008, updated to RCS No. 157–March 2017. Lima: Defensoría del Pueblo.

Defensoría del Pueblo, Adjuntía para la Prevención de Conflictos Sociales y la Gobernabilidad. 2017d. "Caso: Tía María—Islay." Ayuda memoria. RCS No. 116–October 2013, updated to RCS No. 156–February 2017. Lima: Defensoría del Pueblo.

De Jong, Wil, and David Humphreys. 2016. "A Failed Social Licence to Operate for the Neoliberal Modernization of Amazonian Resource Use: The Underlying Causes of the Bagua Tragedy of Peru." *Forestry* 89, no. 5 (September): 552–64.

Delamaza, Gonzalo, Antoine Maillet, and Christian Martínez Neira. 2017. "Socio-territorial Conflicts in Chile: Configuration and Politicization (2005–2014)." *European Review of Latin American and Caribbean Studies* 104 (July–December): 23–46.

Departamento Nacional de Planeación, Colombia. 2005. *Visión Colombia II Centenario: 2019*. Bogotá: Departamento Nacional de Planeación.

Devlin, John F., and Nonita T. Yap. 2008. "Contentious Politics in Environmental Assessment: Blocked Projects and Winning Coalitions." *Impact Assessment and Project Appraisal* 26, no. 1 (March): 17–27.

Díaz Cuellar, Vladimir. 2011. "La minería bajo el dominio de las transnacionales." *PetroPress* 25: 20–26.

Earle, Lucy, and Brian Pratt. 2009. "Indigenous Social Movements and International NGOs in the Peruvian Amazon." Occasional Papers Series No. 49 (March). Oxford: International NGO Training and Research Centre.

Eaton, Kent. 2006. "The Downside of Decentralization: Armed Clientelism in Colombia." *Security Studies* 15, no. 4 (October–December): 533–62.

Eaton, Kent. 2017. *Territory and Ideology in Latin America: Policy Conflicts between National and Subnational Governments*. New York: Oxford University Press.

Eisenstadt, Todd A., and Karleen Jones West. 2019. *Who Speaks for Nature? Indigenous Movements, Public Opinion, and the Petro-State in Ecuador*. New York: Oxford University Press.

Equipo de Investigación de la Organización de Desarrollo de las Comunidades Fronterizas del Cenepa (ODECOFROC). 2009. *Crónica de un engaño: Los intentos de enajenación del territorio fronterizo Awajún en la Cordillera del Cóndor a favor de la minería*. Informe IWGIA 5. Lima: ODECOFROC, Grupo de Trabajo Racimos de Ungurahui, and Grupo Internacional de Trabajo sobre Asuntos Indígenas.

Falleti, Tulia G., and Thea N. Riofrancos. 2018. "Endogenous Participation: Strengthening Prior Consultation in Extractive Economies." *World Politics* 70, no. 1 (January): 86–121.

Flemmer, Riccarda, and Almut Schilling-Vacaflor. 2016. "Unfulfilled Promises of the Consultation Approach: The Limits to Effective Indigenous Participation in Bolivia's and Peru's Extractive Industries." *Third World Quarterly* 37, no. 1: 172–88.

Flores Unzaga, César. 2016. *Conviviendo con la minería en el sur andino: Experiencias de las mesas de diálogo y desarrollo de Espinar, Cotabambas y Chamaca*. Lima: Oxfam America and CooperAcción.

Flórez Flórez, Mario. 2012. "En defensa del Páramo de Santurbán: Cronología de una lucha que apenas comienza . . ." In Catalina Toro Pérez, Julio Fierro Morales, Sergio Coronado Delgado, and Tatiana Roa Avendaño, eds., *Minería, territorio y conflicto en Colombia*, 465–84. Bogotá: Universidad Nacional de Colombia.

Fontana, Lorenza B., and Jean Grugel. 2016. "The Politics of Indigenous Participation through 'Free Prior Informed Consent': Reflections from the Bolivian Case." *World Development* 77 (January): 249–61.

Fulmer, Amanda M. 2014. "The Politics of a Strange Right: Consultation, Mining, and Indigenous Mobilization in Latin America." In George Andreopoulos and Zehra F. Kabasakal Arat, eds., *The Uses and Misuses of Human Rights: A Critical Approach to Advocacy*, 65–88. New York: Palgrave Macmillan.

Gálvez Aldana, Ramiro. 2014. "Alcance de las consultas populares en Colombia." *Boletín el topo* 17 (May).

Gamboa Balbín, Aída Mercedes. 2017. *Gobernanza en las APP: Lecciones aprendidas del Gasoducto Sur Peruano*. Lima: Derecho Ambiente y Recursos Naturales.

Gamu, Jonathan Kishen, and Peter Dauvergne. 2018. "The Slow Violence of Corporate Social Responsibility: The Case of Mining in Peru." *Third World Quarterly* 39, no. 5: 959–75.

Gandarillas G., Marco. 2014. "La Ley Minera: Una amenaza a la democracia y los derechos humanos." *PetroPress* 33 (February–August): 30–34.

Glave, Manuel A., and Juana Kuramoto. 2002. "Minería, minerales y desarrollo sustentable en Perú." In Equipo MMSD América del Sur, eds., *Minería, minerales y desarrollo sustentable en América del Sur*, 529–91. London and Geneva: International Institute for Environment and Development, World Business Council for Sustainable Development.

Gobierno Regional Moquegua. n.d. *Mesa de diálogo: Resumen de las doce primeras sesiones*.

Goldfrank, Benjamin. 2011. *Deepening Local Democracy in Latin America: Participation, Decentralization, and the Left*. University Park: Pennsylvania State University Press.

Gómez Isa, Felipe. 2014. "Cultural Diversity, Legal Pluralism, and Human Rights from an Indigenous Perspective: The Approach by the Colombian Constitutional Court and the Inter-American Court of Human Rights." *Human Rights Quarterly* 36, no. 4 (November): 722–55.

Gonzalez, Yanilda. 2016. "Varieties of Participatory Security: Assessing Community Participation in Policing in Latin America." *Public Administration and Development* 36, no. 2 (May): 132–43.

Griffiths, Tom. 2007. *Holding the IDB and IFC to Account on Camisea II: A Review of Applicable International Standards, Due Diligence and Compliance Issues.* September. San Francisco: Amazon Watch.

Guasti, Laura. 1983. "The Peruvian Military Government and the International Corporations." In Cynthia McClintock and Abraham F. Lowenthal, eds., *The Peruvian Experiment Reconsidered*, 181–205. Princeton, NJ: Princeton University Press.

Gustafsson, Maria-Therese. 2016. "Private Conflict Regulation and the Influence of Peasant Communities over Natural Resources." *Latin American Research Review* 51, no. 2: 86–106.

Gustafsson, Maria-Therese. 2018. *Private Politics and Peasant Mobilization: Mining in Peru.* London: Palgrave Macmillan.

Guzmán-Gallegos, María A. 2017. "Between Oil Contamination and Consultation: Constrained Spaces of Influence in Northern Peruvian Amazonia. *Third World Quarterly* 38, no. 5 (May): 1110–27.

Haarstad, Håvard, and Cecilia Campero. 2011. *Participation in the Bolivian Hydrocarbon Sector: The "Double Discourse" and Limitations on Participatory Governance.* URBECO-Report 04/11. Bergen: Center for Urban Ecology and the University of Bergen.

Hacker, Jacob S., Paul Pierson, and Kathleen Thelen. 2015. "Drift and Conversion: Hidden Faces of Institutional Change." In James Mahoney and Kathleen Thelen, eds., *Advances in Comparative-Historical Analysis*, 180–208. Cambridge: Cambridge University Press.

Helmke, Gretchen, and Steven Levitsky. 2006. "Introduction." In Gretchen Helmke and Steven Levitsky, eds., *Informal Institutions and Democracy: Lessons from Latin America*, 1–30. Baltimore, MD: Johns Hopkins University Press.

Henao, Juan Carlos, and Ana Carolina González Espinosa, eds. 2016. *Minería y comunidades: Impactos, conflictos y participación ciudadana.* Minería y desarrollo, vol. 4. Bogotá: Universidad Externado de Colombia.

Hernández Marín, Edison Alonso. 2018. "Los impactos y el conflicto socioambiental por el fracturamiento hidráulico: Caso de estudio en el municipio de San Martín, Cesar–Colombia." Master's thesis, Universidad Nacional de Colombia.

Herrera, Veronica. 2017. "From Participatory Promises to Partisan Capture: Local Democratic Transitions and Mexican Water Politics." *Comparative Politics* 49, no. 4 (July): 479–99.

Hindery, Derrick. 2004. "Social and Environmental Impacts of World Bank/IMF-Funded Economic Restructuring in Bolivia: An Analysis of Enron and Shell's Hydrocarbons Projects." *Singapore Journal of Tropical Geography* 25, no. 3 (November): 281–303.

Hinojosa, Leonith, Anthony Bebbington, Guido Cortez, Juan Pablo Chumacero, Denise Humphreys Bebbington, and Karl Hennermann. 2015. "Gas and Development: Rural Territorial Dynamics in Tarija, Bolivia." *World Development* 73 (September): 105–17.

Hochstetler, Kathryn. 2011. "The Politics of Environmental Licensing: Energy Projects of the Past and Future in Brazil." *Studies in Comparative International Development* 46, no. 4 (December): 349–71.

Human Rights Watch. 2010. *Paramilitaries' Heirs: The New Face of Violence in Colombia*. New York: Human Rights Watch.

Jaskoski, Maiah. 2012. *Resource Conflicts: Emerging Struggles over Strategic Commodities in Latin America Phase II*. Monterey: Naval Postgraduate School Center on Contemporary Conflict, October.

Jaskoski, Maiah. 2013. *Military Politics and Democracy in the Andes*. Baltimore, MD: Johns Hopkins University Press.

Jaskoski, Maiah. 2014. "Environmental Licensing and Conflict in Peru's Mining Sector: A Path-Dependent Analysis." *World Development* 64 (December): 873–83.

Jaskoski, Maiah. 2020. "Participatory Institutions as a Focal Point for Mobilizing: Prior Consultation and Indigenous Conflict in Colombia's Extractive Industries." *Comparative Politics* 52, no. 4 (July): 537–56.

Jaskoski, Maiah. 2021. "Conflicto y estrategia social en la minería y los hidrocarburos peruanos: Los usos variados de la participación en la evaluación de impacto ambiental." *Revista de Ciencia Política* 41, no. 3 (December): 587–609.

Jiménez Jiménez, Magda Catalina. 2016. "El Páramo de Santurbán: '*Accounability*' social exitoso." In Juan Carlos Henao and Ana Carolina González Espinosa, eds., *Minería y comunidades: Impactos, conflictos y participación ciudadana*, 465–512. Minería y desarrollo, vol. 4. Bogotá: Universidad Externado de Colombia.

Johnson, Andrea E. 2005. "Participation through the Pipeline: Assessing the Role of Civil Society in Peru's Camisea Natural Gas Project." Master's thesis, Yale School of Forestry and Environmental Studies.

Kaup, Brent Z. 2010. "A Neoliberal Nationalization? The Constraints on Natural-Gas-Led Development in Bolivia." *Latin American Perspectives* 37, no. 3 (May): 123–38.

Lanegra Quispe, Iván. 2014. "Consulta previa, minería y regulación ambiental en la legislación nacional." *Derecho y sociedad* 42: 101–12.

Leifsen, Esben, Maria-Therese Gustafsson, Maria A. Guzmán-Gallegos, and Almut Schilling-Vacaflor, eds. 2017a. "New Mechanisms of Participation in Extractive Governance: Between New Technologies of Governance and Resistance Work." Special issue, *Third World Quarterly* 38, no. 5 (May).

Leifsen, Esben, Luis Sánchez-Vázquez, and Maleny Gabriela Reyes. 2017b. "Claiming Prior Consultation, Monitoring Environmental Impact: Counterwork by the Use of Formal Instruments of Participatory Governance in Ecuador's Emerging Mining Sector." *Third World Quarterly* 38, no. 5 (May): 1092–109.

Levine, Caroline. 2015. *Forms: Whole, Rhythm, Hierarchy, Network*. Princeton, NJ: Princeton University Press.

Levitsky, Steven, and Lucan A. Way. 2010. *Competitive Authoritarianism: Hybrid Regimes after the Cold War*. New York: Cambridge University Press.

Leyva, Ana. 2018. *Consúltame de verdad: Aproximación a un balance sobre consulta previa en el Perú en los sectores minero e hidrocarburífero*. June. Lima: CooperAcción and Oxfam.

Li, Fabiana. 2015. *Unearthing Conflict: Corporate Mining, Activism, and Expertise in Peru*. Durham, NC: Duke University Press.

Lingán, Jeannet. 2008. "El caso de Cajamarca." In Martin Scurrah, ed., *Defendiendo derechos y promoviendo cambios: El estado, las empresas extractivas y las comunidades locales en el Perú*, 31–68. Lima: Instituto de Estudios Peruanos and Oxfam América.

López-Murcia, Julián Daniel. 2017. "Recentralisation and Causes: Colombia, 1994–2014." PhD dissertation, University of Oxford.

Madrid, Raúl L. 2008. "The Rise of Ethnopopulism in Latin America." *World Politics* 60, no. 3 (April): 475–508.

Madrid, Raúl L. 2011. "Bolivia: Origins and Policies of the Movimiento al Socialismo." In Steven Levitsky and Kenneth M. Roberts, eds., *The Resurgence of the Latin American Left*, 239–59. Baltimore, MD: Johns Hopkins University Press.

Mähler, Annegret, and Jan H. Pierskalla. 2015. "Indigenous Identity, Natural Resources, and Contentious Politics in Bolivia: A Disaggregated Conflict Analysis, 2000–2011." *Comparative Political Studies* 48, no. 3: 301–32.

Mahoney, James, and Kathleen Thelen. 2010. "A Theory of Gradual Institutional Change." In James Mahoney and Kathleen Thelen, eds., *Explaining Institutional Change: Ambiguity, Agency, and Power*, 1–37. New York: Cambridge University Press.

Mance, Henry. 2008. "La política de la sostenibilidad: Ascenso y declive del Ministerio del Medio Ambiente colombiano." In Manuel Rodríguez Becerra, ed., *Gobernabilidad, instituciones y medio ambiente en Colombia*, 101–252. Bogotá: Foro Nacional Ambiental.

Marston, Andrea, and Tom Perreault. 2017. "Consent, Coercion and *Cooperativismo*: Mining Cooperatives and Resource Regimes in Bolivia." *Environment and Planning A* 49, no. 2 (February): 252–72.

Martínez, Astrid, and Martha Delgado. 2017. "Estudio sobre el impacto de la actividad petrolera en las regiones productoras de Colombia." Informe de Fedesarrollo a Ecopetrol S.A. September 15. Bogotá: Fedesarrollo.

Massé, Frédéric. 2016. "Minería y post conflicto: ¿Es posible una minería de oro libre de conflicto en Colombia?" In Juan Carlos Henao and Ana Carolina González Espinosa, eds., *Minería y comunidades: Impactos, conflictos y participación ciudadana*, 257–82. Minería y desarrollo, vol. 4. Bogotá: Universidad Externado de Colombia.

Mayka, Lindsay. 2019. *Building Participatory Institutions in Latin America: Reform Coalitions and Institutional Change*. Cambridge: Cambridge University Press.

Mayorga, René Antonio. 2005. "Bolivia's Democracy at the Crossroads." In Frances Hagopian and Scott P. Mainwaring, eds., *The Third Wave of Democratization in Latin America: Advances and Setbacks*, 149–78. Cambridge: Cambridge University Press.

McAdam, Doug, and Hilary Schaffer Boudet. 2012. *Putting Social Movements in Their Place: Explaining Opposition to Energy Projects in the United States, 2000–2005*. New York: Cambridge University Press.

McAdam, Doug, Hilary Schaffer Boudet, Jennifer Davis, Ryan J. Orr, W. Richard Scott, and Raymond E. Levitt. 2010. "'Site Fights': Explaining Opposition to Pipeline Projects in the Developing World." *Sociological Forum* 25, no. 3 (September): 401–27.

McClintock, Cynthia. 2006. "Electoral Authoritarian versus Partially Democratic Regimes: The Case of the Fujimori Government and the 2000 Elections." In Julio F. Carrión, ed., *The Fujimori Legacy: The Rise of Electoral Authoritarianism in Peru*, 242–67. University Park: Pennsylvania State University Press.

McNeish, John-Andrew. 2013. "Extraction, Protest and Indigeneity in Bolivia: The TIPNIS Effect." *Latin American and Caribbean Ethnic Studies* 8, no. 2: 221–42.

McNeish, John-Andrew. 2017. "A Vote to Derail Extraction: Popular Consultation and Resource Sovereignty in Tolima, Colombia." *Third World Quarterly* 38, no. 5 (May): 1128–45.

McNulty, Stephanie L. 2011. *Voice and Vote: Decentralization and Participation in Post-Fujimori Peru*. Stanford, CA: Stanford University Press.

Merino, Roger. 2018. "Re-politicizing Participation or Reframing Environmental Governance? Beyond Indigenous' Prior Consultation and Citizen Participation." *World Development* 111 (November): 75–83.

Montambeault, Françoise. 2016. *The Politics of Local Participatory Democracy in Latin America: Institutions, Actors, and Interactions*. Stanford, CA: Stanford University Press.

Montero, Alfred P., and David J. Samuels, eds. 2004. *Decentralization and Democracy in Latin America*. Notre Dame, IN: University of Notre Dame Press.

Montoya, David. 2018. "Conflictividad social, diálogo y gobernanza territorial." *Ideele revista* no. 278. Lima: Instituto de Defensa Legal.

Moreno Hermoza, Gustavo. 2014. "El caso Las Bambas." In Iván Ormachea Choque, Javier Caravedo Chocano, Gustavo Moreno Hermoza, and César Bedoya García, *Minería, conflicto social y diálogo*, 125–61. Lima: ProDiálogo, Prevención y Resolución de Conflictos.

Munilla, Isabel. 2010. *People, Power, and Pipelines: Lessons from Peru in the Governance of Gas Production Revenues*. Boston: Oxfam America.

Negrete Montes, Rodrigo E. 2013. "Derechos, minería y conflictos: Aspectos normativos." In Luis Jorge Garay Salamanca, ed., *Minería en Colombia: Derechos, políticas públicas y gobernanza*, 23–54. Bogotá: Contraloría General de la República.

Nunes, Rodrigo M. 2010. "Ideational Origins of Progressive Judicial Activism: The Colombian Constitutional Court and the Right to Health." *Latin American Politics and Society* 52, no. 3 (Autumn): 67–97.

Observatorio de Conflictos Mineros en el Perú. 2015. *17o Observatorio de conflictos mineros en el Perú*. Reporte segundo semestre. December. Lima: Observatorio de Conflictos Mineros en el Perú, CooperAcción, Fundación Ecuménica para el Desarrollo y la Paz, Grupo de Formación e Intervención para el Desarrollo Sostenible.

Observatorio de Conflictos Mineros en el Perú. 2020. *27o Observatorio de conflictos mineros en el Perú*. Reporte segundo semestre. December. Lima: Observatorio de Conflictos Mineros en el Perú, CooperAcción, Fundación Ecuménica para el Desarrollo y la Paz, Grupo de Formación e Intervención para el Desarrollo Sostenible.

O'Faircheallaigh, Ciaran. 2017. "Shaping Projects, Shaping Impacts: Community-Controlled Impact Assessments and Negotiated Agreements." *Third World Quarterly* 38, no. 5 (May): 1181–97.

Orduz Salinas, Natalia. 2014. *La consulta previa en Colombia*. Documento de trabajo ICSO No. 3. Santiago: Instituto de Investigación en Ciencias Sociales, Universidad Diego Portales.

Orduz Salinas, Natalia, and Hanna Thiesing. 2016. *La vida es de los arriesgados*. Documentary. Colombia.

Orihuela, José Carlos. 2014a. "Converging Divergence: The Diffusion of the Green State in Latin America." *Studies in Comparative International Development* 49, no. 2: 242–65.

Orihuela, José Carlos. 2014b. "The Environmental Rules of Economic Development: Governing Air Pollution from Smelters in Chuquicamata and La Oroya." *Journal of Latin American Studies* 46, no. 1 (February): 151–83.

Orihuela, José Carlos, and Maritza Paredes. 2017. "Fragmented Layering: Building a Green State for Mining in Peru." In Eduardo Dargent, José Carlos Orihuela,

Maritza Paredes, and María Eugenia Ulfe, eds., *Resource Booms and Institutional Pathways: The Case of the Extractive Industry in Peru*, 97–117. Cham: Palgrave Macmillan.

Paredes, Maritza. 2008. "El caso de Tambogrande." In Martin Scurrah, ed., *Defendiendo derechos y promoviendo cambios: El estado, las empresas extractivas y las comunidades locales en el Perú*, 269–300. Lima: Instituto de Estudios Peruanos and Oxfam América.

Paredes, Maritza, and Lorena de la Puente. 2017. "The Social Construction of a Public Problem: The Role of the Ombudsman in Building Institutions for Extractive Conflict." In Eduardo Dargent, José Carlos Orihuela, Maritza Paredes, and María Eugenia Ulfe, eds., *Resource Booms and Institutional Pathways: The Case of the Extractive Industry in Peru*, 119–51. Cham: Palgrave Macmillan.

Pellegrini, Lorenzo, and Murat Arsel. 2018. "Oil and Conflict in the Ecuadorian Amazon: An Exploration of Motives and Objectives." *European Review of Latin American and Caribbean Studies* 106 (July–December): 209–18.

Pellegrini, Lorenzo, and Marco Octavio Ribera Arismendi. 2012. "Consultation, Compensation and Extraction in Bolivia after the 'Left Turn': The Case of Oil Exploration in the North of La Paz Department." *Journal of Latin American Geography* 11, no. 2: 103–20.

Pérez-Rincón, Mario Alejandro. 2014. *Conflictos ambientales en Colombia: Inventario, caracterización y análisis*. Documento de trabajo. Cali: Universidad del Valle.

Perla, Cecilia. 2012. "Extracting from the Extractors: The Politics of Private Welfare in the Peruvian Mining Industry." PhD dissertation, Brown University.

Perreault, Thomas. 2008. "Natural Gas, Indigenous Mobilization and the Bolivian State." Programme Paper 12. United Nations Research Institute for Social Development.

Perreault, Tom, and Gabriela Valdivia. 2010. "Hydrocarbons, Popular Protest and National Imaginaries: Ecuador and Bolivia in Comparative Context." *Geoforum* 41, no. 5 (September): 689–99.

Pinto Herrera, Honorio. 2013. "Conflicto minero en Santa Ana (Puno)." *Investigaciones sociales* 17, no. 31: 207–20.

Pinto Herrera, Honorio. 2015. "Tintaya: Conflicto socioambiental 2012." *Alma máter* 2, no. 3: 169–86.

Pinto Herrera, Honorio. 2016. "Proyecto minero Tía María: Razones de la protesta." *Investigaciones sociales* 20, no. 36: 199–213.

Ponce, Aldo F., and Cynthia McClintock. 2014. "The Explosive Combination of Inefficient Local Bureaucracies and Mining Production: Evidence from Localized Societal Protests in Peru." *Latin American Politics and Society* 56, no. 3 (Fall): 118–40.

Poole, Deborah, and Gerardo Rénique. 2012. "Peru: Humala Takes Off His Gloves." *NACLA Report on the Americas*, Spring: 4–5.

Postero, Nancy Grey. 2007. *Now We Are Citizens: Indigenous Politics in Postmulticultural Bolivia*. Stanford: Stanford University Press.

Powęska, Radosław. 2017. "State-Led Extractivism and the Frustration of Indigenous Self-Determined Development: Lessons from Bolivia." *International Journal of Human Rights* 21, no. 4: 442–63.

Premauer, Julia, and Fikret Berkes. 2012. "Colombia: Makuira, the Cosmological Centre of Origin for the Wayúu People." In Nigel Dudley and Sue Stolton, eds., *Protected Landscapes and Wild Biodiversity*, 53–60. Gland, Switzerland: International Union for Conservation of Nature and Natural Resources and Gesellschaft für Internationale Zusammenarbeit.

Przeworski, Adam, and Henry Teune. 1970. *The Logic of Comparative Social Inquiry*. New York: John Wiley and Sons.

Quiñones, Patricia. 2013. "Concesiones, participación y conflicto en Puno: El caso del proyecto minero Santa Ana." In Javier Torres Seoane, ed., *Los límites de la expansión minera en el Perú*, 17–71. Lima: Asociación Servicios Educativos Rurales.

Quiroga Ángel, Daniel. 2018. "Minería de carbón y guerra: Una mirada a la economía política del conflicto armado en el Cesar y La Guajira." In Angelika Rettberg, Ralf J. Leiteritz, Carlo Nasi, and Juan Diego Prieto, eds., *¿Diferentes recursos, conflictos distintos? La economía política regional del conflicto armado y la criminalidad en Colombia*, 193–254. Bogotá: Ediciones Uniandes.

Radhuber, Isabella M. 2012. "Indigenous Struggles for a Plurinational State: An Analysis of Indigenous Rights and Competences in Bolivia." *Journal of Latin American Geography* 11, no. 2: 167–93.

Ramírez Cleves, Gonzalo Andrés, and Floralba Alejandrina Padrón Pardo. 2016. "La consulta popular frente a proyectos de exploración y explotación minera." In Juan Carlos Henao and Ana Carolina González Espinosa, eds., *Minería y comunidades: Impactos, conflictos y participación ciudadana*, 415–63. Minería y desarrollo, vol. 4. Bogotá: Universidad Externado de Colombia.

Red Muqui. 2016. *Balance y propuestas para el funcionamiento de los procesos de diálogo en el Perú*. March. Lima: Red Muqui and Oxfam.

Red Muqui and Grupo de Formación e Intervención para el Desarrollo Sostenible (GRUFIDES). 2015. *Paquetes normativos 2013–2015 y su impacto en los derechos de las personas en el Perú: Análisis*. Lima: Red Muqui and GRUFIDES.

Rettberg, Angelika, Juan Camilo Cárdenas, and Juan Felipe Ortiz-Riomalo. 2018a. "Mismo recurso, diferentes conflictos: Un análisis de la relación entre oro, conflicto y criminalidad en seis departamentos colombianos." In Angelika Rettberg, Ralf J. Leiteritz, Carlo Nasi, and Juan Diego Prieto, eds., *¿Diferentes recursos, conflictos distintos? La economía política regional del conflicto armado y la criminalidad en Colombia*, 341–400. Bogotá: Ediciones Uniandes.

Rettberg, Angelika, Ralf J. Leiteritz, Carlo Nasi, and Juan Diego Prieto. 2018b. "¿Recursos diferentes, conflictos distintos? Un marco para comprender la economía política del conflicto armado y la criminalidad en las regiones colombianas." In Angelika Rettberg, Ralf J. Leiteritz, Carlo Nasi, and Juan Diego Prieto, eds., *¿Diferentes recursos, conflictos distintos? La economía política regional del conflicto armado y la criminalidad en Colombia*, 3–45. Bogotá: Ediciones Uniandes.

Rettberg, Angelika, and Juan Diego Prieto. 2018. "Conflicto crudo: Petróleo, conflicto armado y criminalidad en Colombia." In Angelika Rettberg, Ralf J. Leiteritz, Carlo Nasi, and Juan Diego Prieto, eds., *¿Diferentes recursos, conflictos distintos? La economía política regional del conflicto armado y la criminalidad en Colombia*, 135–92. Bogotá: Ediciones Uniandes.

Revelo-Rebolledo, Javier. 2019. "The Political Economy of Amazon Deforestation: Subnational Development and the Uneven Reach of the Colombian State." PhD dissertation, University of Pennsylvania.

Revista jubileo. 2017. "Uno de los tres megacampos de gas del país está en fase de declinación." No. 35 (May): 11–13.

Richani, Nazih. 2005. "Multinational Corporations, Rentier Capitalism, and the War System in Colombia." *Latin American Politics and Society* 47, no. 3 (Autumn): 113–44.

Riofrancos, Thea N. 2017. "Scaling Democracy: Participation and Resource Extraction in Latin America." *Perspectives on Politics* 15, no. 3 (September): 678–96.

Riofrancos, Thea N. 2020. *Resource Radicals: From Petro-nationalism to Post-extractivism in Ecuador*. Durham, NC: Duke University Press.

Roa Avendaño, Tatiana, and Luisa María Navas. 2014. "Introducción o incitación a la lectura." In Tatiana Roa Avendaño and Luisa María Navas, eds., *Extractivismo, conflictos y resistencias*, 17–35. Bogotá: Censat Agua Viva.

Rodríguez, Gloria Amparo. 2011. *Las licencias ambientales y su proceso de reglamentación en Colombia*. Bogotá: Foro Nacional Ambiental.

Rodríguez, Gloria Amparo. 2014. *De la consulta previa al consentimiento libre, previo e informado a pueblos indígenas en Colombia*. Bogotá: Universidad del Rosario and Gesellschaft für Internationale Zusammenarbeit.

Rodríguez, Gloria Amparo, Claudia Ardila Ibagon, and Alejandro Puentes Vargas. 2010. "El laberinto jurídico de los U'was en ejercicio del derecho a la resistencia." *Diálogos de saberes*: 173–93.

Rodríguez, Gloria Amparo, and Andrés Gómez Rey. 2013. "La participación como mecanismo de consenso para la asignación de nuevos derechos." *Pensamiento jurídico* 37 (May–August): 71–104.

Rodríguez, Gloria Amparo, and Lina Marcela Muñoz Ávila. 2009. *La participación en la gestión ambiental: Un reto para el nuevo milenio*. Bogotá: Universidad del Rosario.

Rodríguez-Becerra, Manuel, and Guillermo Espinoza. 2002. *Gestión ambiental en América Latina y el Caribe: Evolución, tendencias y principales prácticas*. Washington, DC: Interamerican Development Bank.

Rodríguez-Franco, Diana. 2017. "Participatory Institutions and Environmental Protection: Popular and Prior Consultations in Latin America." PhD dissertation, Northwestern University.

Rodríguez-Garavito, César. 2011. "Ethnicity.gov: Global Governance, Indigenous Peoples, and the Right to Prior Consultation in Social Minefields." *Indiana Journal of Global Legal Studies* 18, no. 1: 263–305.

Rodríguez-Garavito, César A., and Luis Carlos Arenas. 2005. "Indigenous Rights, Transnational Activism, and Legal Mobilization: The Struggle of the U'wa People in Colombia." In Boaventura de Sousa Santos and César A. Rodríguez-Garavito, eds., *Law and Globalization from Below: Towards a Cosmopolitan Legality*, 241–66. Cambridge: Cambridge University Press.

Rodríguez-Piñero, Luis. 2005. *Indigenous Peoples, Postcolonialism, and International Law: The ILO Regime (1919–1989)*. Oxford: Oxford University Press.

Ross, Catherine. 2008. "El caso del Proyecto Camisea: Logros y limitaciones de una coalición ciudadana naciente." In Martin Scurrah, ed., *Defendiendo derechos y promoviendo cambios: El estado, las empresas extractivas y las comunidades locales en el Perú*, 199–268. Lima: Instituto de Estudios Peruanos and Oxfam América.

Sanborn, Cynthia A., and Juan Luis Dammert B. 2013. *Extracción de recursos naturales, desarrollo económico e inclusión social: Perú*. Lima: Centro de Investigación de la Universidad del Pacífico.

Sanborn, Cynthia A., Verónica Hurtado, and Tania Ramírez. 2016. *La consulta previa en el Perú: Avances y retos*. Documento de investigación 6. Lima: Universidad del Pacífico.

Sandoval Rojas, Nathalia. 2013. "La movilización social en tiempos de la Constitución: Feministas, indígenas y víctimas de crímenes de Estado ante la Corte Constitucional colombiana." *Colombia internacional* 79 (September–December): 191–217.

Schilling-Vacaflor, Almut. 2013a. "Prior Consultations in Plurinational Bolivia: Democracy, Rights and Real Life Experiences." *Latin American and Caribbean Ethnic Studies* 8, no. 2: 202–20.

Schilling-Vacaflor, Almut. 2013b. "Rethinking the Consultation-Conflict Link: Lessons from Bolivia's Gas Sector." GIGA Working Papers no. 237. Hamburg: German Institute of Global and Area Studies.

Schilling-Vacaflor, Almut. 2017a. "'If the Company Belongs to You, How Can You Be against It?' Limiting Participation and Taming Dissent in Neo-extractivist Bolivia." *Journal of Peasant Studies* 44, no. 3: 658–76.

Schilling-Vacaflor, Almut. 2017b. "Who Controls the Territory and the Resources? Free, Prior and Informed Consent (FPIC) as a Contested Human Rights Practice in Bolivia." *Third World Quarterly* 38, no. 5 (May): 1058–74.

Schilling-Vacaflor, Almut, and Riccarda Flemmer. 2015. "Conflict Transformation through Prior Consultation? Lessons from Peru." *Journal of Latin American Studies* 47, no. 4 (November): 811–39.

Schilling-Vacaflor, Almut, and Annegret Kuhn. 2015. "Interacciones conflictivas Estado-sociedad sobre nuevos proyectos de gas." In Fundación EU-LAC, ed., *Protestas sociales y capacidad de respuesta de la democracia: Evaluando realidades en América Latina y el Caribe y la Unión Europa*, 127–52. Hamburg: Fundación EU-LAC.

Scott, James C. 1998. *Seeing Like a State: How Certain Schemes to Improve the Human Condition Have Failed*. New Haven, CT: Yale University Press.

Shenk, Jamie L. Forthcoming. "Consultations and Competing Claims: Implementing Participatory Institutions in Colombia's Extractive Industries." *Comparative Politics*: https://doi.org/10.5129/001041522X16358097946287.

Silva Montealegre, Diana. 2015. "Informe grupos étnicos corredor fronterizo Puerto Vega-Teteye en el marco de la Resolución 1930 de 2010." July. Puerto Asís: Consultoría para la Comisión Minero Energética y Ambiental del Putumayo.

Sociedad Peruana de Derecho Ambiental (SPDA). n.d.a. "¿En qué casos se presenta el estudio de impacto ambiental?" Legislación ambiental; El sector minero; Normas de protección ambiental; Estudio de impacto ambiental. Website. Viewed January 25, 2021, at http://www.legislacionambientalspda.org.pe.

Sociedad Peruana de Derecho Ambiental (SPDA). n.d.b. "Estudios ambientales para la pequeña minería y la minería artesanal." Legislación ambiental; El sector minero; Normas de protección ambiental; Estudio de impacto ambiental. Website. Viewed January 25, 2021, at http://www.legislacionambientalspda.org.pe.

Sociedad Peruana de Derecho Ambiental (SPDA). 2016. *La participación ciudadana en los procesos de evaluación: Análisis de casos en 6 países de Latinoamérica*. Cuaderno de derecho de acceso No. 4. Lima: SPDA.

Solano, Pedro. 1999. *Hidrocarburos y áreas naturales protegidas: Más allá del suelo y el subsuelo*. Lima: Sociedad Peruana de Derecho Ambiental.

Stallings, Barbara. 1983. "International Capitalism and the Peruvian Military Government." In Cynthia McClintock and Abraham F. Lowenthal, eds., *The Peruvian Experiment Reconsidered*, 144–80. Princeton, NJ: Princeton University Press.

Stetson, George. 2012. "Oil Politics and Indigenous Resistance in the Peruvian Amazon: The Rhetoric of Modernity against the Reality of Coloniality." *Journal of Environment and Development* 1, no. 1: 76–97.

Szablowski, David. 2010. "Operationalizing Free, Prior, and Informed Consent in the Extractive Industry Sector? Examining the Challenges of a Negotiated Model of Justice." *Canadian Journal of Development Studies* 30, nos. 1–2: 111–30.

Tockman, Jason, and John Cameron. 2014. "Indigenous Autonomy and the Contradictions of Plurinationalism in Bolivia." *Latin American Politics and Society* 56, no. 3 (Fall): 46–69.

Toro Pérez, Catalina. 2012. "Geopolítica energética: Minería, territorio y resistencias sociales." In Catalina Toro Pérez, Julio Fierro Morales, Sergio Coronado Delgado, and Tatiana Roa Avendaño, eds., *Minería, territorio y conflicto en Colombia*, 17–34. Bogotá: Universidad Nacional de Colombia.

Torres Wong, Marcela. 2019. *Natural Resources, Extraction and Indigenous Rights in Latin America: Exploring the Boundaries of Environmental and State Corporate Crime in Bolivia, Peru and Mexico*. New York: Routledge.

Tuval Antonio, Riquett Araque. 2017. "Coexistencia del ministerio de ambiente y desarrollo sostenible y de las corporaciones autónomas regionales: Necesidad o burocracia." *Derectum* 2, no. 1: 9–29.

Ulloa, Astrid, and Sergio Coronado, eds. 2016. *Extractivismos y posconflicto en Colombia: Retos para la paz territorial*. Bogotá: Editorial Universidad Nacional de Colombia and Centro de Investigación y Educación Popular Programa por la Paz.

United Nations. n.d. "United Nations Declaration on the Rights of Indigenous Peoples." Web site. Viewed January 1, 2022, at https://www.un.org/development/desa/indigenouspeoples/declaration-on-the-rights-of-indigenous-peoples.html.

United Nations Human Rights Council. 2009. *Informe del Relator Especial sobre la situación de los derechos humanos y las libertades fundamentales de los indígenas, S. James Anaya; Adición: Observaciones sobre la situación de los pueblos indígenas de la Amazonía y los sucesos del 5 de junio y días posteriores en las provincias de Bagua y Utcubamba, Perú*. United Nations. A/HRC/12/34/Add.8. August 18.

Urrea, Danilo, and Tatiana Rodríguez Maldonado. 2014. "Gran minería y conflicto: Una perspectiva socio-ambiental del modelo de desarrollo en Colombia." In Tatiana Roa Avendaño and Luisa María Navas, eds., *Extractivismo, conflictos y resistencias*, 73–106. Bogotá: Censat Agua Viva.

Van Cott, Donna Lee. 2000. "A Political Analysis of Legal Pluralism in Bolivia and Colombia." *Journal of Latin American Studies* 32, no. 1 (February): 207–34.

Velasco Jaramillo, Marcela. 2014. "The Territorialization of Ethnopolitical Reforms in Colombia: Chocó as a Case Study." *Latin American Research Review*, 49, no. 3: 126–52.

Walter, Mariana, and Joan Martinez-Alier. 2010. "How to Be Heard When Nobody Wants to Listen: Community Action against Mining in Argentina." *Canadian Journal of Development Studies* 30, nos. 1–2: 281–301.

Walter, Mariana, and Leire Urkidi. 2017. "Community Mining Consultations in Latin America (2002–2012): The Contested Emergence of a Hybrid Institution for Participation." *Geoforum* 84 (August): 265–79.

Wampler, Brian. 2007. *Participatory Budgeting in Brazil: Contestation, Cooperation, and Accountability*. University Park: Pennsylvania State University Press.

Wampler, Brian and Leonardo Avritzer. 2004. "Participatory Publics: Civil Society and New Institutions in Democratic Brazil." *Comparative Politics* 36, no. 3 (April): 291–312.

Yashar, Deborah J. 2005. *Contesting Citizenship in Latin America: The Rise of Indigenous Movements and the Postliberal Challenge*. New York: Cambridge University Press.

Zeisser Polatsik, Marco. 2015. *La experiencia de la mesa de diálogo en Espinar 2012–2013: ¿Un nuevo modelo de gestión de conflicto socio ambiental?* Lima: CooperAcción.

LAWS, JUDICIAL DECISIONS, EXECUTIVE MEASURES, AND INTERNATIONAL TREATIES AND DECLARATIONS

International Labour Organization (ILO). 1989. *Indigenous and Tribal Peoples Convention, C169*. June 27. Viewed July 29, 2021, at https://www.ilo.org/dyn/normlex/en/f?p=NORMLEXPUB:1.

United Nations. 2007. *United Nations Declaration on the Rights of Indigenous Peoples*. Viewed January 1, 2022, at https://www.un.org/development/desa/indigenous peoples.

Bolivia

Decreto Supremo (DS) 29033. 2007. "Reglamento de consulta y participación para actividades hidrocarburíferas." April 24.

Law 3058. 2005. "Ley de hidrocarburos." May 17.

Regulations, Law 1333. 1995. "Reglamentación de la Ley No. 1333 del medio ambiente: Reglamento de prevención y control ambiental." December 8.

Colombia

Auto 06445. 2018. "Por el cual se ordena el archivo de la solicitud de Licencia Ambiental iniciada a través del Auto 99 del 4 de enero de 2018." Ministerio de Ambiente y Desarrollo Sostenible, Autoridad Nacional de Licencias Ambientales. October 23.

Decree 330. 2007. "Por el cual se reglamentan las audiencias públicas ambientales y se deroga el Decreto 2762 de 2005." Ministerio de Ambiente, Vivienda y Desarrollo Territorial. February 8.

Decree 2041. 2014. "Por el cual se reglamenta el Título VIII de la Ley 99 de 1993 sobre licencias ambientales." Ministerio de Ambiente, Vivienda y Desarrollo Territorial. October 15.

Decree 2820. 2010. "Por el cual se reglamenta el Título VIII de la Ley 99 de 1993 sobre licencias ambientales." Ministerio de Ambiente, Vivienda y Desarrollo Territorial. August 4.

Law 1450. 2011. "Por la cual se expide el Plan Nacional de Desarrollo, 2010–14." June 16.

Law 1753. 2015. "Por la cual se expide el Plan Nacional de Desarrollo 2014–2018 'Todos por un nuevo país'." June 9.

Presidential Directive 01. 2010. "Garantía del derecho fundamental a la consulta previa de los grupos étnicos nacionales." March 26.

Resolution 0331. 2012. "Por la cual se otorga una licencia ambiental y se toman otras determinaciones." Ministerio de Ambiente y Desarrollo Sostenible, Autoridad Nacional de Licencias Ambientales. May 15.

Resolution 1015. 2011. "Por la cual no se acepta un desistimiento por motivos de interés público, se niega una licencia ambiental global y se toman otras determinaciones." Ministerio de Ambiente, Vivienda y Desarrollo Territorial. May 31.

Resolution 01606. 2018. "Por la cual se otorga una Licencia Ambiental y se toman otras determinaciones." Ministerio de Ambiente y Desarrollo Sostenible, Autoridad Nacional de Licencias Ambientales. September 20.

Sentence SU123/18. 2018. Reference: Expediente T-4.926.682. Constitutional Court. November 15.

Sentence T-730/16. 2016. Reference: Expediente T-5.237.384. Constitutional Court. December 19.

Sentence T-769/09. 2009. Reference: Expediente T-2315944. Constitutional Court. October 29.

Peru

Decreto Supremo (DS) 020-2008-EM. 2008. "Reglamento ambiental para las actividades de exploración minera." Ministerio de Energía y Minas. April 1.

Decreto Supremo (DS) 028-2008-EM. 2008. "Aprueban el reglamento de participación ciudadana en el subsector minero." Ministerio de Energía y Minas. May 27.

Directive 001-2014-VMI-MC. 2014. "Lineamientos que establece instrumentos de recolección de información social y fija criterios para su aplicación en el marco de la identificación de los pueblos indígenas u originarios." Ministerio de Cultura, Viceministerio de Interculturalidad. February 25.

Legislative Decree 613. 1990. "Código del medio ambiente y los recursos naturales." September 8.

Report 389-2010/MEM-AAM/CAG/WAL/CMC. 2010. "Asunto: 'Evaluación de la Modificación del Estudio de Impacto Ambiental del Proyecto Quellaveco de la empresa Anglo American Quellaveco S.A.'" Ministerio de Energía y Minas, Viceministerio de Minas. April 20.

Report 531-2009/MEM-AAM/PRN/WAL/EA/WBF/PRR/RC. 2009. "Asunto: 'Evaluación de la Modificación del Estudio de Impacto Ambiental del Proyecto Quellaveco de Anglo American Quellaveco S.A.'" Ministerio de Energía y Minas, Viceministerio de Minas. May 15.

Resolución Directoral (RD) 173-2011-MEM/AAE. 2011. Ministerio de Energía y Minas. June 7.

Resolución Directoral (RD) 225-2010-MEM/AAM. 2010. Ministerio de Energía y Minas. July 6.

Resolución Ministerial (RM) 304-2008-MEM/DM. 2008. "Aprueban normas que regulan el proceso de participación ciudadana en el subsector minero." Ministerio de Energía y Minas. June 24.

Resolución Ministerial (RM) 596-2002-EM/DM. 2002. "Aprueba el reglamento de consulta y participación ciudadana en el procedimiento de aprobación de los Estudios Ambientales en el sector energía y minas." Ministerio de Energía y Minas. December 21.

Resolución Ministerial (RM) 728-99-EM/VMM. 1999. "Aprueban reglamento de participación ciudadana en el procedimiento de aprobación de los estudios ambientales presentados al MEM." Ministerio de Energía y Minas. December 30.

Resolución veinte. 2019. Expediente 14037-2012-0-1810-JR-CI-10. Corte Superior de Lima. April 26.

NEWS SOURCES

News about Bolivia

Achtenberg, Emily. 2014. "Rival Factions in Bolivia's CONAMAQ: Internal Conflict or Government Manipulation?" *NACLA*, "Rebel Currents." February 2.

Barriga, Roberto. 2014. "Guaraníes aprueban inicio de consulta previa para Sísmica 3D San Antonio." *El Páis*. August 19.

Bolivia.com. 2012. "Compensación de $us 37 millones exigida por Takovo Mora inviabiliza construcción de la Planta Río Grande." January 18.

Candela, Gemma. 2015. "Takovo Mora, un mes después: Continúan las secuelas de la represión policial." *La Pública BO*. September.

Centro de Estudios para el Desarrollo Laboral y Agrario. 2011. "Denuncian que petrolera quiere quedarse con tierras de la comunidad guaraní Iguasurenda." Noticias de prensa. June 2.

Educación Radiofónica de Bolivia (ERBOL). 2012a. "Directorio paralelo toma oficinas de la sede de la CIDOB." July 27.

Educación Radiofónica de Bolivia (ERBOL). 2012b. "Gobierno creó cuatro paralelas de la CIDOB para que apoyen la carretera." *Servindi*. November 20.

Educación Radiofónica de Bolivia (ERBOL). 2015a. "YPFB dice que no consultó a guaraníes porque los pozos están en área privada." July 31.

Educación Radiofónica de Bolivia (ERBOL). 2015b. "Denuncian violenta intervención policial a bloqueo guaraní contra pozos petroleros en Takovo Mora." August 18.

Educación Radiofónica de Bolivia (ERBOL). 2015c. "Guaraníes de Takovo Mora se abren a iniciar diálogo." *Correo del sur*. August 21.

Educación Radiofónica de Bolivia (ERBOL). 2015d. "Guaraníes piden hace 19 años titulación de Takovo Mora." August 24.

Eju! 2010. "Pueblo Guaraní aún no decidió ingreso de Petroandina al parque Aguaragüe." November 12.

Eju! 2013. "Indígenas guaraníes traban inversión en megaproyecto gasífero." March 11.

Eju! 2014. "Manejo de recursos millonarios enfrenta a dirigentes guaraníes de la APG IG." September 6.

Eju! 2020. "Perú y Paraguay captan el 94% de las ventas de GLP boliviano." February 3.

El Deber. 2020. "Una de las tres CIDOB eligió nuevo presidente y demanda titulación de territorios indígenas y nuevas dotaciones." November 1.

El Día. 2014. "Gran Chaco inicia operaciones y Yacuiba celebra con suspensión de actividades." October 16.

El País. 2013. "Yaku Igua recibirá Bs 14 millones por construcción de Planta Gran Chaco." May 16.

Equipo Nizkor and Derechos Human Rights. 2013. "La APG IG afirma que el proceso de consulta sobre el Bloque San Antonio está viciado de nulidad." January 18, 2013, letter from Benildo Vaca, head of Natural Resources, APG-Itika Guasu, to the Viceminister of Energy Development, Ministry of Hydrocarbons and Energy. January 21.

Fundación Tierra. 2019. "Bolivia cuenta con un marco legal para la consulta." News section of web site: https://ftierra.org/. June 11.

Instituto Nacional de Reforma Agraria. 2012. "INRA aclara que declaró tierras fiscales 'NO disponibles' en TCO Takovo Mora." News section of web site: http://www.inra.gob.bo. January 13.

La Andalucía boliviana. 2012. "Comunidades guaraníes aprobaron desarrollo del Bloque San Antonio." December 7.

La Razón. 2018. "Aún no se cuenta con una normativa que garantice la consulta previa a los pueblos indígenas." April 30.

López Camacho, Enid. 2018. "21 proyectos ponen en riesgo a las áreas protegidas y a los indígenas." *Los Tiempos*. April 22.

Los Tiempos. 2016. "YPFB Petroandina suma dos fracasos." March 23.

Luksic, Alvaro. 2010. "Guaraníes advierten con paralizar proyecto gasífero boliviano-argentino." *El País*. August 30.

Luksic, Alvaro. 2012a. "Ministerio de Hidrocarburos revela que ya hizo consulta para Separadora del Chaco." *El País*. June 28.

Luksic, Alvaro. 2012b. "APG toman otra vez predios de la planta separadora del Gran Chaco." *El País*. July 3.

Luksic, Alvaro. 2012c. "Indígenas logran 'consulta' para la Planta del Chaco." *El País*. September 30.

Ministerio de Hidrocarburos. 2014. "Concluye con éxito proceso de Consulta y Participación para el proyecto 'Exploración Sísmica 3D, en el Bloque San Antonio'." Press release. November 14.

Observatorio petrolero sur. 2011. "Bolivia: Tribunal Constitucional reconoce derecho a consulta y propiedad de la TCO Itika Guasu." May 19.

Oxígeno. 2015. "Policías intervienen bloqueo de comunarios de Takovo Mora." August 18.

Página siete digital. 2015. "Indígenas de Takovo Mora reanudan bloqueo a planta Gran Chaco." August 14.

Paredes, Jimena. 2013. "Guaraníes exigen una nueva compensación." *La Razón*. April 4.

Seas Yelma, Natalia. 2013. "Guaraníes bolivianos defienden su agua en tierra de petróleo." *IPS Noticias*. January 23.

Servicio de Noticias Ambientales (SENA). 2010. "Indígenas del pueblo guaraní demandan que se respeten los derechos de consulta establecidos por la nueva Constitución." May 21.

Servindi. 2011. "Bolivia: Tribunal Constitucional otorga posibilidad de veto a indígenas." September 6.

Servindi. 2012. "Bolivia: Acuerdan culminar proceso de consulta previa a guaraníes." January 27.

Vásquez, Wálter. 2012. "Declaran cuarto intermedio en lío por Río Grande." *La Razón*. January 19.

Vicepresidencia del Estado Plurinacional de Bolivia. 2015. "García Linera habló de la distribución de tierras, la consulta y participación en la entrega de viviendas en Takovo Mora." News section of web-site: http://www.vicepresidencia.gob.bo. September 26.

Yacimientos Petrolíferos Fiscales Bolivianos (YPFB). 2012. "YPFB y Takovo Mora acuerdan Bs 7 millones como compensación por la Planta Río Grande." Communications section of web-site: http://www1.ypfb.bo. April 10.

Yacimientos Petrolíferos Fiscales Bolivianos (YPFB). 2016. "Campo Caigua aporta nuevos 20 millones de pies cúbicos por día de gas desde enero." News section of web-site: https://www.ypfb.gob.bo/. January 19.

News about Colombia

Agencia Nacional de Licencias Ambientales (ANLA). 2018. "Alrededor de 600 personas asistieron a reunión informativa sobre proyecto petrolero en Caquetá." February 8.

Bermúdez Liévano, Andrés. 2015. "Caquetá se le planta al petróleo." *La silla vacía*. July 1.

Bermúdez Liévano, Andrés. 2017. "La empresa china sin 'licencia social' para sacar petróleo en Colombia." *Semana sostenible*. November 29.

Betancur Alarcón, Laura. 2016. "El milenario arroyo que cambiará de rumbo por una mina de carbón." *El Tiempo*. May 24.

Censat Agua Viva noticias. 2018. "Niegan licencias ambientales para pilotos de fracking en el Magdalena Medio." November 6.

Chato, Pilar. 2016. "¿Por qué los U'wa se han tomado una planta de Ecopetrol?" *Otramérica*. July 21.

Cobb, Julia. 2017. "AngloGold Suspends Colombia Project after Anti-mining Vote." *Reuters*. April 27.

Colectivo de Abogados "José Alvear Restrepo" and Corporación Ambiental y Turística del Río Humadea–CORPOHUMADEA. 2016. "Ecopetrol pretende explorar pozo en Meta incumpliendo fallo de Tutela." April 8.

Comisión Intereclesial de Justicia y Paz. 2008. "Consulta de los Pueblos 24–28 de febrero de 2009." *Parti-sí-pa* 153 (December 23).

Comité por la Defensa del Agua del Municipio de Tauramena–Casanare. 2018. "La odisea que originó la consulta popular de Tauramena–Casanare." *Semillas*. April 4.

Congote Gutiérrez, Nicolás. 2012. "Lucha embera por el cerro de los espíritus." *El Tiempo*. November 29.

Cuevas Guarnizo, Angélica María. 2014. "'La Colosa afectaría páramos del Tolima'." *El Espectador*. January 2.

Dejusticia. 2016. "Corte se estrenó en fallos sobre consultas populares mineras a favor de la participación ciudadana." October 20.

Dejusticia. 2018. "Solicitamos la anulación de la sentencia que le pone límites a las consultas populares." News section of web site: https://www.dejusticia.org. December 5.

Díaz, Karla. 2016. "El caso del bloque petrolero 'El Nogal' en Caquetá." *Semana sostenible*. May 20.

Díaz Parra, Karla. 2018. "'Desapareció el agua': Preocupación en Caquetá por falencias en los estudios técnicos de la empresa petrolera Emerald Energy." *Semana sostenible*. March 20.

Dinero. 2014. "No solo violencia." August 21.

Ebus, Bram. 2017. "World Bank Exits Controversial Angostura Goldmine Project in Colombian Moorland." *Mongabay*. March 23.

El Espectador. 2017. "'Consulta minera en Cajamarca no tiene la capacidad de cambiar la ley': Gobierno." March 27.

El Espectador. 2019. "Tauramena (Casanare) votó contra la explotación petrolera y la justicia anuló su decisión." October 18.

El Tiempo. 2000. "Los indígenas U'wa volvieron a paro de Boyacá." May 23.

El Tiempo. 2011. "Procuraduría pidió revocar título minero en Parque Yaigojé-Apaporis." July 13.

El Tiempo. 2012a. "En Guamal piden que no les perforen la montaña para extraer petróleo." May 13.

El Tiempo. 2012b. "Ecopetrol, con licencia para explorar municipios en el Meta." July 26.

El Tiempo. 2012c. "Cerrejón pospone el proyecto de desviación del río Ranchería." November 9.

El Tiempo. 2013a. "Concepto favorable a perforación en Lorito 1." February 26.

El Tiempo. 2013b. "Se unen las voces en un grito contra la explotación petrolera." March 19.

El Tiempo. 2013c. "Se cumple casi un mes del plantón en Guamal por exploración petrolera." March 21.

El Tiempo. 2013d. "Señales de alarma por descontrolada extracción de petróleo en el Meta." July 24.

El Tiempo. 2013e. "Tribunal ordena detener obras de proyecto petrolero de Ecopetrol." August 29.

El Tiempo. 2013f. "Lista la audiencia de Lorito 1." September 20.

El Tiempo. 2013g. "Ecopetrol: 'Proyecto CPO-9 sí cumple con licencias'." October 2.

El Tiempo. 2013h. "Inconforme ánimo en audiencia pública." October 5.

El Tiempo. 2013i. "En Tauramena no tendrán más proyectos petroleros." December 16.

El Tiempo. 2014a. "Rebelión a proyecto petrolero en el Meta." April 24.

El Tiempo. 2014b. "'Fiebre del oro' enfrenta a dos comunidades indígenas." April 30.

El Tiempo. 2014c. "Corte Constitucional ordena a Ecopetrol suspender operación de pozo." July 31.

El Tiempo. 2014d. "Premio para los indígenas del parque Yaigojé por oponerse a la minería." September 24.

El Tiempo. 2016a. "Corte discute sobre tutela contra 27 pozos petroleros en Putumayo." February 18.

El Tiempo. 2016b. "Preparan estudio ambiental para hacer fracking en Cesar." April 28.

El Tiempo. 2016c. "San Martín, el pueblo que rechaza el 'fracking' en su territorio." October 27.

El Tiempo. 2017. "Tribunal tumbó Acuerdo Municipal que prohibió la minería en Ibagué." December 5.

Flórez Góngora, Miguel Ángel. 2015. "Conflicto en el Caquetá: Mininterior dialoga con comunidades que rechazan sísmica de Emerald Energy." *Inteligencia petrolera*. July 2.

Gómez Nadal, Paco. 2014. "La interminable lucha de los U'wa contra el petróleo." *Otramérica*. April 18.

The Guardian. 2015. "Colombian Tribe Scores 'Historic' Victory versus Big Gas." March 26.

Güesguán Serpa, Óscar, and Sergio Silva Numa. 2016. "'Fracking' genera incertidumbre en San Martín, Cesar." *El Espectador*. April 13.

Guidi, Ruxandra. 2016. "New Law Banning Mining in Colombia's Moorlands Could Draw First Lawsuit." *Mongabay*. March 15.

Hernández Bonilla, Juan Miguel. 2017. "Cajamarca: Golpe a la locomotora minera." *El Espectador*. March 26.

Herrera, Natalia. 2012. "El pulso por el río Ranchería." *El Tiempo*. June 10.

Hidalgo y Costilla, Braulio, and Lucía Ramírez. 2014. "Putumayo, entre la guerra y el despojo." *Seguimos informando*. September 26.

Hill, David. 2014. "Will the U'was Be Forced to Threaten to Commit Mass Suicide Again?" *The Guardian*. June 17.

Jáuregui Sarmiento, David. 2017. "Tribunal del Tolima tumbó prohibición minera a gran escala emitida por Consejo de Ibagué." *Asuntos legales*. December 7.

Koop, Fermín. 2015. "Unidos contra la explotación de petróleo en Colombia." Asociación Ambiente y Sociedad. News section of web site: https://www.ambienteysociedad.org.co. August 15.

La Liga Contra el Silencio. 2019. "Liderazgo ambiental en riesgo: Meta y petróleo." January 16.

Meléndez P., Jorge Enrique. 2006. "U'was perdieron guerra de 14 años." *El Tiempo*. December 16.

Molano Jimeno, Alfredo. 2013. "Tauramena le dice no a la exploración petrolera." *El Espectador*. December 15.

Neira, Oscar. 2016. "Caquetá: Empieza la perforación petrolera." *El Espectador*. October 31.

Observatorio de Conflictos Mineros de América Latina. 2018. "Resistencia al fracking en Colombia." July 31.

Orduz, Natalia. 2012. "Desviación del Río Ranchería, ¿sí o no?" *La silla vacía*. August 20.

Portafolio. 2011. "Proyecto Minero de la empresa Greystar enfrenta problema ambiental." February 22.

Portafolio. 2016. "Tras acuerdo con los u'wa comienzan reparaciones en Gibraltar." July 28.

Portafolio. 2017. "Alcalde de Ibagué dice que la consulta popular minera 'sigue viva'." February 20.

Prensa libre Casanare. 2013a. "Ecopetrol avanza en la socialización del proyecto sísmico Odisea 3D." September 4.

Prensa libre Casanare. 2013b. "Ecopetrol confirmó suspensión del proyecto de sísmica Odisea 3D en Casanare." December 11.

Prensa libre Casanare. 2017. "Ecopetrol comenzó obras civiles para pozo exploratorio Lorito-1, en el Meta." August 14.

Prieto, Jineth. 2016. "Las Vetas de la sentencia sobre páramos." *La silla vacía*. February 14.

Pulido, Julio. 2014. "Putumayo, ¿qué está pasando?" *Semanario voz*. August 29.

Radio France internationale. 2020. "Contraloría da razón a comunidades en disputa con Cerrejón por Arroyo Bruno." July 18.

Radio mundo real. 2018. "Frenar el sacudón: Entrevista a Carlos Andrés Santiago, integrante de CORDATEC, sobre la lucha 'pacífica y contundente' que dan contra el fracking en Colombia." April 3.

RCN radio. 2018. "Anla inició trámite para licencia ambiental de Fracking en Cesar." February 7.

Reuters. 2019. "Eco Oro Pulls Out of Colombia Gold Concession amid Legal Battle: Letter." June 28.

Rojas Hernández, Tatiana. 2020. "Graves hallazgos de la Contraloría sobre arroyo desviado por Cerrejón." *El Tiempo*. July 15.

RPT noticias. 2016. "En San Martín, Cesar, dicen que ANLA miente frente al fracking." April 17.

Rubiano, María Paula. 2017. "La Procuraduría pidió frenar el pozo estrella de Ecopetrol." *El Espectador*. September 4.

Semana. 2011. "El 'Avatar' colombiano." May 21.

Semana. 2017. "La otra cara de las licencias ambientales." May 20.

Semana. 2018. "Corte ordena consultar a los awá para proyecto petrolero del Putumayo." November 19.

Semana sostenible. 2016a. "El fracking se va temporalmente del Cesar." September 22.

Semana sostenible. 2016b. "El petróleo acabó con el agua de Puerto Asís." October 24.

Semana sostenible. 2016c. "La verdad detrás del fallo sobre el Arroyo Bruno." December 21.

Semana sostenible. 2018a. "Denuncian contaminación del agua en donde se haría uno de los primeros pilotos de fracking en Colombia." February 15.

Semana sostenible. 2018b. "Los 9 municipios que le dijeron No a la minería usando la consulta popular." October 12.

UN periódico digital. 2019. "El arroyo Bruno en La Guajira, ¿intereses económicos contra el medioambiente?" July 29.

Valencia, Edilberto. 2018. "Florencia, Morelia, Valparaíso y Milán: Vía libre para las petroleras." *Selva.com.co*. October 2.

Vanguardia. 2011. "Amplia participación en la marcha en defensa del agua." February 26.

W Radio. 2014. "Gobierno logra acuerdo con comunidad U'wa para reparar oleoducto Caño-Limón Coveñas." May 2.

News about Peru

Álvarez, Luis. 2017. "Gasoducto del Sur: Un proyecto que comienza a oxidarse." *La República*. November 26.

Álvarez Rodrich, Augusto. 2012. "Conga post mortem." *La República*. August 23.

Andina. 2009. "Minera Afrodita recibe permiso del MEM para exploración en la Cordillera del Cóndor." December 10.

Andina. 2010. "Hasta el 9 de mayo se recibirán aportes al EIA del proyecto minero de Quellaveco." April 16.

Andina. 2011. "MEM aprobó estudio de impacto ambiental del proyecto minero Las Bambas de Xstrata." March 7.

Bárcena Carpio, Jonathan. 2014. "Arequipa: Policía evitará bloqueos de vías en paro contra Tía María." *La República*. December 15.

Bloomberg. 2019. "Southern Copper espera que Tía María inicie producción en el 2022." *Gestión*. July 24.

Business News Americas. 1999. "Metalfin Transfers Properties to Afrodita." June 30.

Business News Americas. 2020. "Río Blanco planea reubicar relavera y concentradora en proyecto en Perú." November 26.

Castro, Jonathan, and Elízabeth Prado. 2012. "Manifestantes de la Marcha del Agua exigen cambio en política minera nacional." February 9.

Cervantes, María. 2019. "Comisión aprueba proyecto cobre Tía María en Perú, pero gobierno dice que no lo impondrá." *Reuters*. October 30.

Chauca, María. 2013. "Proyecto Tía María cumple con audiencia pública en medio de protesta que dejó tres heridos." *La República*. December 19.

Chauca Castillo, María. 2013. "Hoy se ejecutará el primer taller de proyecto Tía María pese a rechazo de dirigentes." *La República*. October 23.

Coordinadora nacional de radio. 2010a. "Controversia por audiencia sobre proyecto minero Quellaveco." April 9.

Coordinadora nacional de radio. 2010b. "Agricultores moqueguanos se movilizaron contra minería." April 14.

De Echave C., José. 2018. "Qué está pasando en las Bambas?" *Servindi*. January 23.

Del Río, María Luisa. 2015. "Las Bambas: Las dos caras del conflicto por el proyecto minero." *Perú 21*. November 15.

Dirección Regional, Energía y Minas–Moquegua. n.d. "Se realizó taller participativo sobre tercera modificación del EIA de proyecto minero Quellaveco." Online document. Retrieved on April 27, 2012, from http://www.diremmoq.gob.pe.

Dow Jones. 2009. "Peru pushes Southern Copper to Get Community OK for Tia Maria." September 15.

El Comercio. 2010a. "Gobierno canceló audiencia pública sobre proyecto Tía María en Islay." April 17.

El Comercio. 2010b. "Tía María traería US$5 millones anuales de desarrollo social." May 2.

El Comercio. 2010c. "Huelga indefinida contra el proyecto minero Tía María se iniciará este lunes." November 20.

El Comercio. 2011. "Presidente regional de Arequipa pidió cancelar proyecto Tía María." April 7.

El Comercio. 2012. "Peritaje al EIA de Conga propone evaluar la preservación de dos de cuatro lagunas." April 19.

El Comercio. 2015. "Southern inició su campaña de sensibilización por Tía María." September 1.

El Comercio. 2016a. "Presidente de Buenaventura: 'Proyecto Conga ya no es viable'." April 26.
El Comercio. 2016b. "Desfile patrio y antiminero contra Tía María en Cocachacra." July 29.
El Comercio. 2017a. "MEM apela sentencia que termina contrato del Lote 116." April 4.
El Comercio. 2017b. "Corte Suprema confirma sentencia que absuelve a Máxima Acuña." May 3.
El Comercio. 2019a. "Piura: Comuneros reavivan con marcha oposición al proyecto minero Río Blanco." April 24.
El Comercio. 2019b. "Las Bambas: Toda la cronología del proceso de diálogo entre minera y Fuerabamba." May 21.
El Comercio. 2020. "Las Bambas: ¿Cuánto le cuesta a Apurímac el bloqueo de carreteras?" February 10.
El Peruano. 2011. "Proyecto Conga suspendido." November 30.
Enlace nacional. 2007. "Realizan taller previo al inicio de la mina Tía María." November 16.
Estrada, Edy. 2013. "Pronunciamiento de ORPIANP sobre territorio awajún-wampís." Baguapero.com. April 25.
Finlayson, Bryan. 2012. "Conga Mine Protests Continue as Peruvians Await Court Decision." *NACLA*. News. January 19.
Fowks, Jacqueline. 2019. "Un conflicto minero pone a prueba al Gobierno peruano." *El País*. April 11.
García, Elías. 2013. "China Zijin busca iniciar proyecto cuprífero Río Blanco en el 2015." *Gestión*. December 30.
Gorriti, Gustavo. 2011. "De lagunas a desmontes." *IDL reporteros*. November 25.
Grupo de Formación e Intervención para el Desarrollo Sostenible (GRUFIDES). 2004. "Contexto de la crisis del Quilish." Equipo Nizkor and Derechos Human Rights. August 21.
Grupo de Formación e Intervención para el Desarrollo Sostenible (GRUFIDES). 2016. "'QUILISH,' la historia de un conflicto que no termina." September 4.
Hualpa, Eliana. 2011. "Tensión en Huacullani por proyecto minero Santa Ana." *Noticias SER*. March 23.
Huanachín, Wilfredo. 2017. "Bear Creek gana fallo arbitral por expropiación en proyecto Santa Ana." *Gestión*. December 4.
Hurtado, Jonathan. 2015. "Entregan territorio ancestral awajún a empresa minera Afrodita." *Servindi*. December 16.
Inforegión. 2011. "Petrolera presenta estudio de impacto ambiental para exploración de pozos en Amazonas." March 17.
Inoue, Yuko. 2012. "Update 3: Mitsubishi Outbids Rivals to Win Peru Copper Mine Stake." *Reuters*. February 17.
Instituto de Defensa Legal. 2019. "Sentencia definitiva ordena suspensión de actividad petrolera en el lote 116." *Noticias*. August 8.
Jima Chamiquit, Clelia, Augostina Mayan, and Wrays Perez. 2016. "Minera Afrodita tiene permiso de explotación en Cordillera del Cóndor." *Servindi*. August 24.
Kayap Jempekit, Zebelio, and Juan Carlos Ruiz Molleda. 2013. "La captura del Estado por una empresa minera: La 'carta de sujeción' de INRENA a minera Afrodita." *Servindi*. August 29.
Kozak, Robert. 2009. "Peru Locals Vote against Southern Copper's Tia Maria." *Mines and Communities*. September 28.
La Mula. 2012. "La revisión del EIA de Quellaveco." May 2.

La Mula. 2020. "Congresistas de Arequipa se reunieron con Zeballos y hablaron sobre Tía María." July 5.

La República. 2012a. "Southern Copper reanudaría proyecto Tía María el 2015." February 9.

La República. 2012b. "Por qué Conga no va." Suplemento especial. March 4.

La República. 2012c. "Yanacocha todavía evalúa nuevas condiciones al proyecto minero Conga." May 9.

La República. 2014. "Cusco: Pobladores acuerdan levantar paro en La Convención." September 9.

La República. 2016a. "Pobladores del valle de Tambo reinician marchas contra proyecto Tía María." April 27.

La República. 2016a. "Yanacocha anuncia su retiro de Conga en el año 2020." August 11.

La República. 2019. "Paro por el Gasoducto Sur inicia con bloqueo de vías en ingresos a regiones del sur." June 6.

La República. 2020a. "Cusco pide a presidente Martín Vizcarra reactivar el Gasoducto del Sur." March 12.

La República. 2020b. "Comuneros de Cusco presentan demanda para anular estado de emergencia." May 14.

Leyva, Ana. 2013. "Análisis de los D.S. 054 y 060 de la PCM." *Noticias SER.pe*. June 6. Reprinted in "Perú: Gobierno sacrifice patrimonio natural, cultural y derechos por favorecer inversión." *Servindi*. June 7, 2013.

Loayza, Jorge. 2011. "Debate: La posición a favor y en contra del polémico proyecto minero." *La República*. November 20.

Los Andes. 2012. "Instalan mesa de diálogo que analizará problemática minera en Moquegua." March 13.

Machacuay, Michael. 2019. "¿Cuál es el origen del conflicto en Las Bambas?" *La República*. March 27.

Malpartida Tabuchi, Jorge. 2018. "Arequipa: Valle de Tambo en compás de espera por Tía María." *El Comercio*. March 3.

Minería y progreso. 2010. "Southern Perú invertirá $50 millones en planta desalinizadora en Tía María." November 12.

Mining.com. 2011. "Aprueban EIA de Sistema de Transporte Andino del Sur de Kuntur." June 8.

Motta, Rufino. 2010. "Se agudiza conflicto Ilo-Moquegua." *La República*. July 4.

Motta, Rufino. 2012. "ANA ratifica que hay agua para Quellaveco." *La República*. January 10.

Motta, Rufino. 2019. "En una semana se sabrá diseño de Gasoducto Sur." *La República*. May 25.

Movimiento Ciudadano frente al Cambio Climático. 2020. "Ciudadanos exigen justicia por criminalización de defensores ambientales awajún." February 27.

Ordóñez, José Alberto. 2009. "Kuntur garantiza construcción del Gasoducto del Sur." *La Mula*. September 14.

Ortiz, Claudia. 2019. "Las Bambas: Los hechos más importantes para entender el conflicto." *La República*. March 27.

Perú 21. 2009. "Una audiencia pública terminó en batalla campal en Arequipa." August 28.

Perú 21. 2013. "Tía María: Suspenden taller para explicar estudio de impacto ambiental." October 30.

Prado, Elízabeth. 2011a. "Declaran nulo el proyecto Tía María." *La República*. April 9.

Prado, Elízabeth. 2011b. "Diálogo sobre proyecto Conga se entrampa." *La República*. October 29.

Reuters. 2010. "Southern ve viable planta desalinizadora para proyecto Tía María." *El Comercio*. May 24.

Reuters. 2020. "Anglo American paraliza proyecto Quellaveco en Perú por tres meses." *Gestión*. April 23.

Revista la punta. 2009. "Southern relanza proyecto Tía María." July 31.

Rochabrún, Marcelo, and Nicholas Casey. 2018. "Peru's President Offers Resignation Over Vote-Buying Scandal." *New York Times*. March 21.

Romo Espinoza, Vanessa. 2012. "Gregorio Santos sobre Conga: 'Ahora es un tema de licencia social'." *El Comercio*. January 3.

RPP noticias. 2020. "Martín Vizcarra dice que Tía María no va en su gobierno: 'No están dadas las condiciones'." January 29.

Ruiz Molleda, Juan Carlos. 2017. "Caso Ichigkat Muja: Admiten demanda por incumplimiento estatal." *Servindi*. June 6.

Ruiz Molleda, Juan Carlos. 2020. "Pueblos indígenas le ganan batalla a gobierno en defensa de sus territorios indígenas." *Servindi*. June 11.

Salcedo, José Víctor. 2013a. "El sur alista huelga exigiendo el Gasoducto Sur Peruano." *La República*. July 31.

Salcedo, José Víctor. 2013b. "La Convención retira gasoducto 'simbólico' que instaló Humala en 2012." *La República*. September 26.

Salcedo, José Víctor. 2014. "Suman dos muertos y un desaparecido en el marco de huelga en La Convención." *La República*. September 7.

Servindi. 2010. "Perú: Suspenden actividades de minera Afrodita en Cordillera del Cóndor." February 17.

Servindi. 2014. "¡Triunfo de los pueblos! CIDH otorga medida cautelar a defensores de lagunas de Conga." May 9.

Servindi. 2015a. "Perú: Poder Judicial anula norma que dispone de territorios indígenas." March 20.

Servindi. 2015b. "Perú: Defensoría del Pueblo registró 211 conflictos sociales en marzo." April 10.

Servindi. 2017. "Decisión histórica: Poder Judicial ordena consulta del Lote 116." March 31.

Servindi. 2018a. "Piura: Rondas rechazan estrategias de Río Blanco para imponer proyecto minero." July 12.

Servindi. 2018b. "Confirmado: Se suspende Lote 116 por no haber sido consultado." August 23.

Servindi. 2019. "Cien concesiones mineras declaradas nulas por falta de consulta previa." May 18.

Servindi. 2020a. "Cusco: ¿Es justo vivir en permanente estado de emergencia?" May 15.

Servindi. 2020b. "Piura: Organizaciones sociales de Ayavaca denuncian maniobras de minera Río Blanco." June 8.

Servindi. 2021. "TC prohíbe uso indiscriminado de estados de emergencia por protestas." January 6.

SPDA actualidad ambiental. 2015. "Tía María: Southern anuncia 'pausa' de proyecto cuprífero en Arequipa." May 15.

SPDA actualidad ambiental. 2016. "Arequipa: Paro contra proyecto minero Tía María es acatado de forma pacífica." May 11.

Suárez, Cándice. 2008. "Consorcio Camisea inició producción de hidrocarburos de Lote 56 con inversión de US$ 872 millones (ampliación)." *Andina*. October 13.

Tecsi, Zaida. 2015a. "Prometen a La Convención planta de fraccionamiento." *La República*. January 27.

Tecsi, Zaida. 2015b. "Nuevo obstáculo para el Gasoducto Sur Peruano." *La República*. March 25.

Tiempominero.com. 2012. "Próxima semana se reinicia el diálogo en proyecto Quellaveco." April 2.

Uceda, Ricardo. 2014. "Santa Ana: La decisión del mes." *La República*. January 7.

Vega Nieto, Luz. 2008. "Quellaveco inició exposiciones de modificatoria de estudio de impacto ambiental en Moquegua." *Radio uno*. August 22.

INDEX

Printed in the USA
CPSIA information can be obtained
at www.ICGtesting.com
CBHW051947200224
4529CB00003B/94

9 780197 568927